TeenCoder™ Series

TeenCoder™: Game Programming

Student Textbook

Third Edition

Copyright 2013

Homeschool Programming, Inc.

TeenCoder™: Game Programming

Third Edition

Copyright © 2013 by Homeschool Programming, Inc.

980 Birmingham Rd, Suite 501-128

Alpharetta, GA 30004

All rights reserved. No part of this book may be reproduced or transmitted in any form or by any means without written permission of the author.

ISBN: **978-0-9887033-2-2**

Terms of Use

This course is copyright protected. Copyright 2013 © Homeschool Programming, Inc. Purchase of this course constitutes your agreement to the Terms of Use. You are not allowed to distribute any part of the course materials by any means to anyone else. You are not allowed to make it available for free (or fee) on any other source of distribution media, including the Internet, by means of posting the file, or a link to the file on newsgroups, forums, blogs or any other location. You may reproduce (print or copy) course materials as needed for your personal use only.

Disclaimer

Homeschool Programming, Inc, and their officers and shareholders, assume no liability for damage to personal computers or loss of data residing on personal computers arising due to the use or misuse of this course material. Always follow instructions provided by the manufacturer of 3rd party programs that may be included or referenced by this course.

Contact Us

You may contact Homeschool Programming, Inc. through the information and links provided on our website: http://www.HomeschoolProgramming.com. We welcome your comments and questions regarding this course or other related programming courses you would like to study!

Other Courses

Homeschool Programming, Inc. currently has two product lines for students: KidCoder™ and TeenCoder™. Our KidCoder™ Series provides easy, step-by-step programming curriculum for 4th through 12th graders. The Visual Basic series teaches introductory programming concepts in a fun, graphical manner. The Web Design series lets students create their own websites in HTML. Our TeenCoder™ Series provides introductory programming curriculum for high-school students. These courses are college-preparatory material designed for the student who may wish to pursue a career in Computer Science or enhance their transcript with a technical elective. Students can learn C#, Java, game programming, and Android application development.

3rd Party Copyrights

This course uses Microsoft's Visual C# 2010 Express as the programming platform. Visual Studio, Visual Studio Express, Windows, and all related products are copyright Microsoft Corporation. Please see http://www.microsoft.com/visualstudio/eng/products/visual-studio-2010-express for more details.

Instructional Videos

This course may be accompanied by optional Instructional Videos! These Flash-based videos will play directly from a DVD drive on the student's computer. Instructional Videos are supplements to the Student Textbook, covering every chapter and lesson with fun, animated re-enforcement of the main topics.

Instructional Videos are intended for students who enjoy a more audio-visual style of learning. They are not replacements for the Student Textbook which is still required to complete this course! However by watching the Instructional Videos first, students may begin each textbook chapter and lesson already having some grasp of the material to be read. Where applicable, the videos will also show "screencasts" of a real programmer demonstrating some concept or activity within the software development environment.

This Student Textbook and accompanying material are entirely sufficient to complete the course successfully! Instructional Videos are optional for students who would benefit from the alternate presentation of the material. For more information or to purchase the videos separately, please refer to the product descriptions on our website: http://www.HomeschoolProgramming.com.

Table of Contents

Terms of Use 3
Disclaimer 3
Contact Us 3
Other Courses 3
3rd Party Copyrights 3
Instructional Videos 4

Table of Contents 5

Before You Begin 11
Minimum Hardware and Software Requirements 11
Conventions Used in This Text 12
What You Will Learn and Do In This Course 13
What You Need to Know Before Starting 13
Software Versions 13
Getting Help & Course Errata 13

Chapter One: Introduction to Game Programming 15
Lesson One: What You Already Know 15
Lesson Two: Types of Computer Games 20
Lesson Three: What You Will Learn In This Course 22
Lesson Four: Introduction to XNA 24
Chapter Review 26
Activity: Install XNA Game Studio 27

Chapter Two: Game Design 31
Lesson One: The Game Proposal 31
Lesson Two: The Game Engine 33
Lesson Three: Creating a New XNA Game Project 36
Lesson Four: The Game Loop 44

Chapter Review 46

  Activity: Looping Colors 47

Chapter Three: Graphics Concepts 49

  Lesson One: Screen Coordinates 49

  Lesson Two: Full Screen vs. Window Mode 52

  Lesson Three: Colored Pixels 56

  Chapter Review 60

  Activity: Screen Toggle 61

Chapter Four: Working With Images 63

  Lesson One: Surfing the Content Pipeline 63

  Lesson Two: Drawing Images 65

  Lesson Three: Image Transformations 69

  Lesson Four: Drawing Text 74

  Chapter Review 77

  Activity: Starry Night 78

Chapter Five: User Input 79

  Lesson One: Keyboard Input 79

  Lesson Two: Mouse Input 85

  Lesson Three: Xbox 360 Controller 88

  Chapter Review 93

  Activity: Cat and Mouse Chase 94

Chapter Six: Sprites 95

  Lesson One: Introducing Sprites 95

  Lesson Two: The Swarm Game 102

  Lesson Three: Initializing Your Swarm 105

  Activity One: Raising the Swarm 108

  Lesson Four: Sprite Movement 109

  Activity Two: Buzzing Bees 113

    Chapter Review 114

Chapter Seven: Completing Swarm 115

    Lesson One: Adding Player Control 115

    Activity One: Sliding Smoke Gun 116

    Lesson Two: Shooting Stingers and Smoke 117

    Activity Two: Shooting the Swarm 119

    Lesson Three: Collision Detection 120

    Activity Three: Feeling the Sting 123

    Lesson Four: Ending and Restarting the Game 124

    Activity Four: Finishing Swarm 125

    Chapter Review 126

Chapter Eight: Animation 127

    Lesson One: Animation Concepts 127

    Lesson Two: Animation Textures 129

    Lesson Three: Animation in the Sprite Class 132

    Chapter Review 136

    Activity: Animated Swarm 137

Chapter Nine: Music and Sound Effects 139

    Lesson One: Sound Files 139

    Lesson Two: Playing Sound Effects 141

    Lesson Three: Playing Music 144

    Lesson Four: The XACT Tool 146

    Chapter Review 148

    Activity: Audible Swarm 149

Chapter Ten: Game Physics 151

    Lesson One: Velocity and Acceleration 151

    Lesson Two: Gravity and Wind 154

    Lesson Three: Reflection 157

    Chapter Review 160

    Activity: Snowball Fight 161

Chapter Eleven: Maze Generation 163

    Lesson One: Maze Types 163

    Lesson Two: Generating a Perfect Maze 165

    Lesson Three: Solving a Perfect Maze 168

    Chapter Review 170

    Activity: A-Maze-ing Backtracker 171

Chapter Twelve: Menus, Overlays and Deployment 173

    Lesson One: Title Screens and Option Menus 173

    Lesson Two: Handling Different Screens 174

    Lesson Three: Displaying Scores and Overlays 179

    Lesson Four: Distributing Games 180

    Chapter Review 186

    Activity: Tic-Tac-Toe 187

Chapter Thirteen: Multiplayer Games 189

    Lesson One: Handling Multiple Inputs 189

    Lesson Two: Scrolling Games 191

    Lesson Three: Viewports and Cameras 195

    Chapter Review 202

    Activity: Star Racer 203

Chapter Fourteen: Artificial Intelligence 205

    Lesson One: Understanding AI 205

    Lesson Two: Developing an AI Algorithm 207

    Lesson Three: Simple Movement Algorithms 209

    Lesson Four: AI for Star Racer 212

    Chapter Review 214

    Activity: Star Racer AI 215

Chapter Fifteen: Final Project 217
Lesson One: Bumper Cars Overview 217
Activity One: Project Kick-Off 219
Lesson Two: Menus and Controls 220
Activity Two: What's on the Menu? 220
Lesson Three: Adding Cars 221
Activity Three: Start Your Engines 222
Lesson Four: Oil Slicks and Coins 223
Activity Four: Hazards and Rewards 223
Lesson Five: Bumper Cars Sounds Effects 224
Activity Five: Make Some Noise 224
Lesson Six: Add Artificial Intelligence 225
Activity Six: Racing Buddy 227

What's Next? 229
Index 231

Before You Begin

Please read the following topics before you begin the course.

Minimum Hardware and Software Requirements

This is a hands-on programming course! You will be installing Microsoft's Visual C# 2010 Express on your computer, which must meet the following minimum requirements:

Computer Hardware

Your computer hardware must meet the following minimum specifications:

	Minimum
CPU	1.6GHz or faster processor
RAM	1024 MB
Display	1024 x 768 or higher resolution
Graphics Card	Supports DirectX-10 or later
Hard Disk Size	3GB available space
DVD Drive	DVD-ROM drive

Xbox 360 Gamepad controllers are optional input devices that may be used if available, but they are not required for any activity.

Operating Systems

Your computer operating system must match one of the following:

Windows XP (x86) with Service Pack 3 or above (except Starter Edition)
Windows Vista (x86 and x64) with Service Pack 2 or above (except Starter Edition)
Windows 7 (x86 and x64)
Windows 8 or Windows 8 Pro (excluding Windows 8 RT)

Conventions Used in This Text

This course will use certain styles (fonts, borders, etc) to highlight text of special interest.

```
Source code will be in 11-point Consolas font, in a single box like this.
```

Variable names will be in **12-point Consolas bold** text, similar to the way they will look in your development environment. For example: **myVariable**.

Function names, properties and keywords will be in **bold face** type, so that they are easily readable.

This picture highlights important concepts within a lesson.

Sidebars may contain additional information, tips, or background material.

Chapter Review section will highlight key elements from each chapter.

Each chapter includes one or more activities that allow you to practice the concepts you have learned.

What You Will Learn and Do In This Course

TeenCoder™: Game Programming will teach you how to write simple games on your own computer! You will be using Microsoft's C# programming language, the Visual C# 2010 Express development environment, and Microsoft's XNA Game Studio 4.0 development kit. This course is geared for high-school students who are already comfortable with C# and object-oriented programming concepts.

This course will not teach you how to write games by stitching together a few pre-built widgets in a predefined game environment or how to create complex animation or 3D environments. To do those things you are using *someone else's* platform to hide many of the interesting and fundamental concepts required to build games from scratch. Upon completion of this course you will understand many of the techniques used to create a wide range of game types!

What You Need to Know Before Starting

You must have completed the *TeenCoder™: Windows Programming* course prior to starting this course. The Visual C# and object-oriented concepts learned in the first course are prerequisites to learning and enjoying this game programming material.

You are also expected to already know the basics of computer use before beginning this course. You need to know how to use the keyboard and mouse to select and run programs, use application menu systems, and work with the Windows operating system. You should understand how to store and load files on your hard disk, and how to use the Windows Explorer to walk through your file system and directory structures. You should also have some experience using text editors and finding helpful information on the Internet.

Software Versions

You will be using the *Microsoft Visual C# 2010 Express* software and the *XNA Game Studio 4.0* to complete this course. These programs can be freely downloaded from Microsoft's website. Your course will contain links to download and install instructions on our website, http://www.HomeschoolProgramming.com. Microsoft may from time to time change their website or download process, or release newer versions of the product. Our website will contain updated versions of the instructions as needed.

Getting Help & Course Errata

All courses come with a Solution Guide PDF and fully coded solutions for all activities. Simply install the "Solution Files" from your course setup program and you will be able to refer to the solutions as needed from the "Solution Menu". If you are confused about any activity you can see how we solved the problem!

We welcome your feedback regarding any course details that are unclear or that may need correction. You can find a list of course errata for this edition on our website.

Chapter One: Introduction to Game Programming

Welcome to the *TeenCoder™: Game Programming* course! In this course you will learn how to write your own computer games using the C# programming language and the Microsoft XNA Game Studio. The first chapter will review what you learned in the prerequisite *TeenCoder™: Windows Programming* course, examine some different categories of games, and look ahead to the lessons in the remaining chapters.

Lesson One: What You Already Know

You should have already completed the first-semester *TeenCoder™: Windows Programming* course. In that course you learned how to write graphical Windows programs using the C# language and the Microsoft Visual C# 2010 Express development environment. Without a solid understanding of the topics presented in the first semester, you will have difficulty completing this course!

In this lesson we will briefly summarize the key topics you learned in the prior course. The game programming lessons starting in the next chapter will assume working knowledge of each topic.

 **If you do not feel comfortable with any subject listed below, we recommend you review that material before moving on to the game programming lessons!**

History of Windows

Modern personal computer operating systems started with DOS in the 1980s. The first graphical operating system called Lisa was created by Apple. The first Windows operating system quickly followed Lisa and has seen many upgrades and iterations over the last 20 years. Windows is the most commonly used operating system in the home today. A "standard look-and-feel" means users have a consistent experience across different types of Windows applications. The current version of Windows is called Windows 8.

Fundamentals of C#

C# was created to fix the many issues that programmers have with C, C++, and Java languages. C# is easy to learn and simple to use. The C# language is inherently object-oriented which allows for more modern, organized, and robust designs and program code. C# also provides full access to the Microsoft .NET Framework, which is a comprehensive set of libraries and objects providing powerful, easy-to-use interfaces into the Windows environment.

Windows Programming Concepts

The most obvious element in a Windows application is the graphical window itself. C# Windows applications are built around a .NET Framework object called a **Form**. A **Form** represents one screen or dialog window within the application. Controls are graphical widgets that you can place on the **Form** for a person to use. The IDE contains over 60 basic controls in the Controls Toolbox. From the Toolbox you can easily add buttons, toolbars, menus, text boxes, printing controls, pictures, checkboxes, and other controls to a **Form**. Graphical applications are guided by user input, and there is no way to predict exactly which actions the user will choose to perform. This makes it difficult to execute the program in a top-down structured manner. Instead, graphical programs are event-driven, which means that certain functions within the code will execute when specific events occur.

Data Types and Variables

Most programs require data to work. A calculator application needs numbers to calculate, an MP3 player needs music files to play, and an image editor needs pictures to load. Clearly, data can come in various forms or types. The simplest data types are numeric. There are many different types of numbers (large, small, decimal, positive, negative, etc) and C# defines a data type for each kind. A numeric data types is a "value" data type, which means declaring the variable will automatically allocate memory for a copy of that data.

In addition to telling the compiler what kind of data type to use, we need to tell the compiler what name we will use to refer to the data in our program. When you create an instance of a data type and give it a name, that instance is called a *variable*. Variables are places where you store data in your program. You can change a variable's contents while running the program (hence the name "variable").

Some variables are "reference" data types. When declaring a "reference" variable, the computer does not create space for the data in memory. Instead the variable name is merely a reference to wherever the data or object actually lives. When you first declare a variable for a reference data type, the variable's value is **null**, which means "nothing". The variable literally refers to nothing and has no data at all associated with it. You allocate memory for an object by using the **new** keyword and assigning the result to a reference variable.

The C# language has a built-in **string** data type. A string is a series of characters that form a line of text. It can be a short string like someone's name, or a very long string like an entire book. The **string** data type is a reference data type.

Basic Flow Control

The way that a program responds to certain decisions is called *flow control*. Flow control is achieved by testing "logical expressions". Logical expressions evaluate to **true** or **false**. All logical expressions involving two or more components require a *comparison operator*. These symbols (>, <, =, !=, >=, <=) are used in logical expressions to compare values.

Logical expressions can be combined using the logical operators: **and (&&)**, **or (||)**, **exclusive or (^)**, and **not (!)**. Logical operators will combine multiple **true** or **false** inputs into a single **true** or **false** output.

The **if()** statement will execute a block of code when a specific logical expression evaluates to **true**. You can use the **else if** keywords to evaluate expressions only when prior **if** expressions are **false**. You may add a final **else** keyword with no logical expression that will run statements when none of the prior **if** or **else if** expressions are **true**.

Loops are often used in a program to execute a series of statements over and over again. One common loop type is a **for()** loop. This loop is typically used to execute a set of statements a fixed number of times. A second type of program loop is called a **while()** loop. This type of loop is used to execute a set of statements *while* a condition is **true**. You may not know in advance how many times the loop will execute, but you know the conditions under which it should continue executing.

User Input

A common user input control is the text box control, which is used to allow the user to enter a string of text into a program. The list box and the combo box are useful input controls that present the user choices from a list of items. Radio buttons and check boxes are similar controls that allow a user to pick from a small set of options.

Math Functions in C#

Math operators are the symbols you use in expressions to perform some math using two operands. You are probably familiar with these operators as C# uses the same symbols you typically see on a calculator. Here is a list of the common math operators:

- addition uses the plus sign (+)
- subtraction uses the minus sign (-)
- multiplication uses the asterisk (*)
- division uses the forward slash (/)
- Modulus (remainder) uses the percent sign (%)

Each operator takes two operands which can be a fixed number, a variable, or the result of evaluating a larger mathematical expression or function. The .NET Framework includes an object called **System.Math**, which contains many useful math constants and functions.

Working with Strings

The **string** data type has a corresponding **System.String** object that can be used interchangeably. Over time a very large number of useful **string** methods have been created. The **string** methods allow you to easily compare, append, and retrieve information for any **string** variable. Each letter in a string is accessed by a numeric value, called an *index*. This value is zero-based, which means that the first letter in a string is letter number 0, the second is number 1, the third is number 2, and so on. In order to access an individual letter in a string, you can use this value between a set of brackets after the string variable name.

To convert any data type to a **string**, you can simply call the **ToString()** method on the variable. To convert a **string** to a numeric data type, you can use the **Parse()** or **TryParse()** method on the data type. These *functions* will convert an input **string** to that data type if possible, and indicate failure in different ways.

Methods

A method (or function) is useful when you have some sort of task that may be repeated during a program, or a task that you want to hide from external code. You must follow certain rules when creating your method names. First, the method's name must consist only of lowercase or capital letters, numbers and underscores ("_"). The first symbol in your method name must always be either a letter or an underscore. If you really want to tap into the power and flexibility of methods, you need to use parameters and return values. Parameters are data that you pass into your method from the calling code. Return values are data that a method can return to a calling program. You can also modify parameters within the method by using the **out** keyword. A statement that invokes a method is often said to be "calling" the method.

Debugging and Exceptions

A *debugger* is a program that will let you observe and analyze your program as it is running. The Visual C# 2010 Express IDE contains an integrated debugger that is very easy to use. The debugger will let you walk step-by-step through each line in your program and observe your program as it runs. This is an extremely powerful tool. While you are observing the running program, you can make sure the program is working as you expect. This includes making sure the statements are executing in the correct order and even watching the contents of your variables to make sure the data is being processed and stored correctly.

Collections

A *collection* is a general term for a data structure that stores groups of items. The .NET Framework defines a number of very useful collections and related objects in the **System.Collections** namespace. Often you will want to walk through each of the items in a collection without knowing anything about the underlying data structure. To do this you can obtain an *enumerator* or *iterator* from the collection object. An enumerator is an object that knows how to access each element of the collection from the beginning to the end, without you knowing anything about the details of the collection. You can conveniently use the **foreach** keyword to loop through all elements in a collection. Some common collection types include arrays and linked lists.

Object-Oriented Programming (OOP)

OOP revolves around the creation of re-usable code *objects*. An object is something that can have both data (properties) and functions (methods) that operate on that data. Ideally, well-coded objects will be useful to many applications and can therefore be shared between different programs.

Classes in C#

In the C# language (and in most languages), an object is called a *class*. A *property* is a variable that belongs to a class. Properties can be any data type (value or reference), including other classes. Class *methods* are functions defined within a class to perform some action. The methods and properties of a class can be **public**, **private** or **protected**. Public methods and properties are available to any program or object that is using the class. Private methods and properties are only available to the class itself and cannot be reached by any external code. The protected access type restricts use to the class itself or any derived subclasses.

Inheritance and Polymorphism

Inheritance means one class can re-use and extend the properties and methods of another class. A *base* class is a class from which other classes can inherit. A *derived* class is a class that inherits from a base class. *Polymorphism* means you can use an object through a base reference and it will behave differently according to its actual derived type.

File I/O

The .NET Framework contains several useful objects for dealing with files and directories. The **Directory** object has methods that will create, move, and navigate subdirectories on a computer's hard drive. A *file* is a data block (or series of bytes) stored on a hard drive. Files have a name (filename), location (directory), as well as other properties. The .NET Framework contains a **File** object which can be used to copy, delete, or otherwise manage the files on a computer. Like the **Directory** object, all **File** methods are **static**, meaning you can call the methods directly on the object type without creating an instance of the object.

To read and write to a text file we use objects from the **System.IO** namespace called **StreamReader** and **StreamWriter**. A *binary* file contains data written as a series of bytes that does not represent textual information. A binary file is very useful when you want to store data in "raw" form, literally copying the bytes from memory into the file. To read and write a binary file we use the **BinaryReader** and **BinaryWriter**.

The **SaveFileDialog** is a pre-built dialog that can be used within a program to allow the user to specify which file name and location to use for saved data. The **OpenFileDialog** is a pre-built dialog that can be used within a program to allow the user to specify which file name and location to use for loading data. Once these dialogs have been called, the program gives control over to the dialog window. When the dialog window is closed, the control falls back to the program.

Lesson Two: Types of Computer Games

Computer games have been around for almost as long as computers themselves. In fact, the first accepted computers emerged in the mid 1940s and by 1952 the first computer game was being played. Granted, the game was just a simple version of tic-tac-toe, and it ran on a vacuum-tube computer, but it was a game!

Computer games have evolved since the early 1950s. Modern computer games are complex, multi-faceted, intense games that involve sound, visual effects and game controllers with tactile feedback. Over the years, the field of computer gaming has branched out into many different *types* of games. The variety of possible computer games is only limited by human imagination. If you can dream it, chances are you can create it!

In this lesson, we will discuss some of the more common types of computer games:

- Arcade games
- Board games
- Role Playing Games (RPG)
- Sports simulators
- Real Time Strategy (RTS)
- First Person Shooter (FPS)
- Massively Multiplayer Online RPG (MMORPG)

Arcade Games

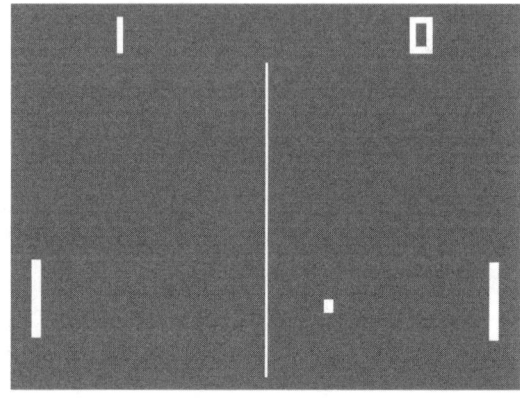

An early popular genre of games in the 1970s was the arcade game. These games were housed in big, upright arcade cabinets and required money to play. The first successful arcade game was a game called Pong, which was a two-player, tennis-like game where each player moved a "paddle" to try to hit a ball back-and-forth. The graphics were very simple: the "paddle" was just a vertical bar on the screen and the "ball" was a small square dot. Nonetheless the game was extremely popular and sparked a whole generation of upright arcade games.

First arcade game: Atari's Pong game from 1979

Arcade games are still popular today. You can find games incorporating elements such as auto racing, fighting, shooting, sports, fantasy, space ships, aliens, food fights, and even angry gorillas.

Board Games

Board games you might play around your family table have been around since well before computers. It wasn't long until gamers realized that computers could be used to automate the tedious tasks involved with traditional board games, like dealing cards, keeping track of money in the bank, or selecting a random event. Nearly all popular table-top games have been converted into computer games, some many times over. These games usually provide a top-down view of the game board and allow multiple players to take turns "rolling" the dice, moving their pieces and interacting with the game. These games tend to be consistently popular, since they mimic familiar games that have been widely known for years and years.

Role Playing Games

"Role Playing Games" or RPGs are popular modern computer games. In an RPG, a player will assume the persona of one or more characters in a game. These characters will then exist and interact within a virtual world over a period of time. There are endless themes for the Role Playing Games: fantasy games with swords and knights, real-world environments with recognizable people and communities, or even futuristic science fiction games with space ships and aliens. The graphics of these games can range from very realistic 3D models to simple text-only displays. You can play these games by yourself or with a few friends.

Sports Simulators

Sports simulation games are especially popular with console game machines. These games allow one or more people to "play" a sport like football, baseball, hockey, golf, racing, etc. These games tend to incorporate a good deal of "game physics". Game physics make objects in the game behave more or less like they would in the real world. Good game physics will make a ball look like it is truly bouncing, a car respond to road conditions in a realistic manner or the snow spray up around your skis as if you were really swooshing down the slopes. We will discuss this important subject in more detail later in this course.

Real Time Strategy

Real-Time Strategy games (or RTS games) are strategy games that occur in real-time. This means that you and your opponents are all attempting to achieve the same results at the same time. These games tend to be very fast-paced, as everything happens at once without taking turns. You may try to build an empire by planting cities, building military and civilian units, and gathering resources like stone, gold or wheat. Once you have built your empire, you can move your military or civilian units across the terrain in a strategic manner and attempt to defeat one or more opponents. You must act quickly and juggle a number of tasks at the same time in order to defeat your opponents or they will overcome you!

First Person Shooter

The "First Person Shooter" (or FPS) game is a type of game that has become very popular in the last two decades. These games give the player a first-person perspective using the high performance 3D graphics. A player interacts with the game as if he or she is standing in the middle of the scene, seeing what their character sees in real-time. FPS games tend to span many different levels filled with monsters, aliens, or other opponents. The objective of the game is usually to survive by shooting the bad guys (or competing players!) with a variety of splashy weapons.

Massively Multiplayer Online RPG

Massively Multiplayer Online RPGs (MMORPGs) are a relatively recent addition to the field of computer gaming. These games are an extension of the traditional RPG. Instead of working individually within a game limited to your own computer, you can play online in a large virtual world with hundreds or thousands of companions. These games will allow you to play with your brother on the computer next to you or with other players in countries all over the world! MMORPGs typically require a high speed internet connection and a monthly subscription to pay for the complex servers maintained by the game company.

Lesson Three: What You Will Learn In This Course

When you buy a professionally produced computer game in a store, you can be sure that behind the scenes an entire team of trained programmers and artists worked to create the finished product. However, a motivated and talented individual can still write creative and enjoyable games by themselves.

As you have seen, there are many different types of computer games. While it would be impossible to completely cover every aspect of computer gaming in one course, we will teach you some key game programming concepts. Along the way you will create several real games. When you are done with the course you will have a set of tools and concepts you can then apply to your own creative efforts.

Course topics include:

XNA Game Studio	<ul><li>Introduction to XNA Game Studio</li><li>Installing the software and creating new game projects</li></ul>
Game Design	<ul><li>Game proposals and design concepts</li><li>Game loops</li></ul>
Graphics	<ul><li>Screen coordinates</li><li>XNA graphics objects</li><li>Managing and displaying game images</li><li>Full screen and windowed modes</li></ul>

Images	<ul><li>Image ordering</li><li>Image scaling</li><li>Image rotating</li><li>Image transparency</li></ul>
User Input	<ul><li>Capturing keyboard events</li><li>Using mouse events</li><li>Using Xbox 360 Gamepads</li></ul>
Sprites	<ul><li>Creating a Sprite library</li><li>Sprite movement</li><li>Collision detection</li></ul>
Animation	<ul><li>Animation concepts</li><li>Animation texture frames</li><li>Creating an animated Sprite</li></ul>
Sound	<ul><li>Playing sound effects</li><li>Playing music</li></ul>
Game Physics	<ul><li>Gravity</li><li>Reflection</li><li>Wind effects</li></ul>
Mazes	<ul><li>Different types of mazes</li><li>Building mazes</li><li>Solving mazes</li></ul>
Multiplayer	<ul><li>Split screens and scrolling games</li><li>Multi-player input</li></ul>
Artificial Intelligence	<ul><li>Understanding artificial intelligence</li><li>Applying AI to a computer game</li></ul>

Within each chapter you will be working on an activity related to the topics in each lesson. In some cases you will create entire games over the course of several chapters. The games that you will create in this course will be fairly simple to start, but you can improvise and expand to your heart's content – the sky's the limit! The final project in the last chapter will incorporate many of the topics into a single game that you produce.

Lesson Four: Introduction to XNA

In the first semester course you learned that the .NET Framework is a collection of pre-built objects that perform many common tasks for you. Programmers like to re-use existing components to create more complex and interesting programs. If they had to reinvent the wheel each time, the final programs wouldn't be as powerful, stable, and predictable.

Similarly, over time game developers have developed common techniques, tips, tricks, and coded widgets specifically to make game programming easier. This body of knowledge is represented in many ways on different programming platforms and languages. Generally speaking, game programmers can rely on some sort of pre-built library, framework, or engine to make their tasks easier. When writing a game you want to focus on the creative aspects and bringing your vision to life.

In this course we have chosen the Microsoft XNA Framework as our gaming library. It is not the only library out there, to be sure. But XNA has a number of significant advantages, including:

- XNA is readily accessible from C# and the Visual C# 2010 Express IDE
- XNA is Microsoft's most modern gaming framework
- XNA has numerous online resources from thousands of XNA programmers
- XNA can be used to write both Windows and Microsoft Xbox 360 games
- XNA is free!

In addition to this course material, you can find useful XNA resources online. Microsoft has founded an online community as a central starting point for downloads, discussion forums, and independent game publishing. This site was originally called the "XNA Creator's Club", was then renamed to the "App Hub", and then renamed again to "Xbox Live Indie Games". The website currently can be found at this location:

http://xbox.create.msdn.com/en-us/

If Microsoft decides to rename the website again, a little bit of searching online should lead you to it.

You are not required to go online to complete this course, other than what we specifically detail in order to download XNA itself! But used correctly the Internet can be a great source of help and inspiration for your games, and we feel comfortable recommending the App Hub website to you. Also, the XNA MSDN help is all located online so your IDE will attempt to pull online reference information if you hit F1 for help on an XNA object. Naturally, use caution when online and always obtain your teacher's permission first.

Chapter One: Introduction to Game Programming

 This course requires online connectivity only to access installation instructions from our website and download the XNA Game Studio from Microsoft. Other online resources and MSDN XNA reference material may be helpful, but always ask permission when going online and only browse websites you know to be safe.

Microsoft XNA Game Studio 4.0

The *XNA Game Studio 4.0* software is a free, downloadable plug-in to the Microsoft *Visual C# 2010 Express* software. The Game Studio includes the XNA Framework and integrates into your IDE. Once installed, the Game Studio allows a programmer to quickly and easily create games for the Windows operating system, the Xbox 360 game console, or Windows Phones. In fact, support for Windows Phones was one of the main focal points of the 4.0 release.

When you go to the XNA download website, you may see the Windows Phone development tool heavily promoted. You do not need to download and install the larger tool set including Windows Phone options for this course! Instead follow the instructions described in the activity at the end of this chapter to get just what you need for Windows and Xbox 360 game development.

Chapter Review

- A Windows "common look-and-feel" gives users the same experience across different applications
- C# was created to fix issues that programmers have with the C, C++, and Java languages.
- A **Form** represents one screen or dialog window within an application.
- *Variables* are places where you store data in your program.
- The way that a program responds to certain decisions is called *flow control*.
- Common user input controls are the textbox, list box, combo box, check box and radio button.
- The .NET Framework includes an object called **System.Math**, which contains many useful math constants and functions.
- A *method* or *function* is useful when you have some sort of task that may need to be performed multiple times during a program.
- A *debugger* is a program that will let you observe and analyze your program as it is running.
- An object is something that can have both data (properties) and functions (methods) that operate on that data.
- In the C# language (and in most languages), an object is referred to as a *class*.
- *Inheritance* means one class can re-use and extend the properties and methods of another class.
- *Polymorphism* means you can use an object through a base reference and it will behave differently according to its actual derived type.
- The field of computer gaming has evolved over the years to include many different types of games.
- The first popular genre of computer games was arcade games.
- Some common types of computer games are board games, role-playing games, sports simulation games, real-time strategy games, first-person shooter games, and multiplayer online games.
- The *XNA Game Studio 4.0* software is a free, downloadable plug-in to the *Microsoft Visual C# 2010 Express* IDE.
- The XNA Framework contains a set of managed libraries designed for game development that are based on the Microsoft .NET Framework.

Chapter One: Introduction to Game Programming

Activity: Install XNA Game Studio

In this activity you will be installing the course files, the Microsoft Visual C# 2010 Express software (if not already present), the XNA Game Studio, and the XNA Help Library on your computer.

Course files	The files that come with this course include material for the student (chapter sample programs, activity starters, instructional documents) and for the teacher (activity solutions, tests, answer keys, etc).
Visual C# 2010 Express	You should have already installed Visual C# 2010 Express on your computer during the first semester course. If you have switched computers or need to re-install the software for any reason, do so during this activity.
XNA Game Studio 4.0	The XNA Game Studio installation will integrate the XNA Framework with your Visual C# 2010 Express software.
XNA Help Library	The XNA Help Library contains reference information about all of the gaming objects contained in the XNA Framework.

Installing the Course Files

The files for this course are installed by a single setup executable that came with your course. The setup file is called "TeenCoder_GameProgramming.exe". Ensure that you are running a Windows account with administrative privileges on your machine when you launch the setup executable.

The setup executable will offer you the choice of installing the Student Files and/or Solution Files. You may install these components on the same computer (if the student should have free access to the solutions) or on different computers (so the teacher can maintain control over the solutions). For a better understanding of the setup process and the files present in the course material, please refer to the "Getting Started Guide" on our website at http://www.HomeschoolProgramming.com.

Go ahead and perform this setup process now. We recommend installing to the default "C:\TeenCoder\Game Programming" directory as we will refer to that directory structure throughout the textbook. You may choose a different location if you want. The setup program will automatically create a "My Projects" directory under the target installation – this is where all of the student projects will go!

TeenCoder™: Game Programming

Once installation is complete you will have a new "TeenCoder" group on your Windows Start Menu. Underneath "TeenCoder" is a "Game Programming" folder. Within that folder are one or two menus for the Student and Solution files (depending on your choices during setup). The look and feel of the Windows Start Menu may change between versions of Windows, but your final Start menu should contain folders and links as shown to the right (assuming both Student and Solution files installed).

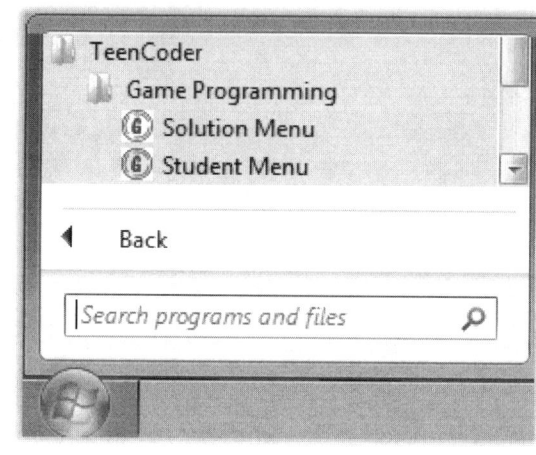

Windows 8 users may see the Solution and Student Menu links appear directly on the desktop.

You can run these menus for convenient, graphical access to all of the instructional documents (PDFs), activity solutions, and other material distributed with the course. You may also simply run Windows Explorer and navigate to your target install directory ("C:\TeenCoder\Game Programming") and launch these files on your own! Use of the Menu systems is optional. Here is an example screen shot from Windows Explorer that shows the directory structure and files in your target directory (details may vary).

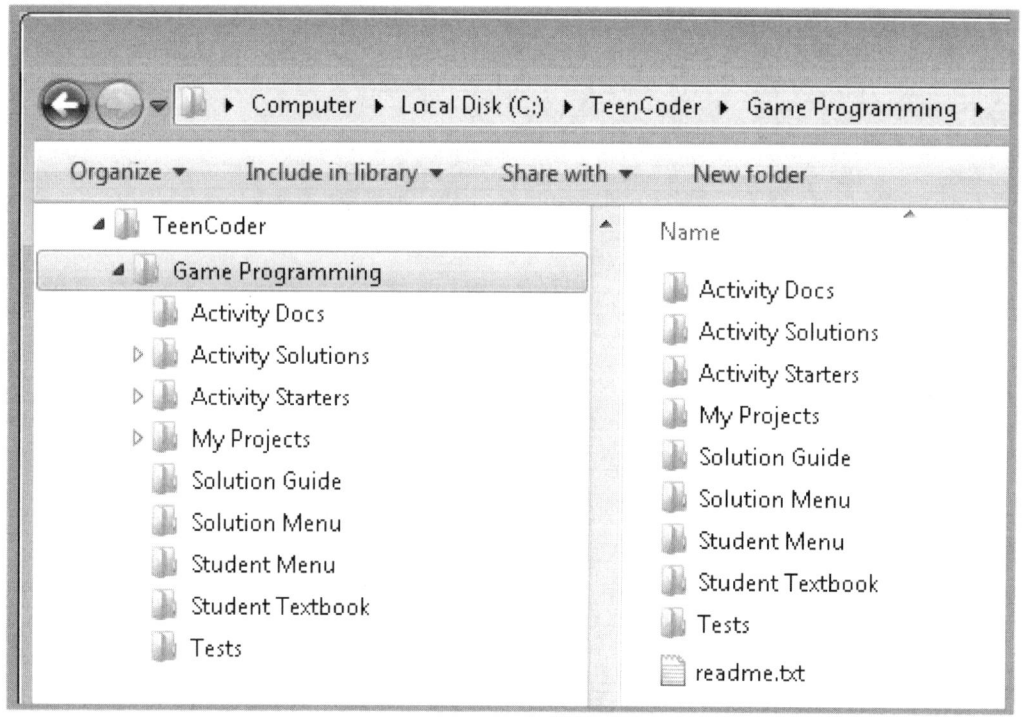

All course descriptions of directory structures will refer to the default installation path. If you choose to install elsewhere, remember to map our instructions to your new location.

Supplemental course documents are in PDF format. A ".PDF" file is a common document format that requires the free Adobe Acrobat program to read. Your computer should already have the Acrobat Reader installed. If you cannot view the PDF documents, you will need to install Acrobat Reader first from http://get.adobe.com/reader/.

Installing Visual C# 2010 Express

You should already have the Visual C# 2010 Express software on your computer if you completed the first semester *TeenCoder^{TM}: Windows Programming* course. If you already have this software, you can skip this part of the activity. If you need to install the software for any reason, that will be your next task. You will need to be connected to the Internet during the download and installation process. Always ask your teacher before doing any activity online. Now, let's get started!

Your Student Menu contains a tab called "Software Install Instructions". Click on that tab and you will see a button called "Get Online Documents". Click that button and you will be directed to a page on our website that contains PDF documents with the current download and installation instructions.

The first document titled "Visual C# 2010 Install Instructions" ("Visual_CS_2010_Install_Instructions.pdf") contains complete, step-by-step instructions on downloading and installing the software. Please use the links from your Student Menu to find and open the Visual C# Install Instructions document now. Follow the instructions to install the IDE on your computer. You can also directly access all install documentation from our website, http://www.HomeschoolProgramming.com.

Within 30 days of installation you also need to register the software with Microsoft (a free process), so we recommend you do that now. Our online document page contains "Visual C# Registration Instructions" ("Visual_CS_2010_Registration_Instructions.pdf"). Open that document now and complete the instructions to register your software with Microsoft.

Getting Help for C#

If you have previously installed the Visual C# 2010 Express software on your computer, then you likely already configured your Help Library and you can skip this section. Otherwise, you will want to configure your Help Library in order to get help on an error, or function description, or some other part of the C# programming language. The MSDN (Microsoft Developer Network) Help Library can be configured for use from within Visual C# 2010 Express. Then, to get help on any topic, just position the mouse in the IDE on the item in question (like a compiler error number or function name) and hit the F1 key. If help files are not installed locally the help library can go online to get help for you.

On our online documents page, please find the document titled "Visual C# 2010 MSDN (Help Library) Install Instructions" ("Visual_CS_MSDN_Install_Instructions.pdf"). Follow those instructions now to install the MSDN Help Library.

You can also use many online resources to help find solutions to error messages or understand the meaning of certain Visual C# topics. Any of the major search engines will lead you to dozens of topics on programming and Visual Studio. Some well-established sites such as Wikipedia (http://www.wikipedia.com) also offer good articles on many programming concepts.

TeenCoder™: Game Programming

XNA Game Studio 4.0

Your last task is to install the XNA Game Studio 4.0 kit on your computer. Find the "XNA Game Studio 4.0 Install Instructions" ("XNA_Game_Studio_Installation_Instructions.pdf") document from our online documents page. These instructions detail how to download and install the XNA Game Studio 4.0. Please open that document now and follow the instructions to install the XNA Game Studio on your computer.

Getting Help for XNA

The XNA Framework includes a large number of new classes and game programming concepts. If you have configured your Help Library for online access as described in the previous section, then you will automatically have access to the online XNA reference material as well. From within your IDE you can select any XNA component and hit F1 to get immediate online help.

All XNA help material is located online, so you cannot choose to install XNA Help Library components locally. If you have locally installed other Help Library components, you may wish to bookmark the XNA Help website in your browser as described in our XNA Game Studio installation instructions document.

 **The Microsoft download website or installation procedure may change over time. Newer versions of Game Studio or Visual C# Express may also be released. If your download and install experience does not match our online instructional documents, please contact us for updated instructions!**

The Working Directory for Student Projects

After installing the Student Files, a "My Projects" directory was automatically created for you. This directory will be the location where you will save all of your projects for this course. The default installation directory is 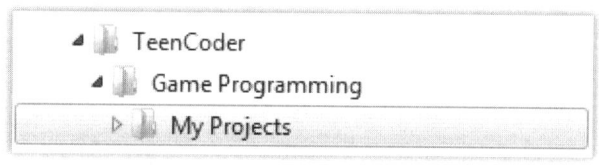 "C:\TeenCoder\Game Programming\", so "My Projects" will be within that hierarchy. Each project you create should be placed in a new sub-folder within your working directory. You may select a different working directory or even create additional working directories on your own; just remember your directory location when you want to save and load your projects. Multiple students may use the same computer for this course by creating different working directories! Use the Windows Explorer program to create new directories.

Chapter Two: Game Design

In this chapter we will discuss some strategies for designing your own computer games. You will also create your first XNA Game Studio project and take a look at the main XNA objects used in the project.

Lesson One: The Game Proposal

A computer game takes a great deal of planning before any code is written. A programmer needs to think about how the game should work from beginning to end, answering some very important questions along the way. What type of computer game is it? What pieces are involved? What kind of graphics and sound will it need? Once you have the answers to these and other questions, you can start to think about the detailed code.

Writing computer games can be a more creative process than most types of programs. Brainstorming ideas and concepts for your game is a very useful tool. However, a good deal of organization and planning are also required to complete a successful game. The first thing you will need to write is your *game proposal*, or set of requirements. A good, solid description will help solidify your ideas. Try and think about some of the following questions:

- What general kind of game do you want to make? Will it be a puzzle game? An arcade game? Or something completely different?
- What will your game screens look like? Will the player see a game board? A country scene? A field of stars in outer-space? Putting some of your visual ideas on paper by sketching out example screens is a good way to get a feel for the graphical components of your game.
- How will your players interact with the game? Will they use a mouse and keyboard? Will they use a game controller or game pad?
- Will your game be one-player or multi-player? How would you create a convincing computer opponent?
- What kind of sound effects will be necessary?
- Is there a back-story to your game? Should the player understand any important information before they start to play?

As you start to answer these questions, you will come up with others on your own. This brainstorming session is very important to the design of your game. Some aspects of a game may not be obvious until you start planning. Once you start writing down your ideas, chances are you will find yourself modifying some parts of the game to make others work better.

 **Every good computer game starts with a series of questions. Answers to these questions form a *game proposal* or sketch of what you want to do in a game program.**

After a few sessions of brainstorming you should have a solid idea how your game will come together. Your ideas should be written down into a series of organized game requirements. These requirements will give you the basis for the game design. During the game design phase you should plan, in detail, how you will write all of the program code to implement your ideas.

Content Planning

Most games require lots of audio and visual *content*. Audio content may come in the form of WAV or MP3 files and will serve as sound effects, background music, or perhaps an audio read-along complement to scrolling text. Visual content consists of graphics files like JPG or PNG. Each of the game objects you see on the screen is represented by an image (or possibly an animated series of images). You might need small images that can move around or images that cover your entire screen for background scenery.

It is not required that you finalize all of your content up-front. In fact, you might spend so much time making nice images and sound effects that you never get around to writing the game! You also might not feel like much of an artist, and don't want to learn how to make polished images. That's OK. You should only plan and build *placeholder* content at first. You just need audio and video files that are good enough to represent what you want in the game so that you can begin coding. A stick figure is just as good as a photo-realistic image when you are writing the game logic. If you want to make sure your logic for playing background music works, just throw in any old recording of your brother or sister trying to sing and worry about picking out that perfect song when the game is nearly done.

Part of content planning is determining how you will get your audio and image files. Do you want to make them yourself? There are free image editor and sound editor programs online that you can download, or you might have already purchased something for your home computer. You might also decide not to dabble at all with making new content and instead focus on finding pre-made content that fits your needs. You can purchase CDs filled with clip art and sound effects, or find free content online. Just remember to use caution and adult supervision when downloading any online application or content.

All of the content you need to complete the games in this course will be provided for you. But you will want to start thinking about how you will obtain content for your own games later on.

Baby Steps

Even simple games may require hundreds of lines of code. For this reason, you should plan to write your game in small stages. This allows you to test certain sections of the game as you go along. This process avoids the classic "big-bang" programming problem, which involves writing all of the code from start to finish without testing – then having to compile, run and debug the entire program at once. It is much easier and more productive to break your program into smaller, easier to manage pieces!

Lesson Two: The Game Engine

If you have ever read any articles or books on game programming, you have probably heard the term: *game engine*. Simply defined, a game engine is the brain of a computer game. The engine is typically a collection of libraries, data and program code that will help to make your game work. Game engines handle everything from playing sound effects to processing user input, dealing with game timers and drawing graphics on the screen. A game engine can even simulate an "intelligent" computer opponent.

A game engine is very important for several key reasons. First, when you plan your game engine as a concrete component with well-defined parts, you will be able to complete the design phase of the program quickly and easily. In fact, just understanding the parts and features of your game engine will become a helpful starting point when you are staring at that first empty source file!

The second reason for well-defined game engines is that they may be re-used in more than one game. Games in the same general category (i.e. FPS, RPG or board games) often share the same design needs and coding elements. The ability to re-use the same game engine with different graphics and storylines is a great time-saver. In this course we will not re-use any game engine because each game program demonstrates a different concept. However, we will build a useful library to handle common tasks that will be shared across most of the course games and that library can be used in your own games too!

Game engines can be divided into several general sections: game state, game logic, and user interactions.

Game State

All games require some sort of data. If you need to keep track of a player's score, you will need a numeric data type. If you have items moving around the screen, you will need to know where these items are positioned and what direction they are heading. If you have multiple players, you will need to track who has the current "turn" in the game. Your game requirements should make all of these data needs obvious and straightforward. You should be able to make a detailed list of many necessary data variables and types from your game requirements.

The part of your game engine that holds the game data is called the *game state*. The game state helps to manage and control all of the information that is needed in game. If you want to be able to save your game to disk and resume game play later, it is the data within the game state that must be saved! When you re-load your game state from disk the game can then continue from where it left off. In this course the game state, generally speaking, will consist of the member variables of the main program class.

Game Logic

A game's logic controls the different components of the game. Are you creating a board game with individual "pieces" that need to move around the screen? What rules need to be enforced at each turn? Will any moving items bounce around the screen? How will the user control the game? Will your players have any time limits? Will anyone or anything be shooting at objects on the screen? What happens when an object is hit by a player's "shot"? The game logic will address these questions based on the requirements for your game.

The game engine's controlling logic will apply the user input to the game state according to the rules of the game. A computer game often has many things happening at the same time in different areas of the game. A player could be shooting from a spaceship, while meteors are spinning around the screen with alien ships racing through the scene at random times. The game logic acts like a traffic cop, managing the behavior of all of these busy components and enabling a smooth gaming experience.

Your game logic may encompass:

- Enforcing the rules of the game
- Interpreting the user input as a move or command that may affect the current game state
- Direct the overall program flow
- Moving the user from screen to screen
- Implementing game physics and artificial intelligence
- Directing all of the graphical and audio elements in the game
- Keeping track of time and making things happen without specific user input

Of course your game logic may perform many more tasks depending on the game! In our games the game logic will be executed within a well-defined method called by the XNA framework many times a second.

User Interactions

The final conceptual part of the game engine is the user interface. This section manages the human input and output for the game. Typically, a user gives input with the keyboard, mouse or game controller. The XNA framework makes it very easy to determine when keys are pressed or mouse buttons are clicked! Part of your game design should specify what specific actions are taken when keys are pressed or mouse movements or clicks are detected.

Output is given through graphics on the screen or audio sound effects and music. You will write well-defined methods to draw images on the screen that represent your game objects, according to your game state. The XNA framework will automatically call your methods when the screen needs to be repainted.

Example Game Engine

To give you a better idea of how the game engine pieces will work together, let's take a look at a simple Tic-Tac-Toe game example. The game engine might be implemented as follows:

Game State	The game state consists of a 3x3 grid representing the 9 cells on the Tic-Tac-Toe board. Each cell in the grid can be either blank or contain an X or O. The game state would also contain a variable to keep track of which player will make the next move.
Game Logic	The game logic would examine each player's move to determine if it is valid. If a user tries to put an X or an O on the board, the logic will first make sure that the square is blank, and then will update the game state to contain an X or an O in the square. Once the X or O is added, the controller will also check to see if there are now 3 Xs or 3 Os in a row which would complete the game.
User Interactions	The user input may consist of mouse clicks on the Tic-Tac-Toe board. The mouse clicks must be detected and translated to determine which square (if any) was clicked. User output would include drawing the game board based on the current game state, and displaying an indication of the current player's turn.

Now that we have designed the game engine, we have a pretty good idea of how to start writing the game! We know which sort of variables to declare. We know we'll need to write several methods dealing with input validation and translation, move verification, and game-over detection. We also know we'll need to have images available to draw the game board and represent the X and O symbols.

Lesson Three: Creating a New XNA Game Project

In this course (as in the first semester *TeenCoder^{TM}: Windows Programming* course), we will be using the Visual C# 2010 Express software. This software is also referred to as an IDE (Integrated Development Environment), which is a single place where you can create your screens, type in your code, and run and debug your program. Everything you need as a programmer can be found in your IDE.

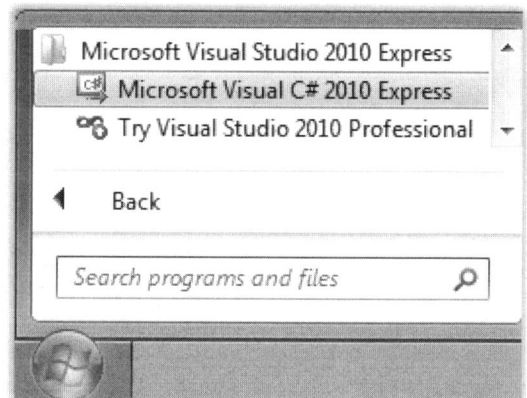

Let's take a look at your Visual C# IDE, which you should have installed in the last course or in the first chapter activity. To start this application, click on your Windows Start button, and then click on "Programs". You should see an icon for "Microsoft Visual C# 2010 Express". This is the Visual C# IDE, so go ahead and run it!

In this lesson, we will walk through the creation of your first XNA game project. Follow along in your Visual C# software! Once your IDE is running, click on "File" and then "New Project".

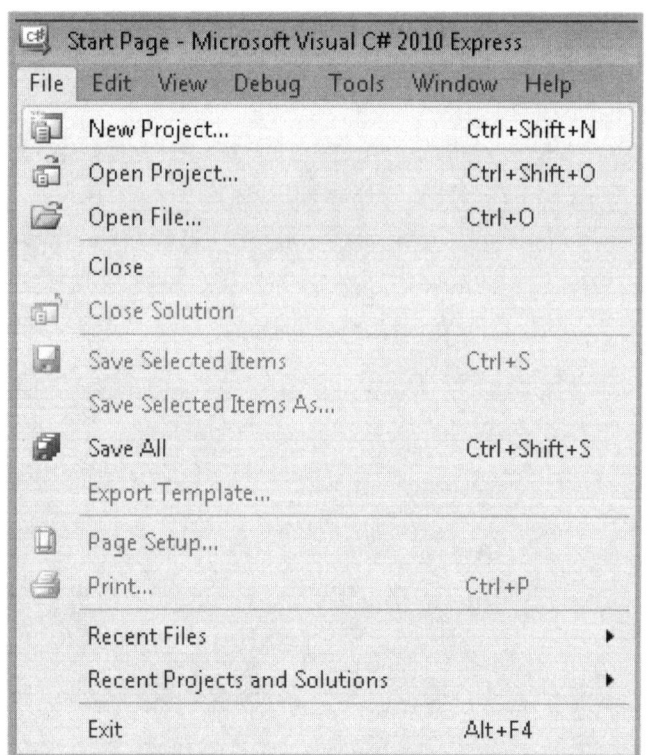

So far, these screens should seem very familiar to you. These are the same screens you would see for any other C# program.

Once you have chosen to start a "New Project", you should see the following screen:

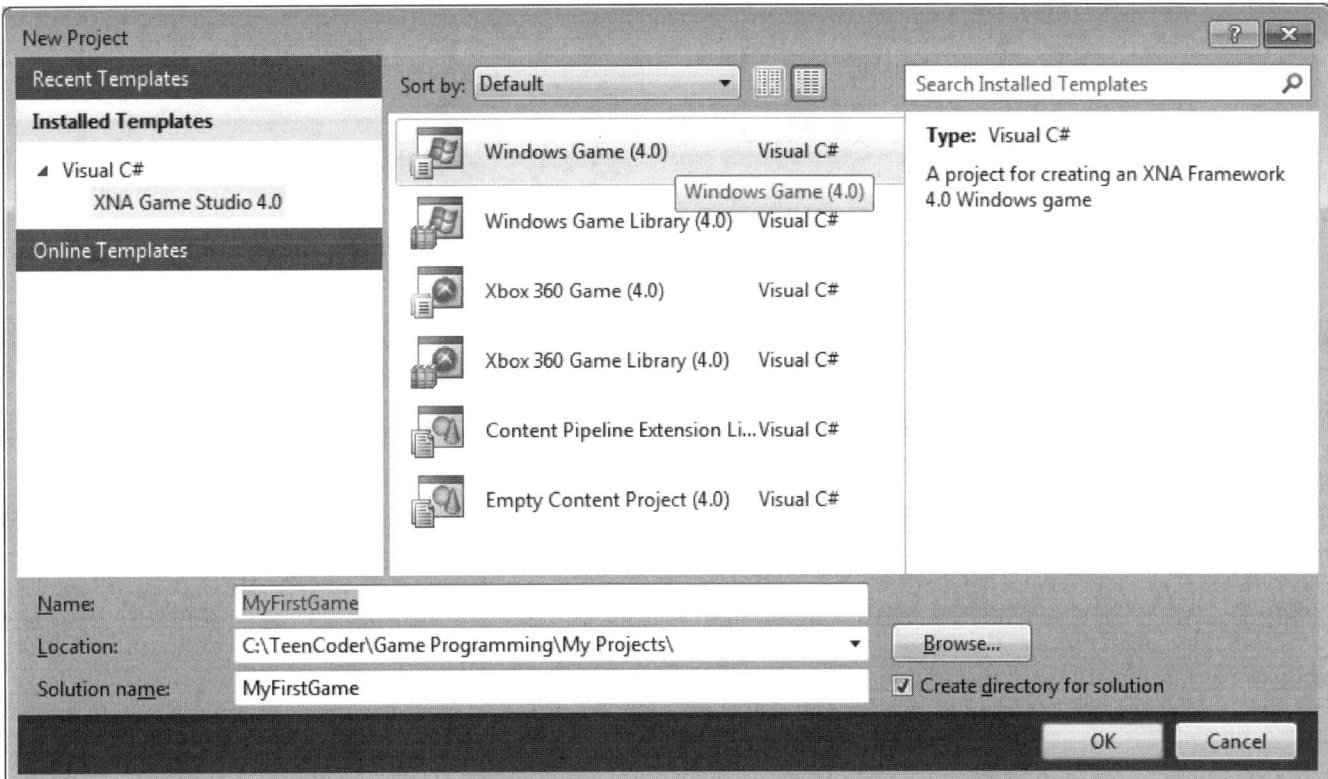

This screen should also look familiar, with a few notable additions! On the left side of the screen is an expandable menu that is titled: "Visual C#". If you click on "Visual C#", you will see the choices for creating a standard C# forms-based Windows program. In the menu below "Visual C#" is another item titled "XNA Game Studio 4.0". Click on this item to display the XNA Game templates as shown in the image above. These are the different types of XNA games that you can create with the XNA Game Studio libraries.

For this course we will be using the "Windows Game (4.0)" template. This will allow us to create games for the Windows operating system. In addition, you can create a project for the Xbox 360 game console with the "Xbox 360 Game (4.0)" template.

Notice that we have given our project a meaningful name ("MyFirstGame") and have changed the location to reflect the directory structure that we are using ("C:\TeenCoder\Game Programming\My Projects"). The default Location listed is likely some other folder, so make sure you have changed the Location field to match your "My Projects" directory.

Finally, we have allowed the IDE to use a Solution Name that is the same as our project name and we have told the software to create a directory for this solution in our "My Projects" directory. You should always create a separate directory for each of your projects to keep the files organized. Make sure your Solution Name does not contain any commas, apostrophes, or other special characters! Just use some combination of letters, numbers, and spaces to ensure your project compiles properly.

Once you click on the "OK" button, your new project will be created and you will see the following screen:

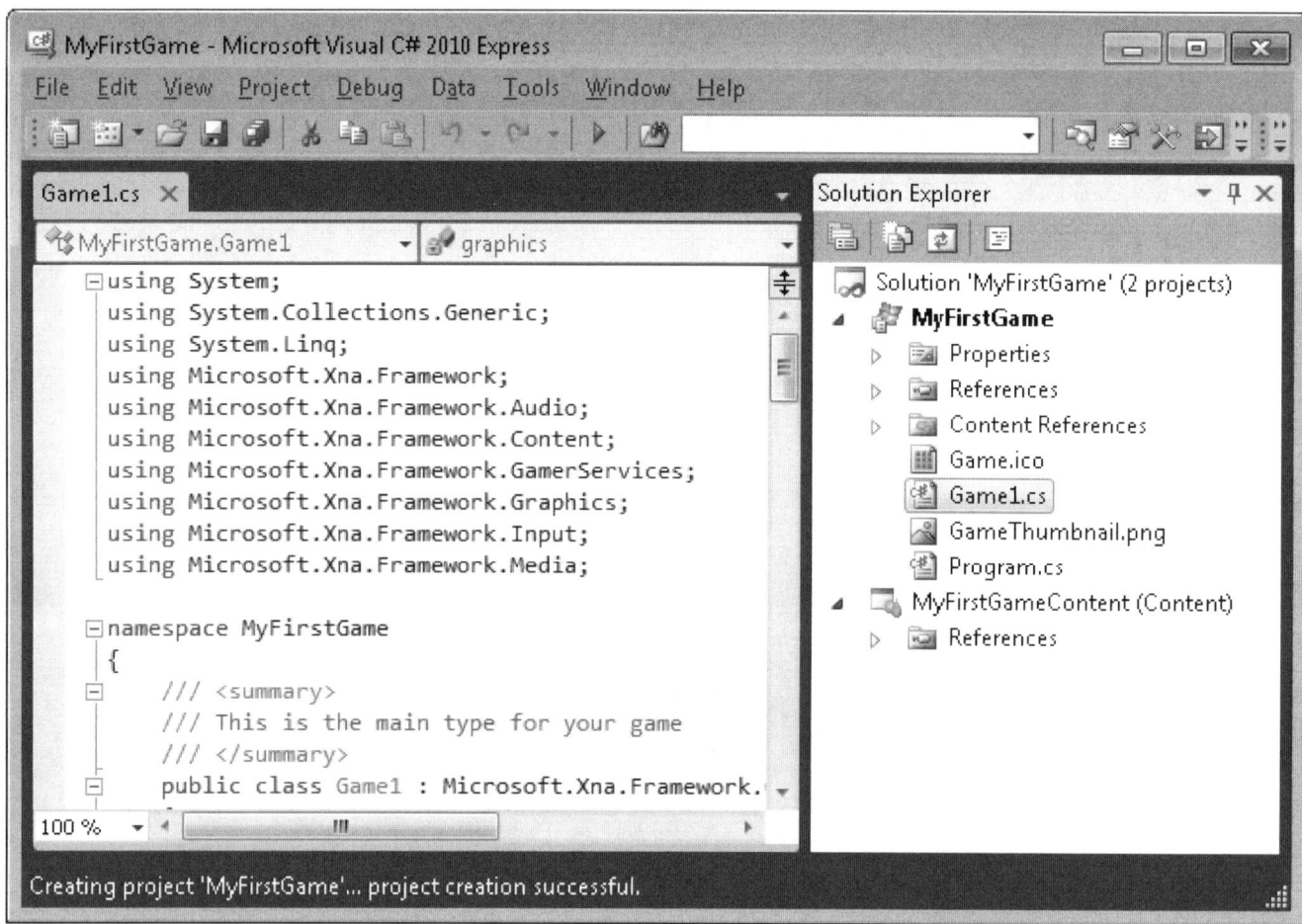

Since this is the same IDE window that you used many times in the previous course, we won't spend much time looking at each pane in detail. You can see that the main code file is called "Game1.cs" and is open in the code editor portion of the screen. The right side of the screen contains the Solution Explorer and perhaps a Properties window, and the bottom of the screen may show any information about errors or output from the project. Each of these panes can be moved or hidden to suite your personal tastes, so your IDE may not look exactly like the image shown. If any pane is hidden you can re-enable it from your "View" Menu.

Unlike a forms-based Windows program, in an XNA game project there is no **Form** object and no Form Design tab! Your entire game lives in the "Game1.cs" file, which you can of course rename and expand into other files. The default source code is preconfigured to use the XNA game libraries, events and functions. Let's take a tour of the important parts of this file now!

The Microsoft.Xna.Framework Namespace

At the very top of your "Game1.cs" file you see a series of **using** statements for XNA namespaces:

Chapter Two: Game Design

```
using Microsoft.Xna.Framework;
using Microsoft.Xna.Framework.Audio;
using Microsoft.Xna.Framework.Content;
using Microsoft.Xna.Framework.GamerServices;
using Microsoft.Xna.Framework.Graphics;
using Microsoft.Xna.Framework.Input;
using Microsoft.Xna.Framework.Media;
using Microsoft.Xna.Framework.Net;
using Microsoft.Xna.Framework.Storage;
```

These statements will import all of the things from the .NET framework and the XNA framework that you will need to complete your game. All XNA objects we discuss throughout the course live somewhere in the **Microsoft.Xna.Framework** namespace hierarchy. In the IDE you can hold your mouse over the name of an object and a tool tip should show the full hierarchy to you. It's possible you won't use objects from every namespace listed, but there is no reason to remove the unused statements so leave them alone.

Later as we develop enhancements in our own library you'll want to add an additional **using** statement to bring in the namespace of our new widgets. You may develop some nice components on your own that you'd like to share between your games, so you can bring those in as well with more **using** statements.

Game Class

The main class representing your overall program is derived from the XNA **Game** object:

```
public class Game1 : Microsoft.Xna.Framework.Game
```

A normal graphical Windows program would have a main class derived from the **Form** object. However in XNA game programming we aren't using **Forms** at all! The **Game** class provides the fundamental infrastructure needed for your game. Your main program class inherits from **Game**.

The main program class defaults to the "Game1" name, but you can change that name to better reflect your actual game. To rename your **Game1** main class, right-click on the "Game1.cs" file in your 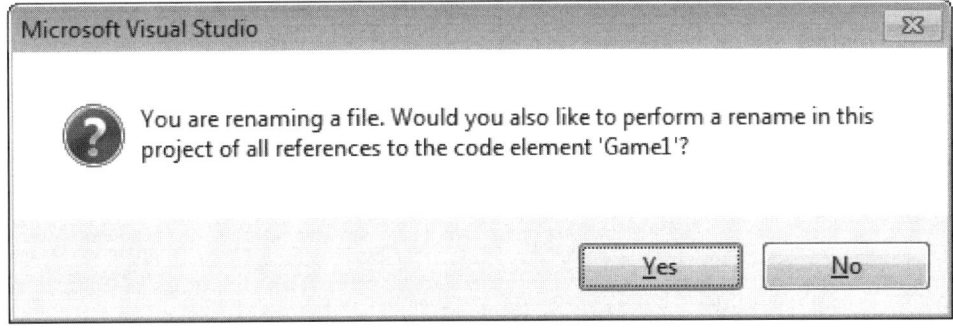 Solution Explorer. Select "Rename" and then type in your new class name, such as "MyFirstGame.cs". Click "Yes" on the next pop-up to rename your main class and other references to the new name! It's that easy!

Default Member Variables

Two member variables of your **Game1** subclass are automatically declared for you in the default project:

```
GraphicsDeviceManager graphics;
SpriteBatch spriteBatch;
```

The **GraphicsDeviceManager** class provides information and management about the graphics capabilities of your computer screen. The **SpriteBatch** class will allow you to draw images on the screen when the window needs to be repainted. We'll cover these objects in more detail later.

The **Game1** constructor has been automatically created for you. It will create a **GraphicsDeviceManager** and specify the directory where your content (images, fonts, and audio) can be found.

```
public Game1()
{
    graphics = new GraphicsDeviceManager(this);
    Content.RootDirectory = "Content";
}
```

The first line creates a new **GraphicsDeviceManager** based on this instance of the game program and assigns it to your `graphics` variable for later use. The second line establishes the directory where your content can be found. The **Content** object is a member of the **Game** class, and by setting the **RootDirectory** property to "Content" we are saying that the audio, image, and font files will be in a subdirectory called "Content". You will learn how to use the Content directory in the next chapter. That's all the default constructor contains, though you may add other initialization code for your game if needed.

Initialize() Method

The next method you'll see in the default project is the **Initialize()** method.

```
protected override void Initialize()
{
    // TODO: Add your initialization logic here
    base.Initialize();
}
```

Initialize() is called automatically by the XNA framework at the start of the game program just after the call to the **Game()** constructor. This is a good place to perform any other setup tasks your program requires. Make sure there is a call to the base class's **Initialize()** method to complete internal XNA setup tasks, such as loading Content files.

LoadContent() Method

The next method you'll see in your project is **LoadContent()**. The XNA framework will call this method automatically to give you a chance to load your game's image, sound, and font files from your Content directory. The method will also initialize the **spriteBatch** member variable declared in your main class in order to enable drawing of images (also known as *textures*).

```
protected override void LoadContent()
{
    // Create a new SpriteBatch, which can be used to draw textures.
    spriteBatch = new SpriteBatch(GraphicsDevice);

    // TODO: use this.Content to load your game content here
}
```

UnloadContent() Method

The **UnloadContent()** method is called just before the game exits. If you have performed any custom content management outside the XNA framework, this will give you a chance to release those resources.

```
protected override void UnloadContent()
{
    // TODO: Unload any non ContentManager content here
}
```

However all of the content we will use from **LoadContent()** is tracked by the XNA framework and automatically released, so there typically isn't anything to do here!

Update() Method

The **Update()** method is one of the two most important methods in your game! This method will be responsible for executing all of your game logic. Here, you can update your on-screen object positions and images to simulate movement, process user input, and so forth. The XNA framework will call this method at regular intervals. The default frequency is 60 times a second but you can adjust the rate as needed.

The **Update()** method contains a few lines of code when a new project is created:

```
protected override void Update(GameTime gameTime)
{
    // Allows the game to exit
    if (GamePad.GetState(PlayerIndex.One).Buttons.Back ==
                                                ButtonState.Pressed)
        this.Exit();

    // TODO: Add your update logic here

    base.Update(gameTime);
}
```

The first line will check to see if the player has pressed the Back button on the Xbox 360 game pad (if any), and will exit the game if pressed. Although you may use a game pad if you have one, it is not required for this course! We will demonstrate mouse and keyboard input in later chapters. Next you should perform all of your game logic. When finished, call the **base.Update()** method at the very end to allow the XNA framework to perform all internal housekeeping.

Draw() Method

The **Draw()** method is the second important function that will be called automatically by the XNA framework. This method handles all of the drawing (sometimes called *rendering*) in the game program. **Draw()** is called just after the **Update()** method. When the **Draw()** method executes, it will clear the screen to a background color, then draw the game graphics on top. This method also contains a few lines of automatically generated code when you create a new project:

```
protected override void Draw(GameTime gameTime)
{
    GraphicsDevice.Clear(Color.CornflowerBlue);

    // TODO: Add your drawing code here

    base.Draw(gameTime);
}
```

The first line will clear the background for the game and will then fill it with a blue color. The second line just calls the base **Draw()** method for the base **Game** class. In between those two lines you will eventually add all of your game rendering code!

Chapter Two: Game Design

Build and Run the Default Project

Build and run your XNA project just like any other Forms-based Windows project. Find and click the green arrow near the top of the IDE, or just hit the "F5" key. When your new project is compiled and run, you will see the screen shown to the right:

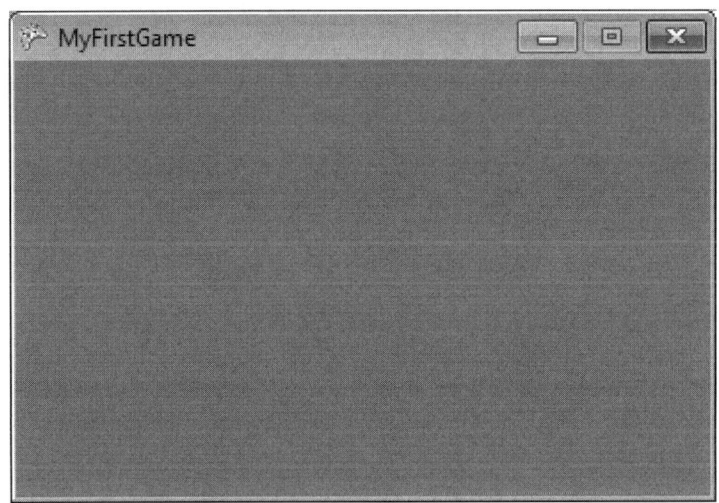

This is the default XNA screen and simply shows the "Cornflower Blue" color that was set in the **Draw()** method for the game.

"HiDef" vs. "Reach" Graphics

Your Windows XNA projects can use one of two graphics modes:

HiDef	This is the default setting, which uses the latest graphics card hardware and DirectX standards.
Reach	This setting is compatible with older graphics cards and some earlier DirectX standards.

If you have a recent computer or updated graphics card, the default "HiDef" setting will work fine. If you receive the message shown on the right when you attempt to run an XNA game, then your hardware is not compatible with HiDef and you need to change to the Reach setting!

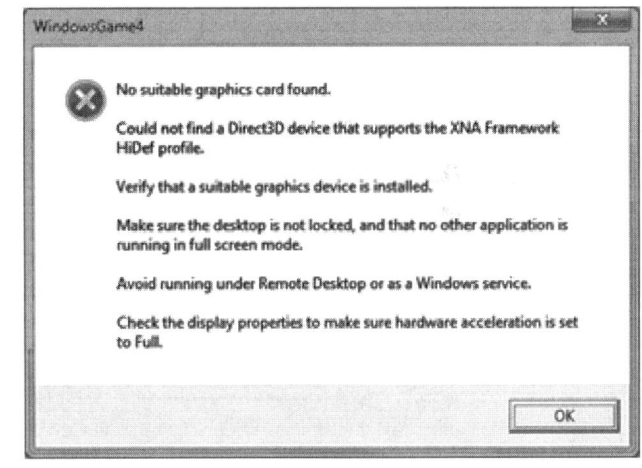

To change your graphics settings, right-click on your project name in the Solution Explorer and select "Properties". On the first "XNA Game Studio" tab, change the "Use HiDef…" setting to "Use Reach…", then save and rebuild your project.

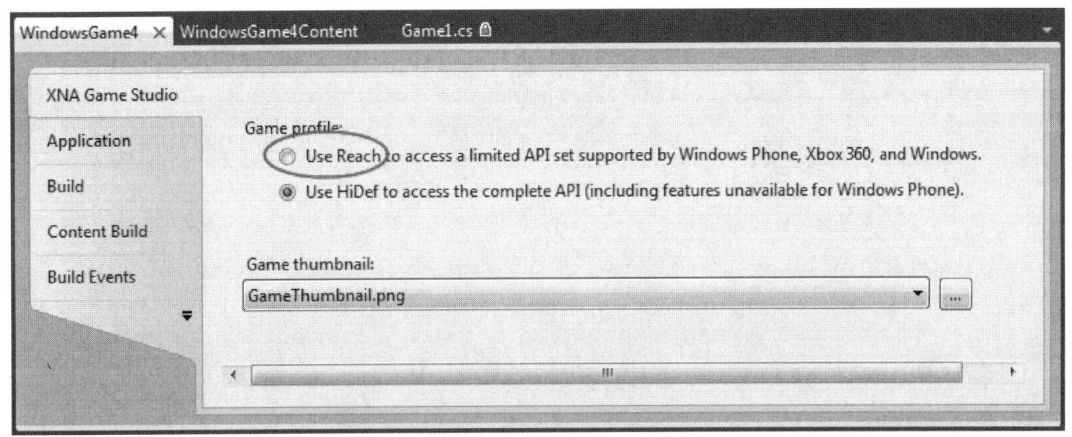

All game projects in this course will work fine with either HiDef or Reach settings.

Lesson Four: The Game Loop

A *game loop* is a function or set of statements that will execute repeatedly while the game is running. Within a game loop you can perform an action that occurs at regular intervals, regardless of whether or not the user is doing anything in the game. For instance, let's say we have an asteroid that needs to fly around the screen, imperiling our little space ship. We cause the asteroid to move by adjusting the asteroid's screen coordinates a small distance at regular intervals. This same theory can also be used to animate an image, detect and handle user input, or play a series of sounds. Everything within the game loop is generally considered to be the "logic" portion of your game engine. Game loops typically run very fast, on the order of 60 times a second!

The XNA framework provides a game loop for you. An XNA game will automatically call the **Update()** and **Draw()** methods that we discussed previously. These methods work together as follows: the **Update()** method is called first. Inside this method you implement your game logic to control all of the elements in your game (updating object positions, etc). Once **Update()** is complete, XNA will call the **Draw()** method.

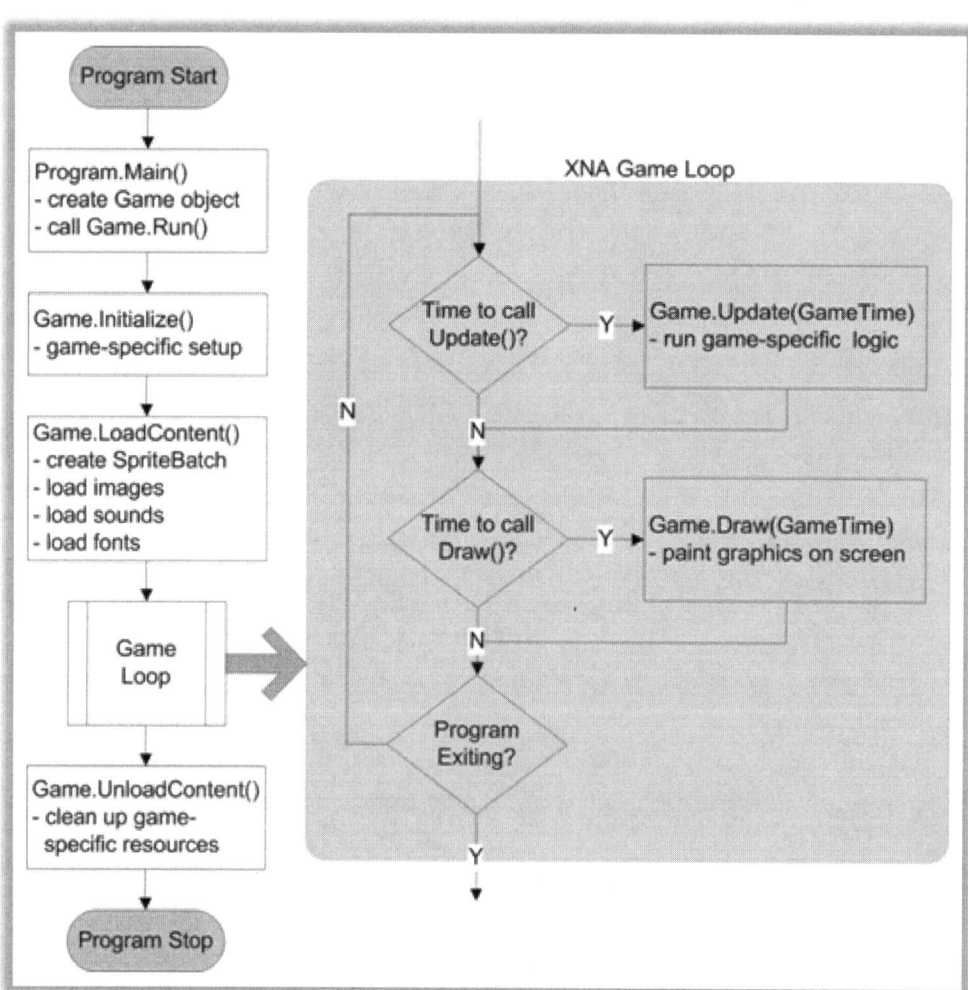

The **Draw()** method will erase the screen and re-paint it with the graphics information you specified during the **Update()** logic.

This **Update** – **Draw** cycle continues until the user decides to exit the game. It all happens very quickly, so if you make small changes to your game state each cycle you'll create the illusion of smooth movement and animation on screen.

Review the flowchart to the right to understand the overall flow of an XNA game. Each step from "Program Start", through **Game** initialization, loading content, entering the game loop, and exiting the program should now be familiar to you after learning about the default methods (**Initialize()**, etc) provided in each XNA game project. The XNA Framework handles the game loop shown in the shaded gray area; you simply need to implement the **Update** and **Draw** methods!

Game Loop Timing Control

The timing for the XNA game loop can be controlled within your code. The default rate is 60 cycles per second, which is fast enough to smoothly animate graphics on the screen without any jerky side effects. However, it is possible to change this rate either faster or slower to meet the needs of your program. To do this, simply add the following line of code within your **Initialize()** method:

```
this.TargetElapsedTime = TimeSpan.FromSeconds(1.0f);
```

You have now changed the time interval for the game loop to once per second. This is extremely slow, and wouldn't be very useful for most games, but it could be useful to watch the game in slow motion to debug a problem. You can also speed up the interval, like this:

```
this.TargetElapsedTime = TimeSpan.FromSeconds(1.0f / 100.0f);
```

Now you have caused the game loop to run 100 times per second (or once every 1/100th of a second). This is extremely fast, but you need to be very careful! If you speed up the interval too much, you could run into a situation where the **Update()** and **Draw()** methods can't finish their tasks in time and the next cycle will be delayed regardless of your **TargetElapsedTime** setting. In most situations the default 60 cycles per second loop rate is fine – you shouldn't adjust it unless you have a very good reason for doing so!

Chapter Review

- Creating a computer game is a very creative process, but organization and planning are also required to complete a successful game design.
- Creating a game in "baby steps" helps to break the game into manageable tasks and makes the testing and debugging phase much easier.
- The computer game "engine" is the brain responsible for controlling all aspects of the game.
- Game engines can be divided into several general sections: game state, game logic, and user interactions.
- Our XNA games are created in the C# language, using the Visual C# 2010 Express software and XNA Game Studio 4.0.
- The **Game** class is the base for your main class representing the overall program.
- When an XNA game is created, several methods and variables are automatically added for you, including the game constructor, **Initialize()**, **LoadContent()**, **UnloadContent()**, **Update()** and **Draw()** methods and the `spriteBatch` and `graphics` member variables.
- A *game loop* is a set of code that will execute repeatedly while the game is running.
- XNA automatically forms a game loop by calling your **Update()** and **Draw()** methods.
- The default XNA game loop executes approximately 60 times a second.

Activity: Looping Colors

In this activity you will create a program that will simply change the background color for the screen once per second. This will demonstrate your ability to create a new XNA game project, control the game loop rate, perform some **Update()** logic, and paint the screen from within the **Draw()** method.

Your activity requirements and instructions are found in the "Chapter_02_Activity.pdf" document located in your "TeenCoder\Game Programming\Activity Docs" folder. You can access this document through your Student Menu or by double-clicking on it from Windows Explorer.

Complete this activity now and ensure your program meets the requirements before continuing!

Chapter Three: Graphics Concepts

In this chapter you will learn how computer screen images are handled within your game code. We will discuss changing the windows size and toggling between windowed and full-screen mode. Finally, you will learn how colors are represented numerically.

Lesson One: Screen Coordinates

Computer screens are all made of individual dots called *pixels*. These pixels are arranged on the screen in a grid pattern. You may have heard a screen's size described in terms of its resolution: 800x600, 1024x768, or 1920x1080. These numbers describe the screen width and height in terms of pixel counts. A screen that has a resolution of 800x600 is displaying a grid of 800 pixels across and 600 pixels down.

Each pixel on a screen is capable of displaying a single color at a time. The actual color can change, depending on what the program wants to display, but a single pixel can only show one color at a time. The grouping of different colored pixels is what creates the vibrantly-colored images you see on a screen.

Each pixel on the screen is uniquely identified by a pair of numbers. This two-coordinate system contains a column number or width (the X-coordinate) and a row number or height (the Y-coordinate). The X-coordinate tells us how far the pixel is from the left of the screen. The Y-coordinate tells us how far the pixel is from the top of the screen. These two coordinates are often grouped into a "coordinate pair" that looks like this: **(x, y)**.

The upper-left coordinate on a computer screen is always (0, 0). As you move across the screen to the right, the X-coordinate (first number) increases. The next pixel over from (0, 0) would be (1, 0) and the next would be (2, 0). As you move down the screen, the Y-coordinate (second number) increases. The next pixel down from (0, 0) would be (0, 1) and the next down would be (0, 2). To the right you see a small grid demonstrating some coordinate pairs.

X →		
0,0	1,0	2,0
0,1	1,1	2,1
0,2	1,2	2,2

Y ↓

Programs running within a window on the screen don't really care about any of the graphics outside the window. The program logic also doesn't care where the window is positioned on the screen. The only thing the program logic needs to do is update the *client area* – the area within the window underneath any title bar, system menu, or dialog border. For this reason, when programming, you will almost always treat the upper-left corner of your client area as the (0, 0) point! Don't worry about where your window lies on the screen or what absolute (physical) screen coordinates correspond to the client area. The operating system will take care of that translation for you.

 **Computer Y-coordinates are backwards from the standard Cartesian coordinate system! Always remember when working with computer graphics that "up" is a negative Y direction and "down" is a positive Y direction! The Math library's trigonometric functions treat Y as positive in the "up" direction, however, so you will have to account for that change if you compute angle from screen coordinates.**

Images

A complete image contains many pixels in a rectangular group. For convenience the position of an image on the screen is identified using a single coordinate pair, usually the upper-left corner of the image. This location is called the *origin* of the image. The XNA drawing functions know how to position all of the pixels in the image given just that one coordinate pair.

The boundaries of an object or image on the screen are typically identified in one of two ways:

- The top-left coordinate pair plus a width and a height
- The top-left coordinate pair and a bottom-right coordinate pair.

Here are examples of both types of identifiers:

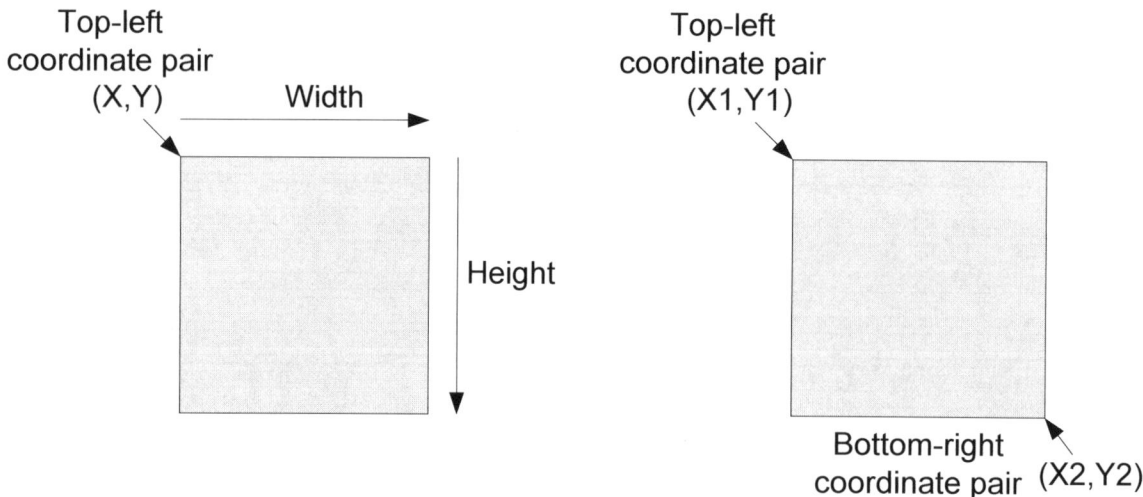

The diagram on the left shows an image with the upper-left coordinates plus a width and height. With this information we can use some simple math to determine the bottom-right point:

- The square's bottom-right X-coordinate = (upper-left X-coordinate) + (width of the square) - 1.
- The square's bottom-right Y-coordinate = (upper-left Y-coordinate) + (height of the square) - 1.

The diagram on the right shows an image with its upper-left coordinate pair and its bottom-right coordinate pair). Given this information you can easily figure out the width and height of the image as follows:

- The square's width = (bottom-right X-coordinate) – (upper-left X-coordinate) + 1.
- The square's height = (bottom-right Y-coordinate) – (upper-left Y-coordinate) + 1.

Vectors

Any code that involves graphics on the screen needs to make use of coordinate pairs on a regular basis. For this reason, the XNA Framework has defined an object called Microsoft.Xna.Framework.**Vector2**, which can be used to easily store a pair of X and Y-coordinates.

The **Vector2** has two numeric properties: **X** and **Y**. You can use a **Vector2** to represent either a location (X- and Y-coordinates of a pixel) or a size (width and height, in pixels) of an object. This data type is usually more convenient to use than keeping track of two separate numbers for X and Y or width and height.

You declare and initialize a **Vector2** variable just like any other reference object, and then you set the X and Y properties just like any normal class property:

```
Vector2 myVector = new Vector2();
myVector.X = 100.0f;
myVector.Y = 100.0f;
```

We will use the **Vector2** data type often in our game programs. In addition to pixel coordinates or width and height, you can use a **Vector2** to represent any two related pieces of numeric data. For instance, you may track an object's speed in the up/down and left/right directions by using a **Vector2**.

Why Floating Point?

Sharp-eyed readers notice that the **Vector2** X and Y properties are **float** instead of **int** data types. Pixels are represented by integer coordinates – it's impossible to position something on-screen at (2.5, 3.7)! Image widths and heights are also integers since images are formed from discrete numbers of pixels in each direction. Why then would a **Vector2** keep track of floating point numbers?

One good reason is that you may be attempting to move an image slowly across the screen. Let's say you want to start an image at X-coordinate 50 and move it 1 pixel to the right every 10 cycles through the game loop. You would naturally want to add 0.1 to the image location each time through the game loop. However if you stored the position as an integer, and then added 0.1 to it, the resulting value of 50.1 would be rounded back down to 50 when storing into an integer. So your object would never move!

Storing floating point numbers to track image positions gives you very fine control over the location of the image. Returning to the preceding example, if you moved your object from location 50 by 0.1 every time through the game loop, the position would be updated to 50.1, 50.2, 50.3, and so on up to 51. When you pass that floating point number into the various graphics drawing methods it will always be automatically rounded up or down to the nearest integer in order to be placed in the correct location. So you would see the image in this example stay at location 50 for the first 5 cycles of the game loop, and then nudge over to location 51 for the next 5 cycles.

Lesson Two: Full Screen vs. Window Mode

So far you have created all of your programs in *window mode*. This means that each program runs within the bounds of a window on the screen. You can see multiple windowed programs on the screen at one time, and the operating system will take care of allowing the user to switch between applications, moving and resizing the windows, showing the title bar at the top, etc.

Game programs, however, are often run in *full screen mode*. This means that the program encompasses the entire monitor screen with no visible title bars, menu bars, status bars, or window border. Full screen mode is popular for computer games for several reasons. First, by using the full screen for the game, we have more space to draw graphics and animations. Second, a player is less likely to accidentally change the focus from the game to another window on the screen. Third, a full screen game promotes immersion in the game experience for the game player. This mode makes them feel more like they are part of the game without any other applications lurking in the background as a distraction.

The XNA Windows game template will automatically generate a game running in window mode. In this lesson we will discuss how to programmatically change the size of your window and switch between windowed mode and full-screen mode.

GraphicsDeviceManager

In XNA game programming, the display screen (a computer monitor, television, or Windows phone) is referred to as a *graphics device*. In order to control the various features and options for these devices, we use a class called the **GraphicsDeviceManager**. As you saw when you created a new project, the default code contains a variable at class level called **graphics** of type **GraphicsDeviceManager**:

```
GraphicsDeviceManager graphics;
```

This variable is then initialized in your game's main constructor:

```
graphics = new GraphicsDeviceManager(this);
```

You will use the **graphics** object to perform actions like toggling between full-screen and windowed mode and setting the current size of the game window.

Chapter Three: Graphics Concepts

 Changing between full-screen and windowed mode isn't something that happens very quickly, so don't plan a lot of switching around in your game. It's usually best to pick a mode and stick with it!

Changing the Window Size

When in window mode you can set the size of your window (in pixels) like this:

```
graphics.PreferredBackBufferWidth = 300;
graphics.PreferredBackBufferHeight = 400;
graphics.ApplyChanges();
```

You have now set your window's width to 300 and the height to 400. Notice you need to call the **graphics**.ApplyChanges() in order to make the window actually resize itself. The width and height you set using these properties is for the client area of the window only. The title bar, menu, and window border all require a bit of extra space!

Getting the Window Size

You can read the current window size out of the **GraphicsDevice** object. The **GraphicsDevice** object has a property called **Viewport**, which represents the viewable area of the window. The **Viewport** property has two useful sub-properties you can read:

```
GraphicsDevice.Viewport.Width    // the width of the window, in pixels
GraphicsDevice.Viewport.Height   // the height of the screen, in pixels
```

You will use these properties frequently later on to determine the boundaries of your window when moving images around on the screen!

Display Modes

The graphics card in a computer is capable of displaying a limited set of screen resolutions. It may be able to support 1024 x 768 pixels, 1280 x 1024 pixels, and so on. The set of available display modes may be further limited by the type of monitor you have – normal or wide screen. If you want to write a game to operate in full screen mode, you will want to determine which modes to support. You could select one simple mode that you think everyone will have (e.g. 1024 x 768) or perhaps a limited subset that allows players with better graphics hardware to pick a wide screen or higher resolution. The nature of your game will determine how hard it is to support additional modes. Your images may or may not scale well as you go to higher modes, or your code may be simpler to write if you assume one mode with fixed width and height. Some games might naturally support all available modes as the graphics and game logic will adapt easily to any dimensions.

Once you decide to go to a full screen mode, the first task is to determine what modes are actually available! You can do this by querying an object called the **GraphicsAdapter**. This object provides some useful information about the current settings on the user's video card. On the **GraphicsAdapter** is a property called **DefaultAdapter** which represents your primary graphics adapter. That **DefaultAdapter** contains a collection of **DisplayMode** objects. The **DisplayMode**, as you might expect, specifies information about one particular mode such as width and height. Let's look at an example that will examine the available modes:

```
foreach (DisplayMode mode in
        GraphicsAdapter.DefaultAdapter.SupportedDisplayModes)
{
    // mode.Width contains the width of this mode, in pixels
    // mode.Height contains the height of this mode, in pixels
}
```

If your game has chosen one or more specific modes to support, at runtime you can query the available modes in this manner and ensure that at least one has a width and height equal to a mode you support.

Even when your game is not actually running in full-screen mode (or running at all!) the operating system has chosen a display mode for the Windows graphical environment. You can find out your current display mode resolution by querying the **DefaultAdapter.CurrentDisplayMode** property. This property will tell us the current height and width of the entire screen.

```
int width = GraphicsAdapter.DefaultAdapter.CurrentDisplayMode.Width;
int height = GraphicsAdapter.DefaultAdapter.CurrentDisplayMode.Height;
```

You may choose not to set any specific mode at all and just go into full-screen mode using whatever resolution the user has currently set.

Entering and Exiting Full Screen Mode

If you want to enter full-screen mode using whatever screen resolution the user has currently set, you simply set a flag on the **graphics** object and then apply the changes:

```
graphics.IsFullScreen = true;
graphics.ApplyChanges();
```

Alternatively, if you want to pick a specific mode and you are sure the computer's graphics adapter supports your chosen width and height, set the preferred back buffer dimensions first:

```
graphics.PreferredBackBufferWidth = 1024;
graphics.PreferredBackBufferHeight = 768;
graphics.IsFullScreen = true;
graphics.ApplyChanges();
```

Now if you were to compile and run our program, it would show up as a true full screen program. But wait! You're not done yet! At this point, if you run the game, you will have no way to exit, since there is no longer a title bar with an "X" icon. Full screen applications require that we set up some other means for the user to exit the application. For now we will simply define a key the user can press that will exit the program.

To respond to a user key press, in your **Update()** function you can add these few lines. You will learn more about keyboard handling in a later chapter, but this should get you started.

```
KeyboardState currentKeyboard = Keyboard.GetState();
if (currentKeyboard.IsKeyDown(Keys.Space))
    this.Exit();
```

The first line retrieves the current state of the keyboard, which includes what keys are being pressed down or released. The second line checks to see if the user is pressing the space bar key. If they are pressing this key, we call the game's **Exit()** method, which will end the game program.

Alternatively you can switch back to window mode, perhaps in response to a key press, and then allow the user to close the window in the normal manner.

```
KeyboardState currentKeyboard = Keyboard.GetState();
if (currentKeyboard.IsKeyDown(Keys.Space))
{
        graphics.IsFullScreen = false;
        graphics.ApplyChanges();
}
```

Changing back to windows mode is as simple as setting the **graphics**.IsFullScreen flag back to **false** and then applying the changes.

Toggling Between Full Screen and Windowed Game

The **GraphicsDeviceManager** object has defined a convenient method called **ToggleFullScreen()**. This method will switch a program into full-screen mode if currently a window, or switch into window mode if currently full screen. You do not need to apply the changes afterwards, this is done automatically. With the following code we allow the user to switch between modes each time the space bar is hit:

```
    KeyboardState currentKeyboard = Keyboard.GetState();
    if (currentKeyboard.IsKeyDown(Keys.Space))
    {
        graphics.ToggleFullScreen();
    }
```

Now when the user presses the spacebar, the game will automatically change from full screen to window mode and back again. You will find that each mode switch takes several seconds, so it's not something you want the user to do that frequently.

Because switching to full screen mode takes a bit of extra effort, including special keys to exit the game, we won't make any of the games in this course use the full-screen mode. However you are welcome to enable full screen for any game using the switching techniques outlined above!

Lesson Three: Colored Pixels

As you now know, computer screens are made up of many tiny dots called pixels. You have learned how to identify a pixel by unique coordinate pair. Each pixel can be made to show one color. When you group many pixels of different colors on the screen, you get an image! In this lesson we will take a closer look how pixel colors are defined.

Color Models

To understand how an individual pixel gets its color, let's take a look at the two most common color models: Additive and Subtractive. Most people are familiar with the Subtractive color model. This model creates colors with paints, pigments or inks. In this model, yellow and blue make green, red and blue make purple, and when you mix all the colors together, you get black. The Subtractive model starts with a white background and, as you add colors, the result gets darker and darker. Professional printers will typically use three main colors: cyan (C), magenta (M), and yellow (Y). Add in some black ink (K) and these CMYK colors can be blended together to create almost any color in nature.

Chapter Three: Graphics Concepts

A computer cannot use paints or inks to display an image on the screen. Instead, the colors on a computer screen are created with projected lights. This color model is called the Additive color model. In this model you start with a black screen and add light of different colors (frequencies). As you add colors the result gets lighter and lighter. The three main colors in Additive color models are red (R), green (G), and blue (B); this is commonly known as the RGB color mode. You can mix red and green to make yellow, red and blue to make magenta, and so on. Mixing all the colors together produces white.

An example of these two color models is seen below. The Subtractive model is on the left and the Additive model is seen on the right.

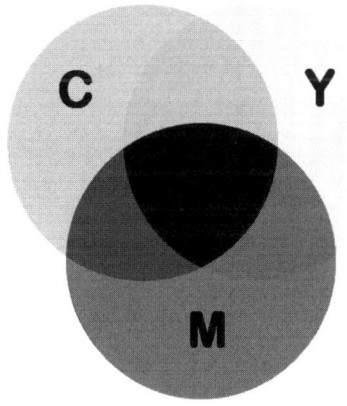 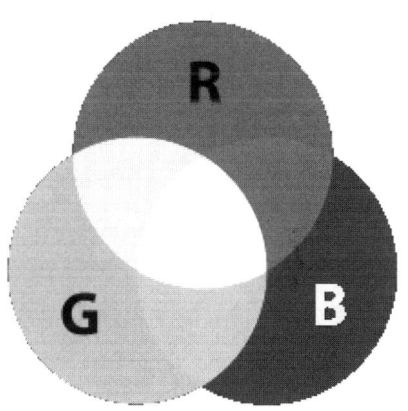

Since our eyes also use projected light to view the world, the Additive color model is how your eyes naturally view color!

RGB Pixels

Each pixel on a computer screen has the ability to emit finely controlled amounts of red, green and blue light. This is why a computer's color scheme is often referred to as "RGB Color". The intensity at which each of these colors projects will determine the final color of the pixel. Each color's intensity can be represented by a number between 0 and 255 (one byte or 8 bits). For the three colors together you would require 3 bytes or 24 bits to show all possible combinations. When you calculate the different possible color combinations for these values, the results are amazing! In a 24-bit color system, there are over 16 million possible colors for each pixel on the screen.

 **24-bit color is often referred to as "true color" because pixels with that high definition can represent photographic-quality images.**

Color Class

So how do we tap into the power of all of these possible colors? The .NET Framework has a built in class called **Color**. You can declare variables of type **Color** and then assign specific colors to them, like this:

```
Color myColor = Color.Blue;
```

Or you can create your own color, by using three RGB values between 0 and 255:

```
Color myColor = new Color(80,50,255);
```

The **Color** constructor will accept individual intensities for the red, green and blue colors. In the above example, the first value is the intensity for the red color (80), the second is for the green color (50) and the last is for the blue intensity (255). The values noted above will give us a bluish-purple color. The input data type is **byte**, so be sure to downcast if you are using a larger integer.

Alpha Channel

A **Color** object also keeps track of one other value – the *alpha* channel value. The alpha channel controls the transparency for a color. If a color has an alpha channel value of 0, it is fully transparent, meaning it will not show up at all. If the value is 255, the pixel is opaque, meaning the actual color will show in full. This is extremely useful if you want an image to have a transparent background. Let's take a look at an example!

We have created an image of a tree and a landscape image, and then drawn the tree on top of the landscape. In the left example, neither of the images have any transparency. Thus you can see the white background parts of the tree image have blocked the underlying landscape. In the image on the right we used transparency in the tree image. All of the white background pixels have an alpha value of 0. This means the tree, when drawn on top of the landscape, will allow the underlying landscape to show through wherever the tree image has an alpha of 0. This gives us a much more natural-looking composite image!

You can set a **Color** object's alpha channel by using a slightly different form of the constructor that takes four bytes instead of three:

```
myColor = new Color(80,50,255,255);   // the color is opaque
myColor = new Color(80,50,255,128);   // the color is semi-transparent
myColor = new Color(80,50,255,  0);   // the color is completely transparent
```

It is not likely that you'll have to manually adjust the alpha values for individual pixels or colors in your game. You should understand how the alpha channel works, however, since you'll want to choose an image editing program and/or image format that supports transparency when relevant.

Putting Transparency to Work

Not all types of image formats support an alpha channel. The most popular formats that support transparency are GIF and PNG. The JPG (JPEG) format does not support transparency! If you are planning a game that requires image transparency make sure all of your images come in GIF or PNG format.

It can be a bit confusing to work with transparent images in a graphics editor or painting program. Often the program itself will support transparency when you're working with the image on the screen. But, when you save the file, you will lose that transparency if you choose a format like JPG that does not support the alpha channel. Make sure you choose PNG or GIF when saving your image files if you care about preserving the transparency in the image.

Chapter Review

- Computer screens are all made of individual dots called pixels.
- Each pixel on a screen is capable of displaying a single color at a time.
- Pixels have two main properties: position and color.
- A two-coordinate system contains an X-coordinate (column) and a Y-coordinate (row).
- A **Vector2** object contains two floating point numeric properties: an X and Y coordinate.
- A **Vector2** can be used to represent any point on a computer screen.
- To change the size of your window, set the **Graphics.PreferredBackBufferWidth** and **Graphics.PreferredBackBufferHeight** and then call **Graphics.ApplyChanges()**.
- A full-screen game is a game which takes up the entire computer screen.
- Set the screen mode using the **GraphicsDeviceManager.IsFullScreen** property and then calling **Graphics.ApplyChanges()**.
- The **GraphicsDeviceManger.ToggleFullScreen()** method can be used to toggle between full screen and windowed mode while a game is running.
- There are two common color models: Additive and Subtractive. The Additive model is used to show colors on a computer screen.
- Computer pixels are given color values according to the RGB (red, green, blue) color system.
- The alpha channel value is used to set the transparency for a color.
- GIF and PNG image formats will support transparency settings with the alpha channel.

Chapter Three: Graphics Concepts

Activity: Screen Toggle

In this activity you will create a program that will define some custom colors and then allow the user to toggle between full-screen and windowed mode.

Your activity requirements and instructions are found in the "Chapter_03_Activity.pdf" document located in your "TeenCoder\Game Programming\Activity Docs" folder. You can access this document through your Student Menu or by double-clicking on it from Windows Explorer.

Complete this activity now and ensure your program meets the requirements before continuing!

Chapter Four: Working With Images

Games are usually very image-centric. Players spend most of their time viewing and interpreting the graphics you put on the screen. The user's experience can be greatly impacted by the quality of the images you use and your skill with making them behave as needed. In this chapter you will learn how to add images to a game, how to draw them on screen, how to scale and rotate images, and how to draw text.

Lesson One: Surfing the Content Pipeline

In XNA the images, sounds, and text fonts that make up the multi-media portion of your game are called *content*. In order to streamline and simplify the loading and use of this content, the XNA Framework contains a resource called the Content Pipeline. The Content Pipeline enables automatic loading of any supported media type. This includes many different kinds of image and sound files plus any font defined on your system.

The Content Node

In the Visual C# 2010 Express software you have a side pane entitled "Solution Explorer". An XNA project will include a node called "Content". This is where you will add all of your images, sounds, and fonts for your game program. Once these files have been added, they are automatically compiled into a file called an XNB (XNA Binary File) which contains relevant information about the content and the game platform on which it will be played. This preprocessing allows the content files to be loaded quickly during the game.

When a project is first created, the Solution Explorer pane should look something the example to the right. You will notice that we have a Content node already created for us, and it is empty except for a folder called "References". If you expand the References folder you'll see a list of several XNA Content Pipeline objects that will be used. You can leave these references alone; there will never be a reason to change anything in this folder during this course.

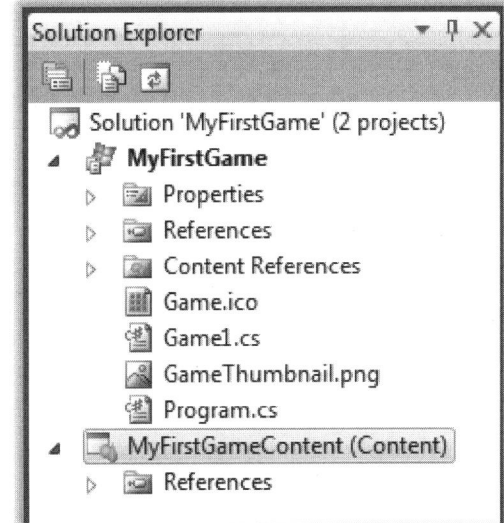

All of your image, sound, and font files will be added to the Content node so they can be used in your game.

Adding Files and Folders to the Content Node

The Content node allows you to add content files directly to the root, or you can create sub-folders in order to help keep your files organized. For very small games with few content files you might want to just put all of the content in the root. However as your games grow in complexity you'll have many content files, and it's good coding practice to organize content into as many sub-folders as needed ("Audio", "Image", etc). This will keep your game files from becoming too cluttered and unmanageable.

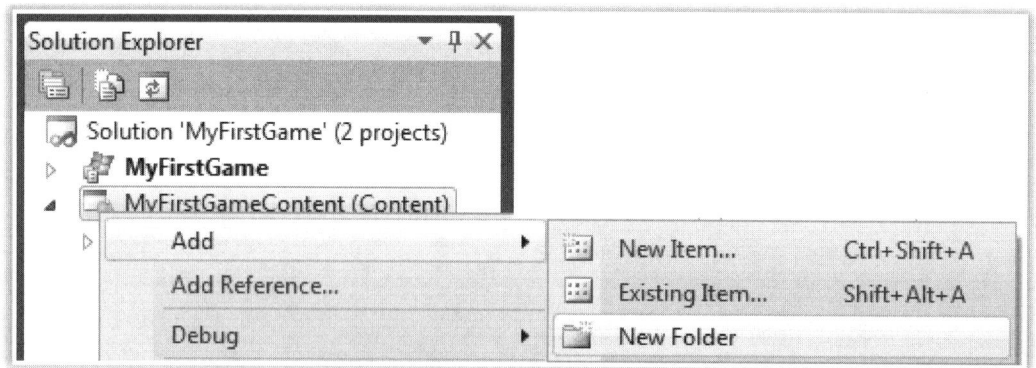

To add a sub-folder, right-click on the "Content" node and then choose "Add" and "New Folder":

This will add a sub-folder named "New Folder", which you can rename to something more meaningful like "Images":

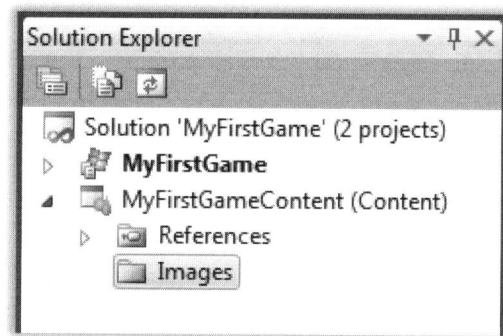

Now let's say you want to add an image called "MyImage.png" to the game. The first step is to add the file to the Content "Images" folder. To do this, right-click on the "Images" folder and choose "Add" and then the "Existing Item" option. The "Add Existing Item" dialog box will be shown:

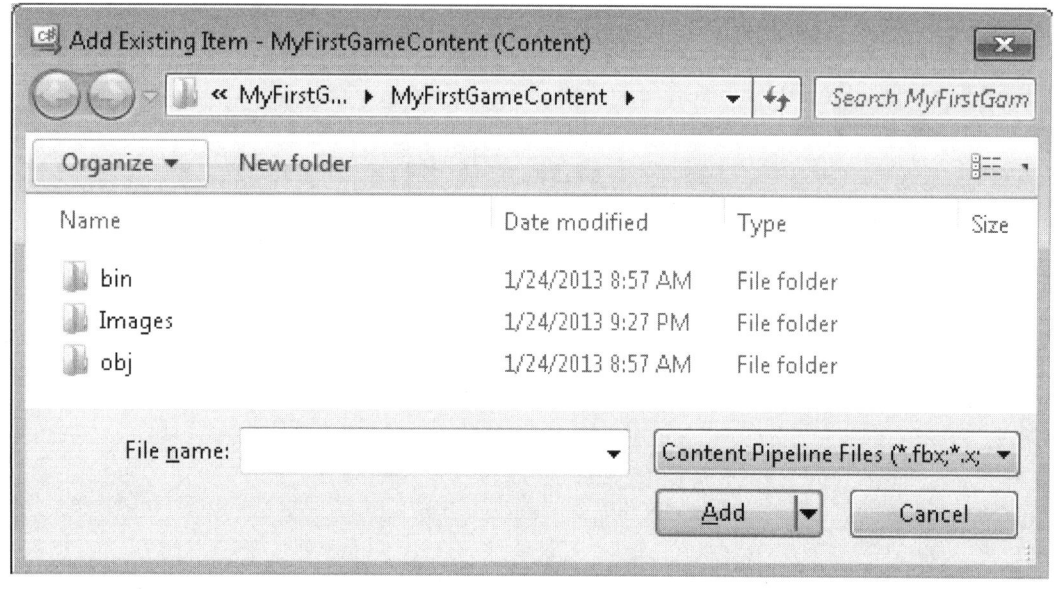

Now you can navigate to the location of your image file on your hard drive, select the file and then click on the "Add" button. Once you have done this, you should see your filename in the Images folder under the Content node.

Once the image file is loaded into the Content node, it is available for use at any time in the game program. In our next lesson, we will discuss how to load and draw images on the screen.

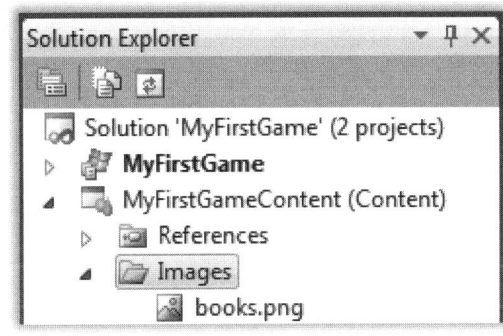

Lesson Two: Drawing Images

Once you have added images to your game Content folder, they are available to be loaded into a variable within your code and then drawn on the screen.

Loading Images

The XNA Content Pipeline uses a **Texture2D** object to load and store images in a game program. You will declare a **Texture2D** object just like any other reference variable:

```
public class Game1 : Microsoft.Xna.Framework.Game
{
    GraphicsDeviceManager graphics;
    SpriteBatch spriteBatch;
    Texture2D myTexture;        // add a Texture2D variable as class member
```

You want to declare the texture object at the top of your main game class so that it will be available whenever it is needed in the game. In other words, don't make it a local variable within your **Draw()** method that must be reinitialized 60 times a second! Declare it somewhere that will prevent it from getting repeatedly recreated.

You can load images from the game Content tree using, unsurprisingly, the **Content** object. The **Content** object is always available; you don't have to declare or initialize it to call static methods. To load an image into the **myTexture** variable, use the **Content.Load()** method:

```
myTexture = Content.Load<Texture2D>("\\Images\\MyImage");
```

Let's take a closer look at the **Load()** method. The first item after the word "Load" is the phrase "<Texture2D>". This tells the compiler exactly what kind of content we are loading – in this case, a **Texture2D** object. The same method is used to load images, sounds, and any other type of multi-media file. For this reason, the **Load()** method requires us to indicate what kind of file we are loading.

The **Load()** method takes only one parameter: the string name of the content resource that we are loading into the game program. This corresponds to the image file that we moved into the "Images" folder in the Content node in our project. Notice that we did not specify the extension of our file. The XNA compiler makes a note of the file extension as soon as the file is added to the Content node. You should not add the file extension to the filename in the **Load()** method call. In fact, the program will not work if you do!

Where should you load your textures into game variables? The **LoadContent()** method will be automatically called by XNA at startup and is an excellent place to load all of your content.

```
protected override void LoadContent()
{
    // Create a new SpriteBatch, which can be used to draw textures.
    spriteBatch = new SpriteBatch(GraphicsDevice);

    // load our image into our Texture2D object
    myTexture = Content.Load<Texture2D>("Images\\MyImage");
}
```

We'll discuss the **SpriteBatch** object in the next section.

Drawing Textures

All of your drawing activity will be accomplished through the **SpriteBatch** object. The **SpriteBatch** provides methods and properties necessary to draw textures in the game window. Every XNA game contains one **SpriteBatch** variable, which is typically declared as a member of the main game class:

```
SpriteBatch spriteBatch;
```

As you saw above, the **SpriteBatch** variable is initialized in the **LoadContent()** method:

```
spriteBatch = new SpriteBatch(GraphicsDevice);
```

Finally, in the game's **Draw()** method, the **SpriteBatch** object is used to draw your textures on the screen. This procedure requires at least three method calls:

- **SpriteBatch.Begin()**, which tells XNA that we are about to draw some images
- One or more calls to **SpriteBatch.Draw()**, which will draw the textures on the screen
- **SpriteBatch.End()**, which tells XNA that we are done drawing that group of images.

Always match a call to **SpriteBatch.Begin()** with a call to **SpriteBatch.End()** when you are done. Each call to **SpriteBatch.Draw()** will display one image at a time and **Draw()** can be called as many times as needed.

"SpriteBatch" is a funny name; why is such a crucial drawing object called "SpriteBatch"? In game programming a *sprite* is not a fizzy soft drink. "Sprite" is a common term for an image on the screen that behaves as some distinct game object such as a critter, ball, wall, car, person, etc. As you will see in later chapters, a sprite object encompasses more than just a texture. However the terminology is still used by the XNA framework in the drawing infrastructure. So, wherever you see "Sprite" within the built-in XNA objects, you can mentally think "texture" or "image" instead! The "Batch" portion of the **SpriteBatch** name comes from the fact that the object can be used to draw groups of textures with similar characteristics.

Using SpriteBatch.Draw()

The **SpriteBatch.Draw()** method is *overloaded*, which means there are several versions with different parameters. The version you use depends on how much control you want over an image drawn on the screen. A simple version of the **Draw()** method is shown below:

```
SpriteBatch.Draw(Texture2D texture, Vector2 position, Color modColor);
```

The first parameter is the **Texture2D** object representing the image to be drawn. The second parameter is a **Vector2** specifying the location (upper-left corner) of the image on the screen. The final parameter is a **Color** modulator value, which has the ability to change the tint of the image. You usually set the modulator value to **Color.White**, which will not change the image's colors at all.

The version of **Draw()** above is nice and simple and can be used when you want to take an image as-is and display it somewhere on the screen. But if you want to do some fancier output including rotating and scaling, or perhaps draw only a portion of the image, you can use a more complex version shown below:

```
SpriteBatch.Draw ( Texture2D texture,
                   Vector2 position,
                   Rectangle sourceRectangle,
                   Color color,
                   float rotation,
                   Vector2 origin,
                   Vector2 scale,
                   SpriteEffects effects,
                   float layerDepth)
```

This version offers us a wealth of choices for drawing the image. The texture, position, and color parameters are identical to the previous version of **Draw()**. Let's look at all of these parameters one-by-one.

Parameter	Description
Texture2D texture	The source image to be drawn on screen
Vector2 position	The location of the image on the screen

Rectangle sourceRectangle	The part of the source image to be drawn. Use **null** if you want to draw the whole image. Otherwise you can define a **Rectangle** specifying some portion of the source image that will be drawn.
Color color	The color modulator (tint) to be applied to the image. Use **Color.White** to draw the image with its normal colors.
float rotation	Specifies an angle, in radians, to which the image should be rotated. The image will be rotated about an origin point specified below. Use 0.0 to draw the image without rotation.
Vector2 origin	Specifies the point around which any rotation will take place. This value will allow us to rotate around the uppermost point, or the center point, or any other point on the screen. The origin is specified relative to the texture's upper-left corner. So a value of (0, 0) will rotate around the upper-left corner, and a value of (width/2, height/2) would rotate around the center.
Vector2 scale	Specifies values by which to grow or shrink the image in the X and Y directions. A vector of (1.0, 1.0) would keep the image at the original size. A vector of (0.5, 2.0) would shrink the image by 50% in the X direction and grow it by 200% in the Y direction.
SpriteEffects effects	Specifies some special effects for the image. Effects can be one of the following values, which do exactly what you expect: **SpriteEffects.None**, **SpriteEffects.FlipHorizontally**, **SpriteEffects.FlipVertically**.
float layerDepth	A value between 0.0 and 1.0 that controls the ordering of images on the screen. A value closer to 0 will place the image toward the top; a value closer to 1 will place the image behind other images. For instance, texture drawn with depth 0.5 would be placed on top of a texture drawn at depth 0.7.

Even if you only want to use one particular special effect (such as rotation), you'd still use this version of **Draw()** and just provide the default values for the other parameters to avoid the other special effects.

We've now spoken at length about **SpriteBatch** and the **Draw()** method. Let's take a look at an example!

```
protected override void Draw(GameTime gameTime)
{
    GraphicsDevice.Clear(Color.CornflowerBlue);
    spriteBatch.Begin();  // begin the SpriteBatch drawing

    // draw myTexture at the location 50,50 without any special effects
    spriteBatch.Draw(myTexture, new Vector2(50, 50), null, Color.White,
            0.0f, new Vector2(0,0), new Vector2(1.0f,1.0f),
            SpriteEffects.None, 0.0f);
```

```
            spriteBatch.End();      // end the SpriteBatch drawing

            base.Draw(gameTime);
    }
```

Assuming your **myTexture** image was loaded with a race car, the above sample code would draw that race car at location (50, 50):

Lesson Three: Image Transformations

The **SpriteBatch.Begin()** method has several different versions. So far we have seen the simplest version:

```
SpriteBatch.Begin();
```

This version does not take any parameters, so the images are just drawn on the screen without any special processing. If you do not need to worry about image depth (ordering), or saving the graphics device settings from batch to batch, this method will work just fine. However, if you want more control over how the images appear, you can use one of the overloaded versions of **Begin()** that take some additional parameters. All images drawn within the **Begin()** / **End()** pair will obey the control parameters specified in the **Begin()** call.

Image Sorting and Blending

You can call **SpriteBatch.Begin()** with two parameters that control how images drawn on top of each other will behave.

```
SpriteBatch.Begin(SpriteSortMode myOrder, BlendState myBlend);
```

Images can be given a "layer depth" (*Z-order*) setting between 0.0 and 1.0 when drawn. Images with a smaller layer depth should be considered "closer" to the front and thus drawn on top of any images with a larger layer depth. Z-ordering is especially helpful when blending together near and far objects in a realistic manner. A tree image in the same location as a distant cloud should appear in front of the cloud, not behind it!

The **SpriteSortMode** enumeration controls the order in which images are drawn on the screen. The enumeration has five possible values, but we're only really concerned with two modes in this course.

SpriteSortMode.Deferred	Images are drawn in the order of the **SpriteBatch.Draw()** method calls between the **SpriteBatch.Begin()** and **SpriteBatch.End()** pair. Layer depth (Z-ordering) is ignored. This is the default behavior!
SpriteSortMode.BackToFront	Images are sorted and drawn in order from back (1.0 layer depth) to front (0.0 layer depth), regardless of the order of the **Draw()** calls.

The remaining three **SpriteSortMode** values are used to fine-tune performance in certain scenarios. You won't have to worry about that for this course, so just remember to use **SpriteSortMode.BackToFront** if you want your images to be drawn in order according to their layer depth! **SpriteSortMode.Deferred** is the default sort mode when you use the plain **SpriteBatch.Begin()** method.

The **BlendState** enumeration controls how the colors of images drawn on top of each other are combined on the screen. There are three values for this enumeration that we might want to use:

BlendState.Additive	The **Additive** mode will take the image's pixels and any previously drawn pixels underneath and add them together. This may give an image a glowing effect.
BlendState.AlphaBlend	**AlphaBlend** means that the image's pixels will be blended with any previously drawn pixels underneath according to the alpha value. If the alpha value of a pixel is transparent, then the underlying pixel color will show through. **AlphaBlend** is used when you want to use images with built-in transparency.
BlendState.Opaque	The **Opaque** mode will not apply any blending technique to the pixels at all. With this value, the sprites are drawn one on top of another and alpha-channel transparency values are ignored.

Fortunately, **BlendState.AlphaBlend** is the default setting when you call **SpriteBatch.Begin()** with no parameters. If you just want to use images with transparency then you don't have to do anything special.

Image Scaling

In addition to the drawing options you can specify in the **SpriteBatch.Begin()** method, you may want to scale (shrink or stretch) individual images as you draw them. You can control the scaling factor with the `scale` parameter of the **Draw()** method.

Now let's look at the `scale` parameter in more detail. The `scale` parameter can be used to stretch or shrink an image on the screen in the X and Y directions. So an image that was originally 50 x 50 pixels may be displayed as 25 x 100 or some other stretched shape. The **scale** parameter is a **Vector2**, where the X member specifies the scale factor in the X direction and the Y member specifies the scale factor in the Y direction. The scaling factor is multiplicative, so a value of 1.0 will display the image at 100% of normal size (no stretching or shrinking). A value of between 0 and 1 will shrink the image and a value above 1 will enlarge the image. So, for instance, a scale value of 0.5 will reduce the image by half (50%) its original size. A scale value of 2.0 will stretch the image twice (200%) its original size.

Here is the same example race car we previously demonstrated drawn both normally and scaled:

```
// draw myTexture at the location 50,50 without any special effects
spriteBatch.Draw(myTexture, new Vector2(50, 50), null, Color.White,
            0.0f, new Vector2(0, 0), new Vector2(1.0f, 1.0f),
            SpriteEffects.None, 1.0f);

// draw myTexture at the location 150,50 with scaling of 50% X and 200% Y
spriteBatch.Draw(myTexture, new Vector2(150, 50), null, Color.White,
            0.0f, new Vector2(0, 0), new Vector2(0.5f, 2.0f),
            SpriteEffects.None, 1.0f);
```

The difference between these **Draw()** calls is that we have specified a scale of (1.0, 1.0) in the first call and (0.5, 2.0) in the second call. The first image will be drawn using normal dimensions and the second image will be drawn half-size (50%) in the X direction and double-size (200%) in the Y direction. See for yourself!

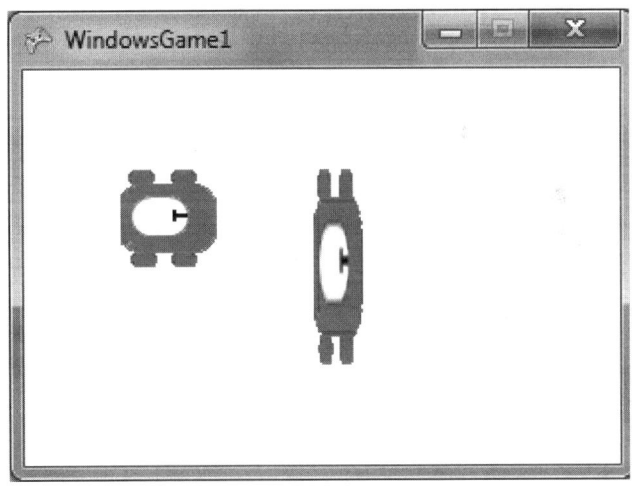

Note: If you are scaling and rotating an image at the same time, some of the **Draw()** parameters get a bit tricky! If your scale vector is anything other than (1.0, 1.0) you should also divide your origin vector by that same scale vector. This is due to the way the **Draw()** method internally processes the transformations.

Image Rotating

XNA provides very powerful image rotation support. If you want an object such as a spaceship to move in different directions on the screen, you only need to create one image of the spaceship and then use XNA to rotate the image as needed to match the direction of travel.

Let's examine the **rotation** and **origin** parameters of the **Draw()** method. The **origin** is the point around which the image will rotate. By default, this point is the upper-left corner (0, 0) of the image. A more common and useful point would be the center of your image. This will let your image rotate "in place" or spin. The **origin** is specified as a **Vector2** object where the X and Y values are relative to the upper-left corner of the image. So if your image is 50 x 50 pixels then the center point would be (25, 25).

Once you have chosen your **origin**, you need to choose the rotation angle. The **rotation** is a floating point number representing an angle in radians (instead of degrees). A radian is simply another measuring system for angles. You can easily convert between radians and degrees using some simple formulas.

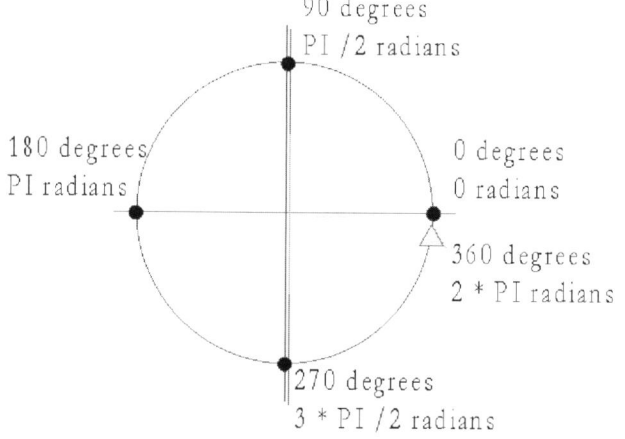

Angles between 0 and 360 in degrees are represented as 0.0 to 2.0 * PI radians. Therefore:

- Angle in degrees = angle in radians * 180 / PI
- Angle in radians = angle in degrees * PI / 180

For example:

- A rotation value of 0.0 radians or 0.0 degrees means the image is not rotated at all.
- A rotation of PI / 2 radians is equal to a rotation of 90 degrees. A rotation of PI radians means half-way around, or 180 degrees.

Note that rotation angles given to the **Draw()** method are backwards from the standard Cartesian concept where positive angles rotate to the left! This is due to that pesky computer screen Y-coordinate reversal where "down" is positive. In this course we stick with the familiar Cartesian standard when storing angles in variables and just put a negative sign on the angles when calling **Draw()**.

The combination of rotation angle and origin gives you very flexible control over your image rotation. You can use it to turn a cannon, spin a wheel, steer a race car, and other limitless possibilities! Here are a couple of examples. We draw the race car un-rotated and then rotated at the same location around an origin of (0, 0). Then we draw the same race car un-rotated and then rotated about its center point.

```
// draw myTexture at the location 50,50 without any special effects
spriteBatch.Draw(myTexture, new Vector2(50, 50), null, Color.White,
                0.0f, new Vector2(0, 0), new Vector2(1.0f, 1.0f),
                SpriteEffects.None, 1.0f);

// draw myTexture at the location 50,50 rotated left 45 degrees around (0,0)
spriteBatch.Draw(myTexture, new Vector2(50, 50), null, Color.White,
                -(float)Math.PI / 4.0f, new Vector2(0, 0),
                new Vector2(1.0f, 1.0f), SpriteEffects.None, 1.0f);
```

```
// draw myTexture at the location 150, 150 without any special effects
spriteBatch.Draw(myTexture, new Vector2(150, 150), null, Color.White,
                 0.0f, new Vector2(0, 0), new Vector2(1.0f, 1.0f),
                 SpriteEffects.None, 1.0f);

// draw myTexture at the location 150, 150 rotated 45 degrees around center
Vector2 origin = new Vector2(myTexture.Width / 2, myTexture.Height / 2);
spriteBatch.Draw(myTexture, new Vector2(150, 150) + origin, null,
                 Color.White, -(float)Math.PI / 4.0f, origin,
                 new Vector2(1.0f, 1.0f), SpriteEffects.None, 1.0f);
```

A key point to notice in the last function call is that in order to rotate "in place" around the center you must add the origin vector to the input location as well! This is due to the order in which XNA applies the various location, scaling, and rotation transformations within the Draw() method.

Here is the resulting output. The first pair shows the top image rotated 45 degrees around the upper-left corner of the bottom image.

The second pair shows the top image rotated 45 degrees around the center of the bottom image. We make it rotate "in place" by adding the origin to the position vector parameter as well.

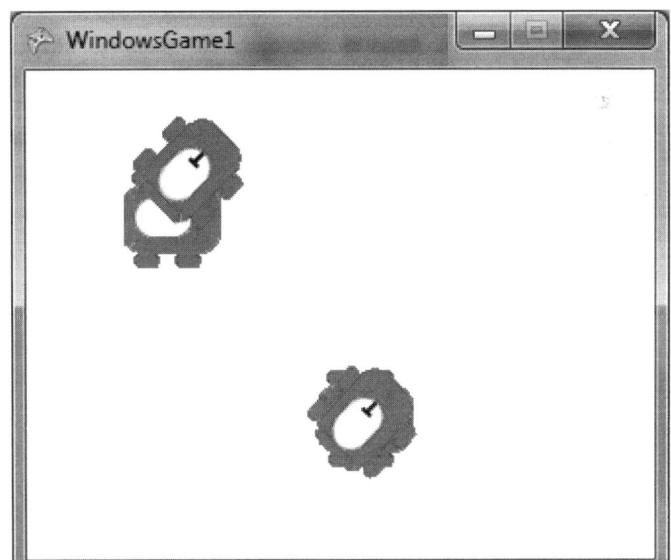

Lesson Four: Drawing Text

In addition to images, games may need some text drawn on the screen. Because XNA games are made to run on multiple platforms (Windows, Xbox 360, and Windows phone) you do not have access to the standard Windows Form controls like a label, text box, or even a pop-up Message Box. Instead, if you need to communicate text to the player, you will need to draw some text onto the screen.

Creating and Loading Fonts

A *font* is a stylized set of characters. The first step to drawing text is adding a font to the Content node in the Solution Explorer. To do this, right-click on the Content node, then choose "Add" and "New Item". Then click on the Sprite Font icon. At this point, you should see the following screen:

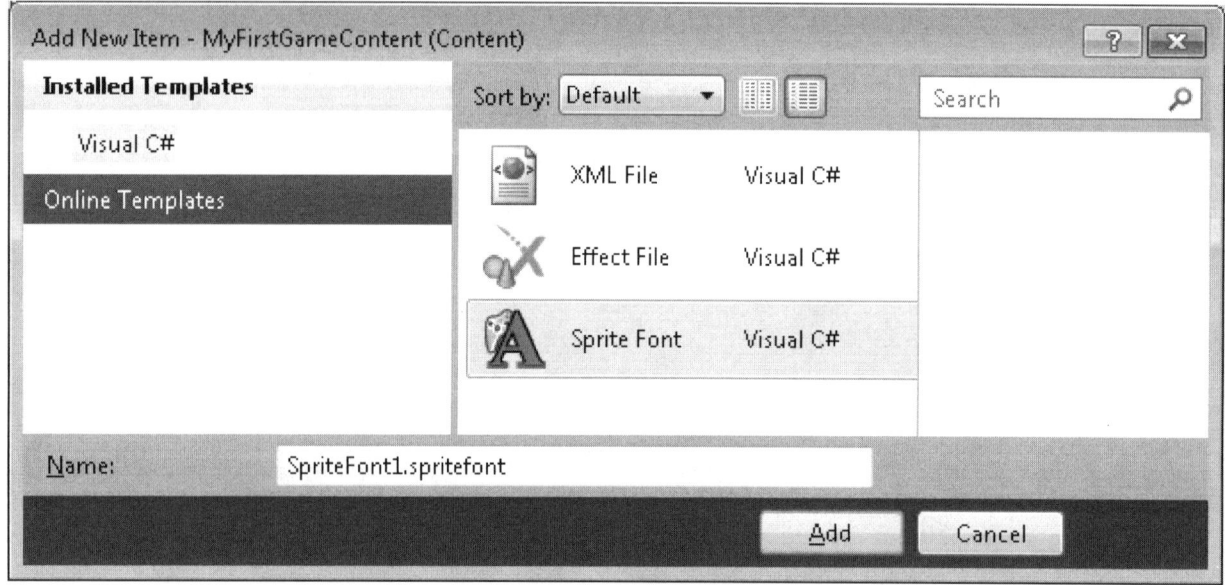

You must give your font a name to the left of the period in the "Name" text box. Replace "SpriteFont1" with some more meaningful name, especially if you want to load multiple fonts into your game and keep them straight later on. We will typically name our font "GameFont" in examples. Make sure to leave the ".spritefont" extension alone. Once you click on the "Add" button, the sprite font will be added to your game's Content.

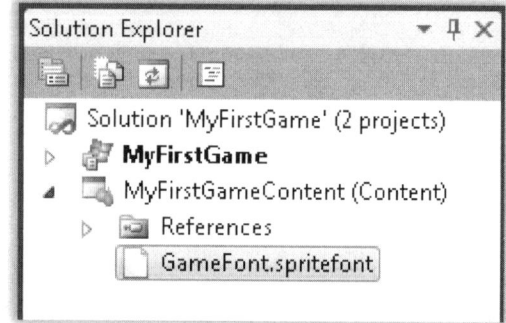

You will also see the new font text file opened in your main editing window. This file can be used to customize the font by choosing the font name, point size, spacing, and so on.

```xml
<?xml version="1.0" encoding="utf-8"?>
<!--
This file contains an xml description of a font, and will be read by the XNA
Framework Content Pipeline. Follow the comments to customize the appearance
of the font in your game, and to change the characters which are available to dra
with.
-->
<XnaContent xmlns:Graphics="Microsoft.Xna.Framework.Content.Pipeline.Graphics">
  <Asset Type="Graphics:FontDescription">

    <!--
    Modify this string to change the font that will be imported.
    -->
    <FontName>Segoe UI Mono</FontName>
```

You can see the default font name in the **<FontName>** element is "Segoe UI Mono". You can leave that as-is or change it to something else like "Arial", "Times New Roman", etc. Just make sure the font name you pick is available on your target platform.

In addition to **<FontName>**, you can see other elements in your font file that you may want to change. Each element such as **<Size>** or **<Style>** has a description in the comments directly above the element. After you make any customizations you want to the font name and other parameters just save and close the file; you won't have to do anything with it again later.

Loading and using a font in your program is very similar to loading and using an image! Instead of **Texture2D** you will use the **SpriteFont** data type. You can declare your **SpriteFont** variable at the main class level for the game just under the **SpriteBatch** variable:

```csharp
public class Game1 : Microsoft.Xna.Framework.Game
{
    GraphicsDeviceManager graphics;
    SpriteBatch spriteBatch;
    SpriteFont myFont;         // declare a variable to hold your font
```

Next, you will need to load the font in the **LoadContent()** method:

```csharp
myFont = Content.Load<SpriteFont>("GameFont");
```

Notice how this **Content.Load()** method call looks a lot like your **Load()** method for textures. The only difference is that here we are telling **Load()** to accept a **SpriteFont** resource type.

TeenCoder™: Game Programming

Drawing Strings with a Font

Once the font is loaded, it is available for use in your program's **Draw()** method. To display a string to the screen use the **DrawString()** method on the **SpriteBatch** object.

```
SpriteBatch.DrawString(SpriteFont spriteFont, string text,
                       Vector2 position, Color color)
```

The first parameter is the **SpriteFont** variable you loaded from your Content pipeline. The second parameter is the text you want to display. The third parameter specifies the location of the upper-left corner of the string. The last parameter determines the color for the text. Simple, right? Let's take a look at some output.

This example draws the race car image with some text underneath.

```
// draw myTexture at the location 50,50 without any special effects
spriteBatch.Draw(myTexture, new Vector2(50, 50), null, Color.White,
                 0.0f, new Vector2(0, 0), new Vector2(1.0f, 1.0f),
                 SpriteEffects.None, 1.0f);

// draw some text underneath the texture
spriteBatch.DrawString(myFont, "Start your engines!",
                       new Vector2(50, 120), Color.Black);
```

There are no surprises to what you'll see from this code. Our text starts at position 50, 120 and is drawn in the font and color specified in the **DrawString()** method.

Much like the **Draw()** method there are many overloads to **DrawString()** that let you do some fancy effects like rotation and scaling. We've only covered the simple version here, so refer to MSDN documentation to see what else you can do!

Chapter Four: Working With Images

Chapter Review

- The images, sounds, and fonts that make up the multi-media portion of your game are called *content*.
- The XNA Content Pipeline enables automatic loading of any supported content type.
- The **SpriteBatch** class provides the methods and properties that are necessary to draw images in the game window.
- XNA uses a **Texture2D** object to represent loaded images in a game program.
- An image is loaded into a **Texture2D** object using the **Content.Load**() method.
- The **SpriteBatch.Draw**() method is used to draw a texture onto the screen.
- The **SpriteBatch.Begin**() method can be used to control the blending and depth ordering of images on the screen.
- Image scaling and rotation can be done through the parameters of the **SpriteBatch.Draw**() method.
- **SpriteFont** objects are used to load and reference fonts from the Content Pipeline.
- Text is drawn on the screen using **SpriteFont** and the **SpriteBatch.DrawString**() method.

TeenCoder™: Game Programming

Activity: Starry Night

In this activity, you will create a rotating field of stars behind a stationary image of the ground and a tree.

Your activity requirements and instructions are found in the "Chapter_04_Activity.pdf" document located in your "TeenCoder\Game Programming\Activity Docs" folder. You can access this document through your Student Menu or by double-clicking on it from Windows Explorer.

Complete this activity now and ensure your program meets the requirements before continuing!

Chapter Five: User Input

The XNA Framework allows games to easily receive input from the three main devices: the keyboard, the mouse, or the Xbox 360™ gamepad controller. In this chapter you will learn how to use all three devices!

All XNA classes related to user input can be found in the **Microsoft.Xna.Framework.Input** namespace. A **using** reference to this namespace is automatically added to the default project created by the IDE.

An input device has a current *state* which is a snapshot that can tell you what buttons or keys are pressed, the position of the mouse cursor on the screen, what triggers are being held down, etc. This state can be queried within your game's **Update()** method. Simply checking the current device state will tell you which keys or input triggers are being activated *right now*. Comparing the current device state to the previous one will tell you which keys or inputs have been pressed or released *since* the last **Update()**.

Lesson One: Keyboard Input

When personal computer games first became popular in the 1980s there was only one way to accept user input: the keyboard. Players used arrow keys and various other keys to control movement and other game details. Even today, when the mouse is the more common input device for most Windows applications, the keyboard is still a primary input source for many Windows games. The keyboard is considered a *digital* input device, which means that each of its keys has only two possible states: on (down) or off (up). Getting and checking the state of any key is extremely simple!

Key Classes

There are several helpful keyboard-related classes and enumerations that we will use to retrieve and process keyboard input. In this section, we will take a look at these objects in detail.

The first important class is the **Keys** enumeration. This enumeration contains a listing of all the possible keys on a keyboard. Each key has a unique name and is referenced in the following manner:

```
Keys.<keyname>
```

The key name property is the name of the physical key on the keyboard. The name can directly represent the letter you see on the key, like **Keys**.A for the "A" key. Names are also defined for non-character keys like **Keys.Space** for the space bar. You can get a list of all defined key names by typing in the keyword **Keys** in your IDE and then entering a period afterwards. A tool-tip pop-up should show you the key naming options. You can also position your editing cursor on the keyword **Keys** and hit F1 to pull up the MSDN help. Here is a short list of some common key values:

	Description
`Keys.A`	The 'A' key
`Keys.Back`	The 'Backspace' key
`Keys.Delete`	The 'Delete' key
`Keys.Enter`	The 'Enter' key
`Keys.Escape`	The 'ESC' key
`Keys.F1`	The 'F1' key

	Description
`Keys.Left`	The left arrow key
`Keys.LeftShift`	The left 'Shift' key
`Keys.NumPad0`	The '0' on the number pad
`Keys.Space`	The space bar
`Keys.Tab`	The 'Tab' key
`Keys.D1`	The number '1' across the top

The **Keyboard** class allows you to retrieve the current state (up or down) of all keys on the keyboard. This class has one main method: **GetState()**. The **GetState()** method will query the keyboard to retrieve the current states for all of the keys on the keyboard. All of the current key states are returned within another object called the **KeyboardState**. When you are ready to process keyboard input, assign the output of the **GetState()** to a **KeyboardState** variable like this:

```
KeyboardState currentKeyState = Keyboard.GetState();
```

Now you can examine your **currentKeyState** variable to find which keys are currently up or down! This class has several useful methods: **IsKeyDown()**, **IsKeyup()**, and **GetPressedKeys()**.

You can call the **IsKeyDown()** method to check and see if a specific key is down:

```
bool KeyboardState.IsKeyDown(Keys key)
```

The only parameter for this method is an enumerated **Keys** value. A **true** or **false** value is returned depending on whether or not the specified key is in a "down" state. Assuming you want to check to see if the space bar is pressed, and you have declared and initialized your **KeyboardState** variable named **currentKeyState**, here's the code to check:

```
if (currentKeyState.IsKeyDown(Keys.Space))
{
  // the space bar is currently down!
}
```

The **IsKeyUp()** method works just like the **IsKeyDown()** method except it returns **true** if the specified key is up instead of down.

```
bool KeyboardState.IsKeyUp(Keys key)
```

Here's an example checking to see if the Tab key is up (not being pressed):

```
if (currentKeyState.IsKeyUp(Keys.Tab))
{
   // the Tab key is currently up!
}
```

Finally, you can use the **GetPressedKeys()** method to retrieve an array of all **Keys** currently being pressed:

```
Keys[] KeyboardState.GetPressedKeys()
```

You can examine all of the currently pressed keys like this:

```
Keys[] pressedKeys = currentKeyState.GetPressedKeys();
foreach (Keys pressedKey in pressedKeys)
{
   // do something with this pressed key
}
```

In most cases we find it simplest to use a combination of **IsKeyUp()** and **IsKeyDown()** to check for specific key presses, but you may find a situation where using **GetPressedKeys()** makes the most sense.

Key Handling Techniques

Processing user input is one of the main tasks you will accomplish from within your game's **Update()** method. When you are ready to process keyboard input, the first step is to get the current **KeyboardState** using **Keyboard.GetState()** and store the result in some variable (e.g. **currentKeyState**) for future use.

If you just need to see if a key is currently held down during this call to **Update()**, regardless of whether or not it was already held down the last **Update()**, then the technique already described works just fine!

```
if (currentKeyState.IsKeyDown(Keys.Space))
{
   // the space bar is currently down!
}
```

This might be useful if you want to keep moving a game object in a certain direction as long as a key is held down. It doesn't matter what the key was doing previously, because right *now* the key is down and the game object needs to move again.

However, if you need to detect distinct key presses (meaning the key is pressed down and then released) this simple technique will not work! Remember the **Update()** method is called around 60 times per second. So if it takes the user a full second to press and release one key, you may have gotten a **true** result back from **IsKeyDown()** 60 times in different calls to **Update()**! If you were using a key press to shoot something, intending for one key press to result in one shot, you might shoot dozens of shots on the screen instead!

In order to detect a distinct key press, regardless of how long the key is held down or how fast your **Update()** method is getting called, you will need to use two different keyboard states: an *old* keyboard state and the current keyboard state. This will enable you to compare the current state to the previous state and see if your key changed from up to down or down to up.

To keep track of the old keyboard state, declare a new class-level **KeyboardState** variable near the top of your **Game** to store the old state from the prior call to **Update()**.

```
public class Game1 : Microsoft.Xna.Framework.Game
{
    GraphicsDeviceManager graphics;
    SpriteBatch spriteBatch;

    KeyboardState oldKeyState;   // keep track of the last keyboard state
```

Now somewhere in your **Update()** method you'll retrieve the current keyboard state as usual. But the first thing you want to do is check to see if your **oldKeyState** variable is **null**, meaning this is the first time **Update()** has ever been called. If so, assign the current keyboard state to the **oldKeyState** variable just to get it started and avoid any possible **null** reference exceptions later.

```
protected override void Update(GameTime gameTime)
{
    KeyboardState currentKeyState = Keyboard.GetState();
    if (oldKeyState == null)
        oldKeyState = currentKeyState;
```

Now we are ready to check and see if the current key state is different than the previous key state. You can check to see if the key has just been pressed or released. It probably doesn't matter which way you choose, just be consistent. You likely don't want to detect a keystroke twice…once going down and once going up.

Let's say we want to determine if the "A" key has just been pressed.

```
if ((oldKeyState.IsKeyUp(Keys.A) && (currentKeyState.IsKeyDown(Keys.A))
{
    // the A key was just pressed down!
}
```

Here we are checking to see if the "A" key was "up" in our previous call to **Update()** and is now "down" in the current state. If this is true then the player must have pressed the key between our last check and our current check. We will therefore only detect the keystroke once when the key is first pressed down. If we wanted to detect the key when it is released instead of pressed, just call **IsKeyDown()** on the "old" state and **IsKeyUp()** on the "new" state.

Your last step in the **Update()** method should be to assign the current keyboard state to the old keyboard state variable. This is how you "remember" what the last state was the next time **Update()** is called.

```
// store current snapshot as old key state for next update
oldKeyState = currentKeyState;
```

Checking for Multiple Key Presses

You might want to know if the user is holding down more than one key at a time. Perhaps you want to have the player move north when the up arrow is being pressed and west when the left arrow is being pressed. But what if you want to move northwest when they are *both* being pressed?

One option would be to use the **GetPressedKeys()** method. During each call to **Update()** you could retrieve an array of all of the currently held down keys and check to see if your particular key combination is present. However looping over the **Keys[]** array many times might become burdensome if you have many interesting combinations to check for. A more straightforward approach would simply call **IsKeyDown()** for each key of interest and make sure the resulting processing of each key makes sense in combination. For instance:

```
if (currentKeyState.IsKeyDown(Keys.Up))
{
    // move north
}
if (currentKeyState.IsKeyDown(Keys.Left))
{
    // move west
}
```

With this logic, if only the up arrow key is down, we will move north. If only the left arrow key is down, we will move west. If both keys are down then we will execute the logic to move both north and west. Just make sure moving one direction doesn't "undo" the effects of having already moved in another direction!

Keyboard Modifiers

Keyboard modifiers are keys that can be held down to alter the interpretation of another key press. The most common modifier keys are the Alt, Ctrl and Shift keys. For example a word processing program would add a lower-case "a" if you just pressed the "A" key, or it would add an upper-case "A" if you held down either Shift key and then pressed "A". In your game you may want to accelerate when the space bar is pressed, or really kick in the afterburners if the left Ctrl key is held down at the same time!

You can easily check for modifier keys by enhancing the **if()** statement that examines both the old and current key states. The following piece of code checks to see if the player has pressed the "Shift-A" combination:

```
if ((oldKeyState.IsKeyUp(Keys.A) && (currentKeyState.IsKeyDown(Keys.A))
{
    // we now know the A key was pressed, now check for Shift...
    if (currentKeyState.IsKeyDown(Keys.LeftShift) ||
        (currentKeyState.IsKeyDown(Keys.RightShift))
    {
        // the A key was pressed with either left or right Shift!
    }
    else
    {
        // the A key was pressed with no Shift!
    }
}
```

Notice that each of the modifier keys Ctrl, Alt , and Shift have "left" and "right" versions of the **Keys** enumeration. Each key is treated separately at the code level even though they both have the same label and tend to behave the same way in most programs.

In game programming it is not uncommon to have only the left or right version of a modifier key do something and reserve the opposite key for another task. If you want them both to have the same effect you need to check for either one being pressed in your program!

Lesson Two: Mouse Input

Although the first mouse appeared in the early 1980s, the use of a mouse did not become popular until the mid 1990s. A mouse offers a fast and flexible way to interact with a computer game. You can move the mouse cursor quickly and nimbly across the screen. Where a set of directional arrows are limited to up, down, left and right, a mouse can move in any direction, at any angle. For this reason the mouse is often used as a directional tool in game programming.

A mouse *cursor* is the arrow or other icon you see on screen that tracks the mouse position. You may have been wondering why the XNA programs you have run so far don't show the mouse within the game window! By default the mouse cursor is not visible in an XNA game because the Xbox console doesn't have a mouse. If you want your players to use the mouse in your game, you will need to make the mouse visible with the following statement:

```
this.IsMouseVisible = true;
```

You can use this line at any point in your code, although it is commonly used either in the constructor for the game class or in the **Initialize()** method.

Mouse Classes

There are several helpful mouse-related classes and enumerations that we will use to retrieve and process the mouse's input. Fortunately they are very similar in style and technique to the keyboard components! In this section, we will take a look at these items in detail.

The first enumeration to understand is **ButtonState**. This enumeration contains only two values: **Pressed** and **Released**. These values will describe the state of any individual mouse button.

The next important class is the **Mouse** class. You use this class to retrieve the current state of the mouse, including its position and states of all buttons. As you might expect, within the **Update()** method you can call **GetState()** on the **Mouse** object and assign the resulting **MouseState** class to a variable:

```
MouseState currentMouseState = Mouse.GetState();
```

The **MouseState** class contains information about all of the mouse's buttons as well as the current cursor position on the screen. The following table describes each of the **MouseState** properties:

MouseState Property	Description
`int X`	The X-coordinate of the mouse cursor, with 0 being the left side of the window. A negative value means the cursor is outside the window to the left. A value greater than the window width means the cursor is outside the game window to the right.
`int Y`	The Y-coordinate of the mouse cursor, with 0 being the top of the window. A negative value means the cursor is above the window. A value greater than the window height means the cursor is below the game window.
`ButtonState LeftButton`	**ButtonState.Pressed** if held down or **ButtonState.Released** if not.
`ButtonState MiddleButton`	**ButtonState.Pressed** if held down or **ButtonState.Released** if not.
`ButtonState RightButton`	**ButtonState.Pressed** if held down or **ButtonState.Released** if not.
`int ScrollWheelValue`	Number representing the current position of the scroll wheel (see below).
`ButtonState XButton1`	The "X" buttons represent the extra buttons beginning to appear on newer mouse devices that can be used for any purpose. They behave just like the left, middle, and right buttons.
`ButtonState XButton2`	

Newer mice have scroll wheels which can be rolled up or down. The position of the scroll wheel is represented by a number that increases or decreases with the position of the wheel. In order to use the wheel you need to compare the current value to the previous value to decide if they are scrolling up or down and how fast the wheel is being scrolled.

Putting the Mouse to Use

Now that we understand the various states of the mouse, let's see how we can put this information to work in a game program. You will find these techniques very similar to keyboard handling and the logic should go in the **Update**() method along with all the other user input processing.

You can check to see if a particular mouse button is held down by examining the button state:

```
MouseState currentMouseState = Mouse.GetState();
if (currentMouseState.LeftButton == ButtonState.Pressed)
{
    // left mouse button is pressed!
}
```

This technique is good for detecting if a mouse button is held down *right now*. But if you want to detect a specific mouse click you need to preserve the old mouse state and compare the current mouse state to it. Sound familiar? You did exactly the same thing to detect key presses on the keyboard.

To detect mouse clicks you will add a class-level **MouseState** variable at the top of our game class, like this:

```
public class Game1 : Microsoft.Xna.Framework.Game
{
    GraphicsDeviceManager graphics;
    SpriteBatch spriteBatch;

    MouseState oldMouseState;   // keep track of the last mouse state
```

Now within the **Update()** method you'll obtain the current mouse state and initialize the old mouse state if it's **null** to avoid any problems:

```
protected override void Update(GameTime gameTime)
{
    MouseState currentMouseState = Mouse.GetState();
    if (oldMouseState == null)
        oldMouseState = currentMouseState;
```

Then you can detect if a button has been clicked by detecting the transition from **Released** to **Pressed**:

```
if ((currentMouseState.LeftButton == ButtonState.Pressed) &&
    (oldMouseState.LeftButton == ButtonState.Released))
{
    // left mouse button was clicked!
}
```

You can reverse the logic if you want to detect the mouse click when it moving from **Pressed** to **Released**.

Finally, of course, at the bottom of your **Update()** method don't forget to save the current mouse state into your old mouse state variable for the next call to **Update()**!

```
// store current snapshot as old key state for next update
oldMouseState = currentMouseState;
```

Getting and Setting the Mouse Position

There are often times in a game when you may need to get the current position of the mouse on the screen. Typically when you detect a "click" of a button you then want to examine the position of the mouse cursor to see just what the user was clicking on!

Retrieving this information is as simple as querying the **X** and **Y** properties of the **MouseState** variable:

```
int x = currentMouseState.X;
int y = currentMouseState.Y;
```

In addition to retrieving the mouse position, you may want to change the mouse position by setting it in your code. To do this, you can call the **Mouse.SetPosition()** method. This method takes an X and Y integer coordinate pair and will change the mouse cursor position to these new values.

```
Mouse.SetPosition(int x, int y);
```

Be careful when designing a game requiring you to set the mouse position. Most users are accustomed to controlling the mouse cursor themselves at all times and might be confused if the mouse cursor begins teleporting around the screen under programmatic control!

Lesson Three: Xbox 360 Controller

The last input device that we will discuss is the Xbox 360 Controller (or gamepad). These are flat-out cool, and are also ideal for bringing the same "feel" of the Xbox game console to a Windows PC. Because an Xbox 360 Controller will work on both a regular PC and an Xbox game console, you can write your game to respond to the same sorts of user input on both platforms.

Keep in mind that all Windows users have a mouse and keyboard, but only some Windows users will also have an Xbox 360 Gamepad. Make sure you support fallback input from mouse and keyboard if the user doesn't have a gamepad!

If you are using an Xbox 360 game console, then the Controller plugs directly into the console. If you are using one on PC, the wired Xbox 360 Controllers have a USB connector which can be plugged into your computer USB port. A wireless Xbox 360 Controller needs a special USB wireless receiver to work on a PC.

You are not required to have an Xbox 360 Gamepad to complete any of the activities in this course. You can learn about Gamepad objects and techniques without actually having a Gamepad device. If you do have a Gamepad you are encouraged to incorporate it into the chapter activities and your own games!

Let's take a closer look at the buttons and features of the gamepad:

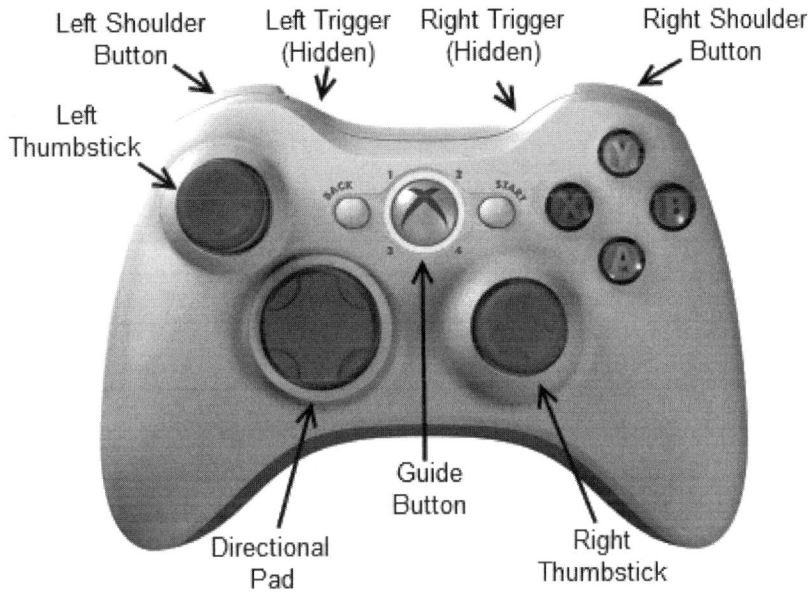

As you can see, a single gamepad has many buttons and controls!

Letter Buttons

The letter buttons are found on the right side of the controller. There are four colored letter buttons: a yellow letter Y, a red letter B, a green letter A, and a blue letter X. You can use these buttons for any purpose in your game, though most games tend to use similar letters for selecting an item, etc.

Start and Back Buttons and the Guide Button

On the top of the gamepad there are two small buttons surrounding a larger circular button. The small left button is labeled "Back" and is mainly responsible for moving back through a set of menus and for ending a game. The small right button is labeled "Start" and is mainly used to move forward through the menus and for starting a game. The Xbox "Guide" button is the large, backlit button in the center of the gamepad. This button is used by the Xbox game console and does not have any functionality on a Windows computer.

Thumbsticks

The gamepad is equipped with two thumbstick controls: one on the lower right and one on the upper left. These controls each work as a kind of joystick. In a typical Xbox game the left thumbstick is used as a movement control. This means the control allows the player to move their character or object around the screen. The right control is often used to change the current view in the game. This feature is often used in 3D games where the player may want to look around in an environment without actually moving. Each thumbstick can also be pressed like a button, giving it both directional and button press capabilities.

Directional Pad

The directional pad has four possible directions: up, down, left, and right. This control is most often used for menu navigation in an XNA game. Although the pad can be used to move characters or objects around the screen, it is rarely used for this purpose. Instead, most programmers opt for the thumbstick controls, which can handle more than four directions.

Shoulder Buttons

There are two buttons on the very top of the gamepad: one on the left and one on the right. These buttons are called "shoulder" buttons because they sit at the "shoulder" of the gamepad. They can be used for any action in a typical Xbox game. However, since they are more difficult to reach than other controls on the gamepad they are most often used for the more un-common game tasks.

Trigger Buttons

Finally, the gamepad has "trigger" buttons. These buttons are on the front of the gamepad (and thus can't be seen in the image above). There are two trigger controls: one on the right and one on the left. These are special controls because they are not simple on/off buttons and do not report a "pressed" or "released" state. Instead they are a sort of dimmer control, which reports a fractional number between 0.0 and 1.0, depending on how far the trigger is pushed. If the trigger is pushed all the way, the gamepad will report a value of 1.0. If it is only pushed slightly, it may report a value like 0.6. These controls are often used to shoot game weapons.

Xbox 360 Controller Classes

There are two main gamepad-related classes that we will use to retrieve and process the controller's input. The **GamePad** class is much like the **Keyboard** class and the **Mouse** class. It has a single method called **GetState()** which will return a **GamePadState** object.

```
GamePadState GamePad.GetState(PlayerIndex index);
```

There is one significant difference between the **GamePad**'s **GetState()** method and that of the **Keyboard** and **Mouse** classes. The **GamePad.GetState()** method takes a single **PlayerIndex** parameter. This parameter specifies which player's gamepad we are checking. You are allowed to connect up to four gamepad devices to either a computer or an Xbox 360 game console. The **PlayerIndex** enumeration contains values representing each possible gamepad: **PlayerIndex.One**, **PlayerIndex.Two**, **PlayerIndex.Three**, and **PlayerIndex.Four**. You will need to separately process the state for each of the gamepads supported by your game.

GamePadState

The **GamePadState** class represents the current state of all inputs on the controller. It contains a mixture of properties and methods that are used to describe the state of each component. Here are the properties:

`bool` `IsConnected`	If the controller at the specified player index is connected this value will be **true**, and all of the other properties are valid. If this property is **false** then the controller is disconnected and no other property should be processed.
`GamePadButtons` `Buttons`	The **GamePadButtons** structure has one **ButtonState** member for each button on the gamepad: **A, B, Back, BigButton, LeftShoulder, LeftStick, RightShoulder, RightStick, Start, X, Y**
`GamePadDPad` `DPad`	The **GamePadDPad** structure has one **ButtonState** member for each direction on the directional pad: **Up, Down, Left, Right**
`GamePadThumbSticks` `ThumbSticks`	The **GamePadThumbSticks** structure has one **Left Vector2** member for the left thumb stick and one **Right Vector2** member for the right thumb stick. Each vector X and Y value will range from -1.0 (tilted all the way left or down) to 1.0 (tilted all the way right or up) with 0.0 representing the midpoint. When combined, the X and Y coordinate pair specify the exact position of the thumb stick, which can be pushed in any direction.
`GamePadTriggers` `Triggers`	The **GamePadTriggers** structure has one **Left float** member for the left trigger and one **Right float** member for the right trigger. Each trigger can have a value between 0.0 and 1.0 to represent how far the trigger is pressed.

While there is quite a bit to digest within this structure, getting individual values out is quite easy! For instance if you wanted to get the horizontal value of the right thumb stick for player one, you could do this:

```
GamePadState myGamePadState = GamePad.GetState(PlayerIndex.One);
if (currentGamePadState.IsConnected)
{
    float xStickDirection = myGamePadState.Thumbsticks.Right.X
}
```

 The IsConnected property is either true or false, depending on whether or not the specified gamepad is actually connected to the PC or the Xbox 360 console. You should always check this property first to see if the gamepad is connected. If it's not connected then none of the other values are valid and should be ignored.

Putting the Xbox GamePad to Use

By now you are very familiar with how to distinguish between an input button being held down and the input being pressed or clicked. The gamepad controller has exactly same behavior as the keyboard and mouse in this regard. To determine if a button has been pressed instead of held down, you should save a copy of the **GamePadState** in an old variable and then compare it to the current state during **Update**().

Gamepad Controller Vibration

All Xbox 360 controllers have the ability to vibrate in a player's hands. This is a really cool feedback effect that often corresponds to crashes and explosions in the game. The vibration makes the player feel more like they are part of the game.

The gamepad controller actually contains two vibration motors, one on the left and one on the right. With a simple line of code, we can turn these motors on and off and even set the intensity of the vibration:

```
GamePad.SetVibration(PlayerIndex index, float leftMotor, float rightMotor)
```

The first parameter in this method is the index of the player whose gamepad we want to vibrate. The second parameter is the amount of vibration for the left motor. The third parameter is the amount of vibration for the right motor. Both motor vibration values should range between 0.0 and 1.0. A value of 0.0 means no vibration and a value of 1.0 means full vibration. Here's how to set both motors to full speed for player one:

```
GamePad.SetVibration(PlayerIndex.One, 1.0f, 1.0f);
```

You can set different values for each motor – they do not have to be the same. If an impact occurs on the left side of the player's character you may want to set a higher value for the left motor, or vice versa for a right-side impact. Remember to set both motor values back to 0.0 when you want the vibration effect to end. Once a vibration is set, it will continue until you set it back to 0.0!

Optional Xbox 360 Gamepad Activities for this Course

You are not required to have an Xbox Gamepad to complete any activities. However, if you do own one or more Xbox 360 Gamepads, we have included some alternate instructions to allow you to use these controls in the game programs you write for this course.

These alternate instructions explain how to incorporate your gamepad(s) into the game program instead of the default keyboard controls. Any activity starter project that contains pre-written input code will have built-in support for both the keyboard *and* Xbox 360 Gamepad(s). The only exception is the Tic-Tac-Toe game, which will only work with mouse input.

Chapter Review

- There are three main methods of input for an XNA game: the keyboard, mouse and Xbox 360 Gamepad controller.
- The **Keys** enumeration represents all of the keys on the keyboard.
- The **KeyboardState** class represents the current state of each of the keyboard's keys and is obtained by calling the **GetState()** method on the **Keyboard** object.
- The **KeyboardState** class has three common methods: **IsKeyDown()**, **IsKeyUp()** and **GetPressedKeys()**.
- Keeping track of the previous keyboard state and the current keyboard state will allow you to process the key only when it is first pressed or when it is released. This prevents multiple actions occurring from one key press.
- The **GetPressedKeys()** method will return an array of **Keys** values, which represent all of the keys currently pressed on the keyboard.
- The Ctrl, Alt, and Shift keys are modifiers that may alter the interpretation of another key press.
- A *mouse* is a common Windows input device that is widely used in many games.
- The mouse *cursor* is not visible by default in an XNA game. You must set the **this.IsMouseVisible** property to **true** to see the mouse pointer.
- The **Mouse** object allows you to retrieve the **MouseState** which represent all of the button states of the mouse as well as the mouse cursor's current position.
- Keeping track of the previous mouse state and the current mouse state will allow you to process the mouse movement or button click only when it is first occurs. This prevents multiple actions occurring from one mouse movement or click.
- Xbox 360 Gamepad controllers can be used on a Windows PC by plugging into a USB port.
- Up to four gamepads can be connected to an Xbox console or PC game at one time.
- The **GamePadState** object is used to keep track of button presses, thumb stick movement, trigger presses, and directional pad input from an Xbox 360 controller.
- Keeping track of the previous gamepad state and the current gamepad state will allow you to process the gamepad input only when it first occurs. This prevents multiple actions occurring from one action on the gamepad.
- You can control the vibration feature of an Xbox 360 gamepad controller using the **GamePad.SetVibration()** method.

Activity: Cat and Mouse Chase

In this project you will use your new mouse and keyboard skills to control a cat and a mouse as they chase each other around the screen. If you have an Xbox 360 gamepad and would like to use that controller instead, alternate gamepad instructions are provided within the activity description.

Your activity requirements and instructions are found in the "Chapter_05_Activity.pdf" document located in your "TeenCoder\Game Programming\Activity Docs" folder. You can access this document through your Student Menu or by double-clicking on it from Windows Explorer.

Complete this activity now and ensure your program meets the requirements before continuing!

Chapter Six: Sprites

In this chapter we will begin formalizing the concept of a *sprite*, which is a useful game object that can move around the screen, animate, collide with other sprites, and so forth. You will also start developing a full-featured game called Swarm!

Lesson One: Introducing Sprites

In order to draw an image on the screen you need to keep track of data such as the texture and screen coordinates. You may also want to track a direction and speed for the object and determine when the object has collided with something else on the screen. Over time game programmers have defined a *sprite* as a conceptual game object that encapsulates these properties and functions. There is no one universal, concrete definition of a sprite as a class. Everyone tends to create their own sprite class that is reflective of their own style of programming. In fact, the XNA framework does not even define sprite class at all – despite having other classes like **SpriteBatch** that seem to be related!

We have created a **Sprite** class for our use in this course. This object is part of the **SpriteLibrary** namespace and can be found in the "Sprite.cs" source file in many of your activity starters. The **Sprite** will allow you to load an image into a texture, set the image position, direction, speed, rotation angle, scale, and other properties. The class will also take care of drawing the image on the screen, determining if it has collided with another **Sprite**, and other useful functions. The **Sprite** will be heavily used throughout the rest of the course, and you are also encouraged to use it within your own games later on. *There is nothing magic about our definition of a sprite – so if you see something you'd like to change or add to the class, go ahead!*

In this lesson we will begin reviewing some of the basic methods and properties in the **Sprite** class. You may want to open the "Sprite.cs" class into the IDE so you can follow along. A copy of this file is located within your "\TeenCoder\Game Programming\Activity Starters" directory.

Initial Look at the Sprite Class

At the top of the "Sprite.cs" file you will find a series of **using** declarations. These declarations bring in the XNA framework objects and **System** objects that will be used internally by the **Sprite**. Next, all classes should belong to some namespace. A namespace is a way of identifying one object as belonging to a related group of objects. Our **Sprite** class belongs to the **SpriteLibrary** namespace. Just like the **Sprite** class itself, this is something we designed and is not a part of the XNA framework. The **Sprite** class definition is **public** because we intend for the class to be used by others.

Here's a snapshot of the top part of the "Sprite.cs" source file:

```csharp
using System;
using System.Collections.Generic;
using System.Linq;
using System.Text;
using Microsoft.Xna.Framework;
using Microsoft.Xna.Framework.Audio;
using Microsoft.Xna.Framework.Content;
using Microsoft.Xna.Framework.GamerServices;
using Microsoft.Xna.Framework.Graphics;
using Microsoft.Xna.Framework.Input;
using Microsoft.Xna.Framework.Media;
using Microsoft.Xna.Framework.Net;
using Microsoft.Xna.Framework.Storage;

namespace SpriteLibrary
{
    public class Sprite
    {
```

All of the properties and methods we will discuss are within the **Sprite** class between the opening and closing brackets for the class.

How to Use the Sprite Class in a Project

If you want to use the **Sprite** class in your game, you will need to do three things. First, copy the **Sprite.cs** file into your game source directory alongside the other *.cs files. Second, add the file to your project in the Solution Explorer. Right-click on your project name, select "Add" and "Existing Item". Then pick the file you just copied into your source directory and add it to your project.

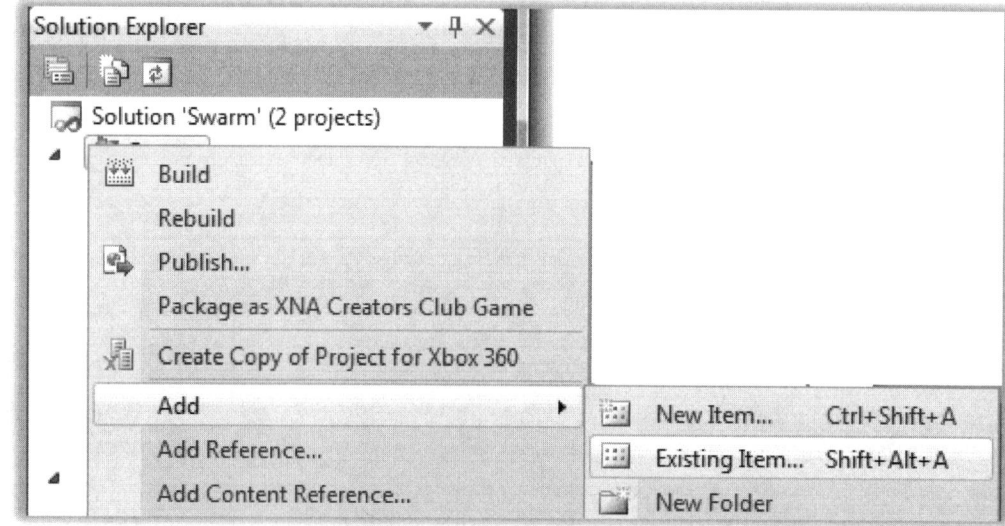

Third, add a **using** statement at the top of your own source code for easy access to the **SpriteLibrary** namespace.

```
using SpriteLibrary;
```

Now you can use the **Sprite** class in your game! Let's take a closer look at some of the useful methods and properties you'll find in the class. Some of these you will recognize clearly as parameters that were described for the **SpriteBatch.Draw()** method. When the **Sprite** draws the image for you it will take all of these parameters into account.

UpperLeft

The first important property is called **UpperLeft** and represents the upper-left location of the sprite image on the screen.

```
public Vector2 UpperLeft;
```

The **UpperLeft**.X and **UpperLeft**.Y members represent the (X, Y) coordinate pair of the upper-left image location. This property is **public** which means you can directly set it to any **Vector2** you like directly from your source code.

Scale

The next property is another **Vector2** value called **Scale**. This property controls the stretching and shrinking factors in the X and Y direction for the sprite's image. Any adjustment to this value can cause the sprite to appear larger or smaller on the screen. The default values (1.0, 1.0) mean the image will appear normal size.

```
public Vector2 Scale = new Vector2(1.0f, 1.0f);
```

Scale is also **public** so you can directly set it to whatever new value you like. Notice that if you set either X or Y scaling factor to 0.0 that means your image will disappear completely!

SpriteTexture

The next property deals with the sprite's image, or texture. The **Texture2D SpriteTexture** value holds the sprite's image once it is loaded by the program.

```
private Texture2D SpriteTexture;
```

This property is **private**, so you will not set it directly. Instead call the **SetTexture()** method, which we will discuss shortly, to give a **Sprite** an image.

IsAlive

The next basic property is a Boolean value called **IsAlive**. This value controls whether or not the sprite is visible on the screen and a candidate for colliding with other sprites.

```
public bool IsAlive = true;
```

By default this value is **true**, since most sprites should be visible on the screen at all times. If you wish to hide the sprite but not get rid of it completely, simply set **IsAlive** to **false**.

RotationAngle and Origin

The **Sprite** class contains built-in support for drawing the image at any rotation angle on the screen! The **RotationAngle** property contains the current angle of the sprite image. This value is stated in degrees using the normal Cartesian sense and can range from 0 to 360. The **Origin** property is a **Vector2** value representing the point around which the sprite will rotate.

```
public double  RotationAngle = 0;
public Vector2 Origin = new Vector2(0, 0);
```

If you want the sprite to spin around its center then you'd set the **Origin** to the center at (image width /2, image height / 2). We will describe methods below that calculate the center point of the image for you.

LayerDepth

The **LayerDepth** property is a **float** value that determines the depth of the sprite, for layering purposes. This value can be used to set the sprite on top of or behind other sprites drawn at an overlapping location.

```
public float   LayerDepth = 0;
```

A **LayerDepth** of 0.0 means the image is all the way in front, and a depth of 1.0 means the sprite is all the way in the back.

Time-To-Live

The time-to-live (**TTL**) property puts a timer on lifespan of a sprite. This is useful when you have a sprite that you want to pop-up on the screen for a short time and then disappear (perhaps a shot fired from a gun lasts 2 seconds).

```
public int TTL = -1;
```

The default "-1" means the TTL feature is disabled. A non-zero value will indicate the sprite is on the TTL timer. Each time the sprite is moved the **TTL** value will be decremented by one, until it reaches zero. When the counter reaches zero the sprite's lifespan has expired and **IsAlive** is set to **false**. If you move the sprite once during each **Update**() call, and **Update**() is being called 60 times a second, then you can do some simple math to figure out what TTL value to start at to make the sprite disappear after a certain time. For instance, at TTL of 120 should cause the sprite to live for 2 seconds.

SetTexture()

One of the first important methods you'll need to call on the **Sprite** is **SetTexture**(). In order to display an image on the screen a texture must specified first! Call **SetTexture**() on each new **Sprite** object you create.

```
public void SetTexture(Texture2D texture)
```

The **SetTexture**() method takes a **Texture2D** object that has already been loaded by your **LoadContent**() method. Note that XNA will call the **LoadContent**() method on startup during the call to **base.Initialize**() that is part of the default **Initialize**() method. So you should not attempt to set any textures into a sprite prior to the call to **base.Initialize**(), otherwise the texture objects will be **null**!

For example, to create a sprite and obtain an image, we could use the following code any time after the call to **base.Initialize**():

```
Sprite mySprite = new Sprite();
mySprite.SetTexture(myTexture);
```

Inside the **SetTexture**() method the **Sprite** will store the texture object in the `spriteTexture` member variable, determine its width and height, and form an initial bounding rectangle. Additional code inside this method has to do with collision detection and animation. This code will be described in a later chapter so don't worry about it for now!

Draw()

The next important method to study is the **Draw**() method. This method will draw the **Sprite** using the current position, rotation, scale and layer depth.

```
public virtual void Draw(SpriteBatch theSpriteBatch)
```

You will call the **Sprite.Draw**() method on each sprite you would like to display on the screen. The method should be called from within your game's **Draw**() method where you have declared a **SpriteBatch** object. Make sure all of your calls to **Sprite.Draw**() happen between **SpriteBatch.Begin**() and **SpriteBatch.End**() in your game's **Draw**() method.

Let's take a peek at how the **Sprite.Draw()** method is written:

```
public virtual void Draw(SpriteBatch theSpriteBatch)
{
    float radians = MathHelper.ToRadians((float)RotationAngle);
    if (IsAlive)
    {
        theSpriteBatch.Draw(spriteTexture, UpperLeft + Origin, imageRect,
                    Color.White, -radians, Origin / Scale, Scale,
                    SpriteEffects.None, LayerDepth);
    }
}
```

The first line will translate the **RotationAngle** property of the sprite into radians. This is important, since the angle of rotation in the **SpriteBatch Draw()** method requires radians and not degrees. The second line makes sure that the sprite is "alive" on the screen. If the sprite is "alive", we can continue with our **Draw()** method. If it is not "alive", we do not want to draw it on the screen.

The next line is where we are calling the **SpriteBatch.Draw()** method. In Chapter Three we studied this method in detail. Here, we have gathered all of the properties of the **Sprite** object together and are passing them into **SpriteBatch.Draw()** with all of the tweaks necessary to make the image behave exactly as desired.

The first parameter is simply the **spriteTexture** property that was initialized during the earlier call to **SetTexture()**. The second parameter is a combination of the sprite's **UpperLeft** and **Origin** properties to position the image on the screen. The third parameter is the "source rectangle" which has been automatically calculated elsewhere in the **Sprite** class (this has to do with animation, which we will cover later). The next parameter is the tint color, which we set to **Color.White** to show the image's normal colors.

The rotation angle in radians is passed in as a negative to correct for the difference beween the normal Cartesian rotation (positive angles rotate left), which the **Sprite** is tracking, and the **Draw()** method's "computer" rotation (positive angles rotate right).

The next two parameters specify the origin and scale for the image. Notice we calculate the input origin from the **Sprite.Origin** property divided by **Sprite.Scale** as described in Chapter Three. The final two parameters are **SpriteEffects.None** (we're not applying any special mirroring effects) and **LayerDepth** value to control the ordering of overlapping images.

Now, when you call the **Sprite.Draw()** method from within your game's **Draw()**, you can be assured that all of the detailed handling of the position, rotation, scaling, and ordering factors are accounted for. When you update any of the **Sprite** properties from within your **Update()** method those changes will be immediately reflected in the image when drawn.

GetWidth() and GetHeight()

The **GetWidth()** and **GetHeight()** methods are used to retrieve the current width and height of the sprite.

```
public int GetWidth()
public int GetHeight()
```

While you could directly access the **SpriteTexture.Width** and **SpriteTexture.Height** properties to get the raw width and height of the texture, these values don't account for any scaling that may be applied!

The **GetWidth()** method contains one line of code:

```
return (int)((float)spriteTexture.Width * Scale.X / (float)numFrames);
```

To calculate the current effective width, we multiply the image width by the scaling factor in the X-dimension. We also divide by the number of frames the are in the image – this is related to animation which we'll cover later. For now your **numFrames** is always 1.

Also notice that we had to do some casting of data types. Since the value of **Scale.X** is a **float** we up-cast the integer **Width** to a **float** (for maximum accuracy) and then do our multiplication. The final result, however, must be cast back to an **int** value, since there is no such thing as a fractional pixel width!

The **GetHeight()** method is almost identical to **GetWidth()**:

```
return (int)((float)spriteTexture.Height * Scale.Y);
```

Here, we are multiplying the image's height by the current scaling factor in the Y-dimension. Also notice that we are doing the same casting as in **GetWidth()** to provide the most accurate result.

GetCenter()

The **GetCenter()** method will return the center of the sprite as a **Vector2** data type. The center is relative to the upper-left corner of the sprite as (0,0) and not the overall screen coordinates.

```
public Vector2 GetCenter()
{
    return new Vector2(GetWidth() / 2, GetHeight() / 2);
}
```

This function gets the center width by dividing the total width by 2 and the center height by dividing the total height by 2. The resulting values are placed into a new **Vector2** value and returned to the calling program.

Lesson Two: The Swarm Game

In this lesson we introduce the first full game you will write: Swarm! Swarm is based on a classic arcade theme where a fleet of enemies try to drop projectiles on the player below. The player in turn is shooting back at the enemy from behind bunkers. In our version, a swarm of angry bees flies back and forth on the screen, shooting their stingers down at the player. The player is represented by a smoke gun, which can move back and forth and shoot smoke at the bees to knock them out. The player can dodge left and right to evade the stingers and hide behind a series of honeycomb "bunkers". But watch out! The bunkers can be slowly destroyed by either the bee stingers or the player's smoke shots.

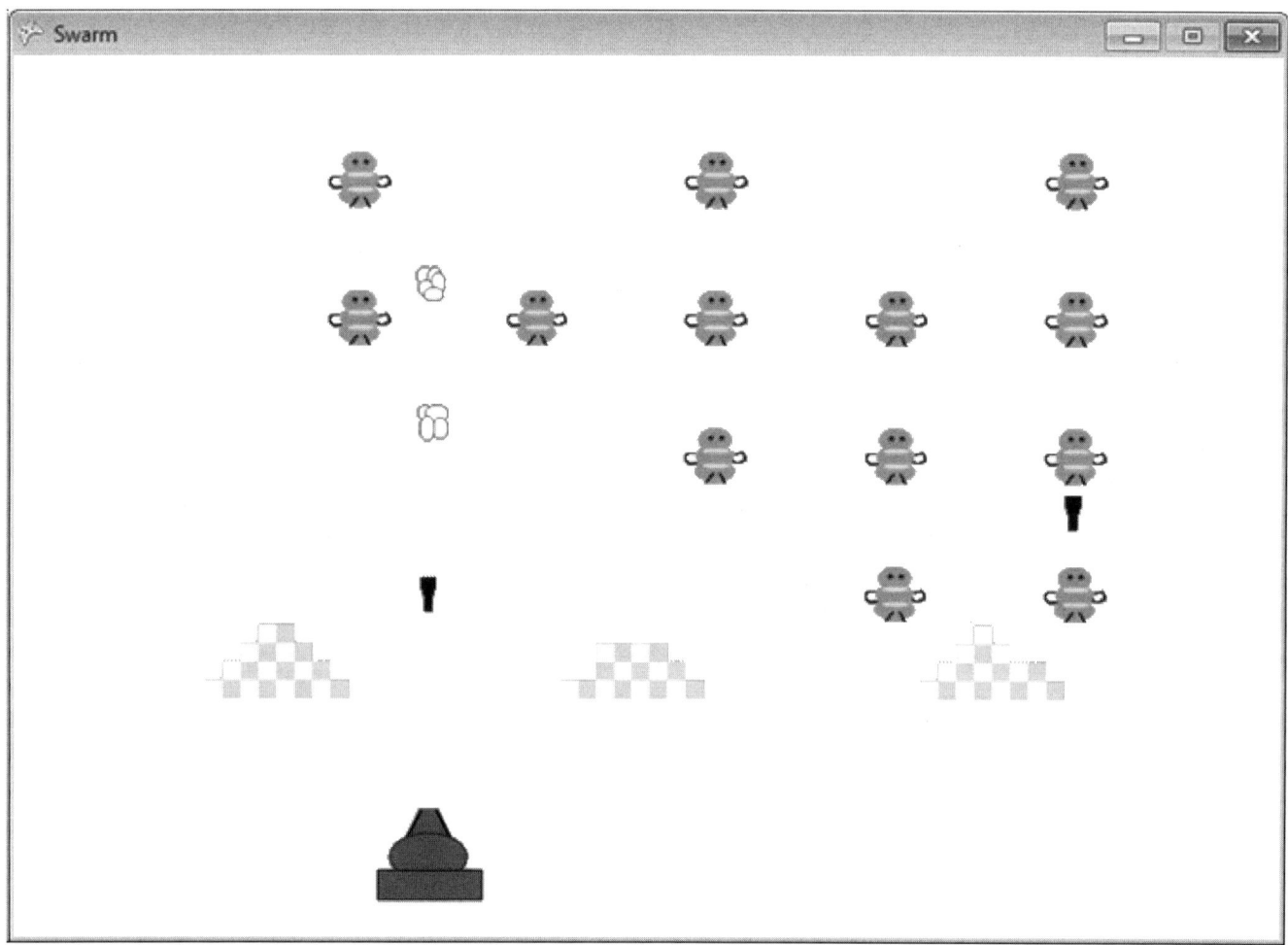

Swarm is a fairly large game and you will be programming all of the important features! We have already created a "starter" project for the game. This starter project can be found in your "\TeenCoder\Game Programming\Activity Starters\Swarm" directory. The name of the solution file is "Swarm.sln". You should copy the "Swarm" directory into your "\TeenCoder\Game Programming\My Projects" directory now. Then go ahead and open this project in the Visual C# 2010 Express IDE.

Chapter Six: Sprites

At this point the Swarm program is merely a shell. You should be able to compile and run the game, but game will only produce an empty screen with the honeycomb bunkers pre-built for you. As you progress through the next couple of chapters you will build more and more functionality into the game.

Checkpoint: Build and run the starter version of the Swarm game from your working directory. You should be able to build without any errors and you should see an empty blue background with three honeycomb bunkers across the bottom.

Your project already contains our **Sprite** class in "Sprite.cs" plus the starter code in "Swarm.cs". Let's take a closer look at the Swarm functions now.

The following functions are completely finished already and you won't have to modify them. We'll provide a brief description here and you can review the code in the activity starter if you are curious about those parts of the game. Don't worry if some of the functions are unfamiliar now; you will understand them all soon!

Function Name	Description
`Initialize()`	This method is automatically created for every XNA game in order to perform basic initialization. Here we will simply call **startGame()** to begin a new game.
`startGame()`	The **startGame()** method will be called whenever a new game is started. This will happen at the beginning of play and when the user starts a new game after finishing the last game. **startGame()** will reset the game state back to the beginning.
`initializeHives()`	This method will handle all of the initialization for the "hive" bunkers that offer some protection. Each section of the hive is an individual **Sprite** with a yellow or orange square image. Since positioning each of the little squares in a bunker arrangement is a bit tedious, we have completed this method for you.
`LoadContent()`	This method is automatically created for every XNA game. Here, we load all of the texture images and other content that will be used throughout the game.
`UnloadContent()`	This method is automatically created for every XNA game. Since all of our game content is loaded through the **ContentManager**, which will take care of unloading it automatically at the end of the game, this method is empty.
`Update()`	This method is automatically created for every XNA game. It is called 60 times a second and will run all of the game's logic. Within the method we make calls to other functions you will write to do things like move sprites and react to collisions.
`findEdgeBee()`	This method will allow us to figure out which bee is currently the furthest to the left or right on the screen. This information will help us to figure out when to change the flight direction of the bees.
`pruneList()`	We track many of the sprites (representing bees, bunkers, stingers, and smoke shots) in linked lists. The **pruneList()** method will remove any "dead" sprites (where **IsAlive** = **false**) from the list.

TeenCoder™: Game Programming

The remaining functions declared in the source code are empty. You will complete these functions during the activities over the next couple of chapters. Here is a brief description of what each function will do:

Function Name	Description
`initializeSmokeSprayer()`	This method will create the smoke gun sprite, set the texture, and position it on the screen at the beginning of the game. The **startGame()** method will call **initializeSmokeSprayer()** automatically.
`initializeBees()`	This method will initialize the bee sprites. Each bee must be given a new **Sprite** with a texture, location, and initial direction.
`stopGame()`	This method will be called whenever the game is completed. This can occur if the player wins or if they are destroyed by a bee sting. The method will display a "game over" message and change the difficulty for the next round.
`checkBeeShots()`	This method will determine when a bee stinger should be "shot" from a random bee, and call **fireBeeShot()** when a new shot is due.
`fireBeeShot()`	This method will determine a random bee from which a new shot will be fired. A new bee stinger shot will be allocated, given an image, initial position, and direction.
`moveSmokeShots()`	This method will move each of the smoke shots up the screen.
`moveBeeShots()`	This method will move each of the bee shots down the screen.
`moveBees()`	This method will check to see if the flight of bees should change direction based on the position of the leftmost and rightmost bees. It will then move each of the bees and check to see if any bee has reached the level of the smoke gun. If the bees reach the smoke gun then **stopGame()** should be called to end the game.
`checkCollisions()`	The **checkCollisions()** method will check for all possible collisions (smoke hits bee or bunker, stinger hits bunker or player, etc) and process the effects of the collision accordingly.
`shootSmokeSprayer()`	This method will cause the smoke gun to "shoot" a smoke shot at the bees.
`Draw()`	**Draw()** is responsible for drawing all of the game elements on the screen.
`handleKeyPress()`	This method will handle all of the player's key presses in the game. The player will use the arrow keys to move the smoke gun left and right and the spacebar to shoot smoke at the bees.

As you can see, there are many different pieces of logic necessary to complete a game! However by breaking the logic down into small methods that can be completed and tested in a series of steps you will not get overwhelmed by having to juggle many details at the same time.

Lesson Three: Initializing Your Swarm

In this lesson we show you how to create and use an instance of a **Sprite** object. Once the lesson is finished you will complete an activity to initialize a few key **Sprite** objects in the Swarm game. Unlike earlier chapters with one activity at the end, you will be completing several activities per chapter, building the game incrementally based on the theory or technique discussed in each lesson.

Initializing Sprites

To use a **Sprite** you first need to declare a variable to hold the **Sprite** object. Here is an example declaration:

```
Sprite mySprite;
```

Now you have declared a variable called **mySprite**, but don't try to use it yet! A **Sprite** is a reference type and therefore must be initialized with the **new** keyword before it can be used. If you tried to use the **mySprite** variable before initializing it, you'd generate a runtime exception because the variable is still **null**.

To initialize **mySprite**, use the **new** keyword like this:

```
mySprite = new Sprite();
```

Of course, you can combine the variable declaration and initialization into a single line, like this:

```
Sprite mySprite = new Sprite();
```

In this game (and most games) we declare the **Sprite** variables as a member variables of the main class because they will be persistent across many method calls. Each **Sprite** variable will be initialized as needed during the game (when the game starts or when the shots are fired).

Using Sprite Variables

Once you have created and initialized a **Sprite** class variable, you can use any of its **public** properties or methods. For instance, if you wanted to position the object at coordinates (100, 100) you'd write this code:

```
mySprite.UpperLeft = new Vector2(50,100);
```

You have now positioned the upper-left corner of the sprite image at a point 50 pixels from the left of the window and 100 pixels down from the top of the window.

Linked List Review

The Swarm game contains several groups of sprites: the bees, bee stingers, smoke shots and hive bunkers. The number of objects in each group will change over time as bees disappear, stingers and smoke shots are launched and vanish, and as hive bunker pieces are destroyed.

Each group of sprites is tracked in the code by a *linked list*. Linked lists are convenient data structures to hold groups of objects where the group may grow or shrink over time and individual group elements are randomly removed or added. We discussed linked lists in detail in our previous course, but let's review them briefly now because they are an important data structure for this game.

A linked list is a data structure that can be visualized as a series of elements, called *nodes*, which are connected to each other like a string of beads. In a doubly-linked list, each node knows how to reach both the next and previous nodes:

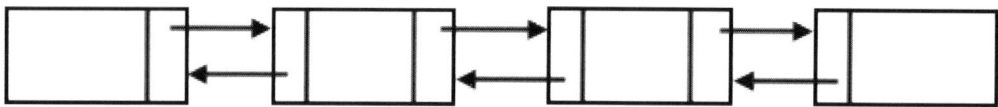

In order to "walk" through the elements in a linked list, you start with the first node in the list and then follow the *next* links until you reach the end of the list. In a doubly-linked list, you can start your "walk" from the first node or the last node and walk either forwards or backwards in the list.

The .NET framework contains a **LinkedList** object that implements a doubly-linked list. To declare and initialize a variable of this data type, use the **new** keyword as follows:

```
LinkedList<int> myList = new LinkedList<int>();
```

The "<int>" parameter shows what kind of data will be stored in the linked list. In this example we use integers but it can be any data type. To add items to the beginning of the list, call the **AddFirst()** method:

```
myList.AddFirst(1); // list = 1
```

Or, to add items to the end of the list, use the **AddLast()** method:

```
myList.AddLast(4);  // list = 1, 4
```

Removing items is just as easy. You can use the **RemoveFirst()** method to remove first item in the list or the **RemoveLast()** method to remove the last item:

```
    myList.RemoveFirst();    // list = 4
    myList.RemoveLast();     // list is empty
```

When you want to remove a specific value from the list, you can use the **Remove()** method, like this:

```
    myList.Remove(4);
```

Finally, to clear the entire contents of the linked list, you will use the following line:

```
    myList.Clear();    // list is empty
```

In the next activity you will begin to work on the Swarm game by implementing two methods: **initializeSmokeSprayer()** and **initializeBees()**. The **initializeBees()** method will create and add bee **Sprite** objects to a linked list. Therefore your list is not tracking numbers as demonstrated above, but **Sprite** objects instead! Here are the four **LinkedList** objects already declared and initialized at the top of the Swarm game:

```
    LinkedList<Sprite> smokeShots = new LinkedList<Sprite>();
    LinkedList<Sprite> hiveSections = new LinkedList<Sprite>();
    LinkedList<Sprite> bees = new LinkedList<Sprite>();
    LinkedList<Sprite> beeShots = new LinkedList<Sprite>();
```

Notice that our linked lists contain **Sprite** objects instead of simple integers.

Activity One: Raising the Swarm

In this activity you will complete the **initializeSmokeSprayer()** and **initializeBees()** methods in the "Swarm.cs" file.

Your activity requirements and instructions are found in the "Chapter_06_Activity1.pdf" document located in your "TeenCoder\Game Programming\Activity Docs" folder. You can access this document through your Student Menu or by double-clicking on it from Windows Explorer.

Complete this activity now and ensure your program meets the requirements before continuing!

Lesson Four: Sprite Movement

Sprites are able to move in any direction on the screen. This means that they can be moving to the right, left, up, down or at some other angle. We will store the sprite's direction as an angle, measured in degrees between 0 and 360. These angles are similar to using a compass to determine your direction.

This circle diagram shows the various angles represented in degrees. 0 degrees is always shown pointing in the right direction, 90 degrees points straight up towards the top of the circle, 180 degrees points directly to the left, and 270 degrees will always point straight down. There are of course many intermediate angles between these points. Angles between 0 and 90 represent some direction pointing up and to the right. Similarly, angles between 90 and 180 point up and to the left, and so on.

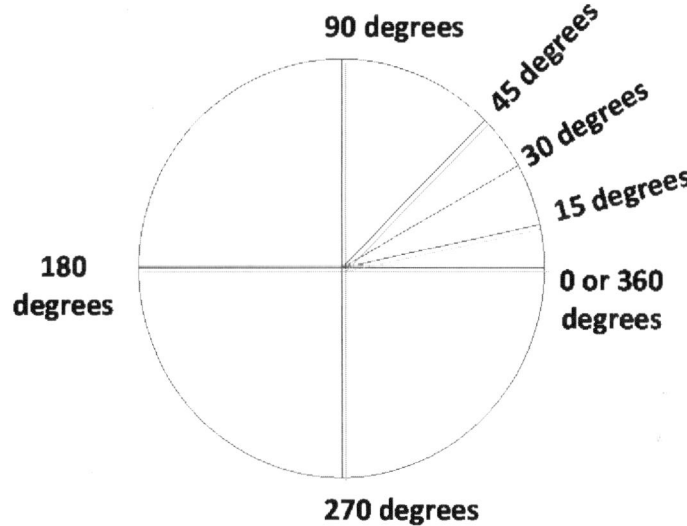

The angles of a circle move from 0 to 360 in a counter-clockwise direction. When you get all the way up to 360 degrees you have reached your starting point directly to the right, and start over at 0 again. This is the standard Cartesian sense for angle direction. As previously mentioned, the XNA functions interpret angles in the opposite direction because a computer's Y-direction is reversed from the Cartesian standard. The **Sprite** will reverse the angle appropriately when calling the **SpriteBatch.Draw()** method.

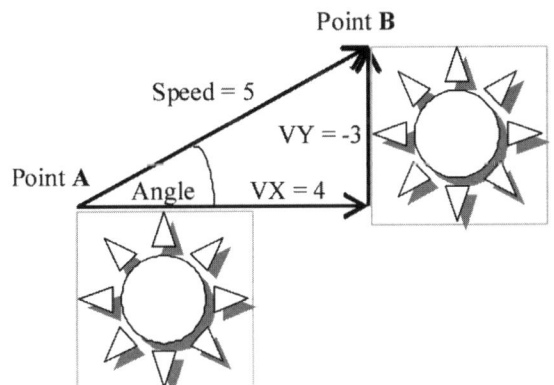

A sprite moving at an angle will experience a change in both the X and Y coordinates. To demonstrate this, consider a sprite that is moving at an angle on the screen.

In order to move from Point A to Point B, we need to move a certain distance in the X direction and a certain distance in the Y direction.

So how do you figure out these individual distances? Using some trigonometric math functions, given an angle and a speed you can calculate the change in X and Y position. Given a change in X and Y position you can also determine the direction angle as well. You do not need to know the exact mathematical details as the **Sprite** class handles all of this for you!

Movement in a certain direction at a certain speed is also called *velocity*. Velocity can be represented either as a speed and direction, or as a change in X and Y coordinates. In the previous diagram the velocity can be specified as (4, -3) since the sprite moved 4 pixels in the X direction and -3 pixels in the Y direction.

Our **Sprite** class will handle all of the trigonometry calculations and conversion functions for you, so you can set the velocity either by speed and direction or by X and Y components. You don't have to worry about the math behind the calculations, but you can look inside the **Sprite** source code if curious about the details.

Now let's take a look at two properties in the **Sprite** class that deal specifically with movement.

MaxSpeed

The **MaxSpeed** property is the maximum possible speed for your sprite. This property is important when the sprite has the ability to change its speed during the course of the game. You never want to create a sprite that moves faster than the player can see or control.

```
public double MaxSpeed = 10;
```

The default **MaxSpeed** value is 10 (pixels per movement). You can adjust that value from your game program at any time.

Velocity

The **Velocity** property is a **Vector2** value that contains the X and Y velocity components.

```
private Vector2 velocity;
```

This property is **private**, meaning you cannot get or set it directly from your game program. Instead call the **SetVelocity()** method to change the velocity or the **GetVelocity()** method to retrieve the current velocity.

```
public Vector2 GetVelocity()
public void SetVelocity(double velocityX, double velocityY)
```

GetVelocity() will return a new **Vector2** containing the current X and Y velocity components.

The **SetVelocity()** method takes two parameters: a value for the speed in the X direction and a value for the speed in the Y direction. The method will calculate the new overall speed value for the sprite, and make sure this value is not greater than the sprite's **MaxSpeed**. This method will also update the direction angle based on your X and Y components.

You can set the sprite's velocity using a speed and angle by calling this method:

```
public void SetSpeedAndDirection(double speed, double directionAngle)
```

This method will convert the speed to X and Y velocity components based on the angle (in degrees).

Chapter Six: Sprites

You can also get or change the current direction angle (in degrees) without changing the speed:

```
public void SetDirectionAngle(double newAngle)
public void ChangeDirectionAngle(double directionAngleDelta)
public double GetDirectionAngle()
```

SetDirectionAngle() will update the sprite's direction to the new absolute angle. **ChangeDirectionAngle()** will add the specified angle offset (either positive or negative!) to the current angle. This can be useful for "turning" right or left. **GetDirectionAngle()** will return the current direction in degrees.

Movement Methods

Once you have set the velocity for your sprite, you will want to move it! There are three different methods that can move your sprite around the screen. The method you choose depends on what you want to happen when your sprite reaches the edge of the window.

```
public bool Move()
public void MoveAndWrap(float screenSizeX, float screenSizeY)
public void MoveAndVanish(float screenSizeX, float screenSizeY)
```

When called, each of the movment methods will add the current velocity to the sprite's position:

```
UpperLeft.X = UpperLeft.X + velocity.X;
UpperLeft.Y = UpperLeft.Y + velocity.Y;
```

Each of the movement methods will also check the Sprite's **TTL** (Time-To-Live) value. If the sprite's **TTL** property is greater than zero then TTL is enabled, and the **TTL** value is reduced by 1. When TTL reaches zero then the **IsAlive** property is set to **false**.

Now, what happens when the sprite reaches one of the sides of the window? If you called **Move**(), nothing special happens; the sprite simply moves off the window and can no longer be seen.

If you call **MoveAndWrap**(), then also provide the window size in the X and Y dimension as parameters. Recall from an earlier chapter that you can get these values from **GraphcisDevice.Viewport.Width** and **GraphicsDevice.Viewport.Height**. The first thing this method does is call the **Move**() method to accomplish basic movement. Next **MoveAndWrap**() will check to see if the sprite has hit the top, bottom, right or left side of the screen. If it has hit any of these sides, the sprite will "wrap" around to the other side of the window and appear to be coming in from the other side.

If you called **MoveAndVanish**(), and provided the same window size in X and Y dimensions, the sprite would vanish when it hits any side of the screen.. This method will internally call **Move**() and then check to see if the sprite has hit any side of the screen. If the sprite has reached an edge it will be marked as dead by setting **IsAlive** = **false**. This method is useful for scenarios like target shooting. If the player misses the target with their shot, you may want to the shot to disappear instead of wrapping around the screen.

Wrapping and Bouncing

You know the screen coordinates are bounded by (0, 0) in the upper left and (window width, window height) in the lower right. How exactly would you determine when a sprite has reached the edge of a screen? It depends! When *bouncing* off the edges you want to change the sprite direction as soon as any part of the sprite hits any edge. The top and left edges are easy. Simply check the sprite's **UpperLeft.X** position to see if it is less than or equal to zero; if so the sprite has reached the left edge! Similarly check the sprite's **UpperLeft.Y** position for less than or equal to zero to see if the sprite has reached the top edge.

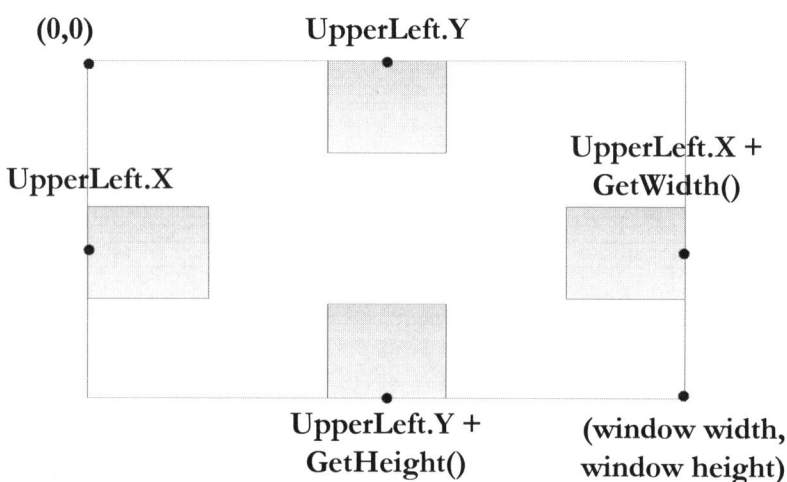

To check the right and bottom edges you need to use the sprite's width and height. The sprite will hit the right edge when **UpperLeft.X** + **Sprite.GetWidth()** is greater than or equal to the window width. It will hit the bottom edge when **UpperLeft.Y** + **Sprite.GetHeight()** is greater than or equal to the window height.

When *wrapping* you may want the sprite to gracefully move all the way off the screen until it's completely invisible, and then appear slowly emerging from just out of view on the far side. In this case along the left edge you need to allow the **UpperLeft.X** value to go negative up to the width of the sprite. Then "wrap" to the other side by setting the **UpperLeft.X** value to the screen width, and the sprite will slowly emerge from the right side. When wrapping from right to left you would allow the **UpperLeft.X** position to reach the screen width so the sprite was all the way off the screen, then wrap the sprite to the left by setting **UpperLeft.X** equal to negative sprite width. Similar operations apply to the top and bottom edge wrapping.

```
    if (UpperLeft.X < (0 - width))    // wrap off left side
        UpperLeft.X = screenSizeX;
    if (UpperLeft.X > (screenSizeX))  // wrap off right side
        UpperLeft.X = 0 - width;
    if (UpperLeft.Y < (-height))      // wrap off top side
        UpperLeft.Y = screenSizeY;
    if (UpperLeft.Y > (screenSizeY))  // wrap off bottom side
        UpperLeft.Y = 0 - height;
```

Chapter Six: Sprites

Activity Two: Buzzing Bees

In this activity you will write the code for the **moveBees**() method in the "Swarm.cs" file. This method will make the bees move left and right on the screen. When the bees reach the left or right edge of the screen, they will shift down toward the player.

Your activity requirements and instructions are found in the "Chapter_06_Activity2.pdf" document located in your "TeenCoder\Game Programming\Activity Docs" folder. You can access this document through your Student Menu or by double-clicking on it from Windows Explorer.

Complete this activity now and ensure your program meets the requirements before continuing!

Chapter Review

- A *sprite* represents a game object and encapsulates useful methods and properties to manage an image on the screen.
- There is no single or formal definition for a **Sprite** class, so we have created one for you to use.
- The **Sprite** class contains properties relating to position and movement such as:
    - The **UpperLeft** property designates the image location on the screen.
    - The **Scale** property controls the stretching or shrinking factors of the sprite image.
    - The **spriteTexture** property contains the loaded **Texture2D** object for the image.
    - The **IsAlive** property is a **Boolean** value which tells us if the sprite is visible on the screen.
    - The **RotationAngle** and **Origin** properties are used to rotate the image around a point.
    - The **LayerDepth** property determines the ordering of the sprite in relation to others overlapped on the same spot.
    - The **TTL** numeric value puts a timer on the visibility of a sprite.
    - The **MaxSpeed** property is the maximum possible speed for your sprite.
    - The **velocity** property is a **Vector2** that holds the X and Y components of the current velocity.
- The **Sprite** class also contains methods to specify images, obtain position and size information, and move the object across the screen:
    - The **SetTexture()** method assigns a loaded image to the **Sprite** from the Content pipeline
    - The **Draw()** method is used to draw the image on the screen.
    - The **GetWidth()** and **GetHeight()** methods calculate the width and height of the sprite.
    - The **GetCenter()** method will retrieve the center-point of the sprite.
    - A variety of methods will allow you to get and set the velocity and determine or adjust the current direction angle.
    - The **Move()**, **MoveAndWrap()**, and **MoveAndVanish()** methods will all move the sprite across the screen according to the current velocity. Each has different behavior when the edge of the screen is reached.

Chapter Seven: Completing Swarm

In the last chapter you made a great start to the Swarm game and learned about the **Sprite** class. In this chapter you will complete the remainder of the Swarm game-play logic including handling of user input, firing of shots, and collision detection.

Lesson One: Adding Player Control

In this lesson you will apply what you have learned about processing keyboard input to the Swarm game. The player will be able to move the smoke gun left and right across the screen by pressing either the left or right arrow keys. They will also be able to shoot the smoke gun by pressing the space bar key.

Recall that in order to accurately detect a key press you need to track the previous keyboard state from the prior **Update**(). By comparing the old keyboard state to the current state you can determine which keys have been pressed or released since the last iteration of the game loop.

A **KeyboardState** variable to track the old state has been declared for you as a member of the main class:

```
KeyboardState oldKeyboardState;
```

All player controls in the Swarm game are handled in the method called **handleKeyPress**(). This method is called from the **Update**() method, which means that it will be executed 60 times per second during game play. In the next activity you will implement the player controls for moving and shooting the smoke gun!

Activity One: Sliding Smoke Gun

In this activity you will allow the player to move the smoke gun back and forth across the screen. Normally the smoke gun is controlled by the keyboard. But you can use an Xbox 360 gamepad instead if preferred.

Your activity requirements and instructions are found in the "Chapter_07_Activity1.pdf" document located in your "TeenCoder\Game Programming\Activity Docs" folder. You can access this document through your Student Menu or by double-clicking on it from Windows Explorer.

Complete this activity now and ensure your program meets the requirements before continuing!

Lesson Two: Shooting Stingers and Smoke

Many computer games have some concept of shooting a projectile on the screen. A game shot has a position, size, direction, and an image and it will need to be moved around the screen and could possibly collide with other objects. For these reasons, a shot is often represented as a sprite. In addition, since most games allow players to shoot more than one shot at a time, shots tend to occur in groups where individual elements come and go frequently. For that reason it may be a good idea to hold your group of shot sprites in a linked list.

Our Swarm game contains two different types of shots: bee stingers and smoke puffs. Since there can be many of these shots on the screen, we have already created linked lists for each type of shot in the starter activity. These lists are declared at the top of the Swarm game class as follows:

```
LinkedList<Sprite> smokeShots = new LinkedList<Sprite>();
LinkedList<Sprite> beeShots = new LinkedList<Sprite>();
```

Maximum Number of Shots

Even though most games allow multiple shots to appear on the screen at once, you will typically want to limit the total number of active shots to some maximum number. This keeps the player from shooting a target by just filling the screen with their shots. Limiting the number of shots and the frequency with which they can be fired is a great way of adding a bit of challenge and realism to the game.

We recommend creating a constant value for the maximum number of shots at the top of your game program. Then use this constant throughout your game logic when deciding if the player is allowed to make another shot. That way if you want to change the number of allowed shots later, you will only need to change the value of the constant in one place and not have to dig through many lines of code!

In our program, we have limited the number of shots with the constant values **MAX_BEE_SHOTS** and **MAX_SMOKE_SHOTS**. These values are initialized at the top of the Swarm game class:

```
const int MAX_BEE_SHOTS = 5;
const int MAX_SMOKE_SHOTS = 2;
```

Shot Movement

You have several options for controlling the lifespan of a projectile on the screen. You might allow the shot to wrap around the screen or bounce off the side of a screen. In that case you should use the TTL feature to make the shot disappear after a while, otherwise it will continue on forever until something gets hit! You may also choose to make the shot vanish when it reaches the edge of the screen. We will be using the vanish option in our Swarm game.

Of course, any shot on the screen should probably stop moving as soon as it collides with another sprite, unless your game calls for some sort of super-shot that goes through things! We will discuss *collision detection* in the next lesson.

Bee Shots

The bee shots in the Swarm game will occur from random bees, at a rate of once every second of game time. Game time in XNA can be measured with an object called **GameTime**. A **GameTime** object is passed into the **Update()** method every time it is called.

```
protected override void Update(GameTime gameTime)
{
}
```

This object has several useful properties:

- **ElapsedGameTime** – the amount of time since the last call to the **Update()** method.
- **TotalGameTime** – the amount of time since the start of the game.

Each of these properties contain a sub-property called **TotalMilliseconds**. This is a double data type that will contain the number of milliseconds that have elapsed. The bee shots will occur once every 1000 milliseconds (1 second) of total game time. This means that we will have to keep track of the last time (in milliseconds) that we fired a bee shot. In this example we've declared **lastBeeShotFired** as a double in the main class, and then update it when a shot is fired:

```
lastBeeShotFired = gameTime.TotalGameTime.TotalMilliseconds;
```

Every time we shoot a bee shot, we will save the total game time, in milliseconds. Then we can compare this value to the current game time during each **Update()** to determine when the next shot should occur.

Activity Two: Shooting the Swarm

In this activity, you will implement the code which will make the bees shoot their stingers and allow the player to shoot the smoke gun.

Your activity requirements and instructions are found in the "Chapter_07_Activity2.pdf" document located in your "TeenCoder\Game Programming\Activity Docs" folder. You can access this document through your Student Menu or by double-clicking on it from Windows Explorer.

Complete this activity now and ensure your program meets the requirements before continuing!

Lesson Three: Collision Detection

A typical game will involve many different sprites moving around the screen at the same time. So what happens when two sprites collide with each other? Maybe a race car has crashed into a side rail, or a shot has hit a target, or a ball has been hit with a bat. When any of these things happen, we need to detect the condition so we can execute the appropriate response. The process of determining if any two sprites have collided with each other is called *collision detection*.

Bounding Rectangle Collision Detection

The simplest method of collision detection is called *bounding rectangle* collision detection. A sprite's bounding rectangle is defined as a box from the upper left coordinate to the lower right coordinate determined by the image's width and height. In this type of collision detection we decide that two sprites have collided if any part of each bounding rectangle overlaps!

Consider the series of three drawings below. Each contains a rocket and a space ship. The lines around the edges represent the bounding rectangles.

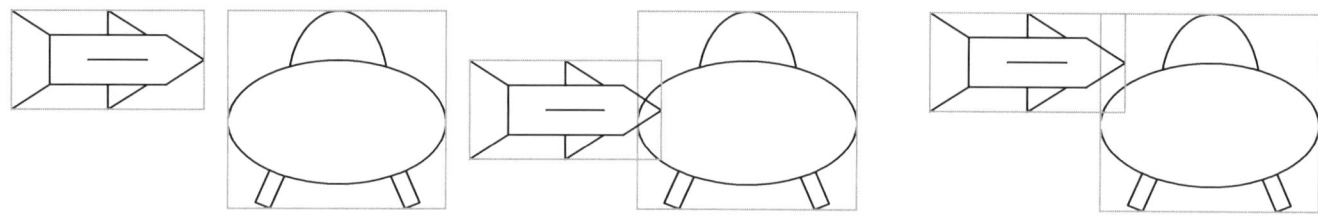

In the first picture the bounding rectangles clearly do not intersect, so there is no collision. In the second picture the rectangles do intersect, so there has been a collision. In the third picture notice that the rectangles intersect yet no part of the rocket image touches the space ship. Nonetheless we still declare this a collision!

You may or may not be able to use bounding rectangle collision detection in your game. It depends on whether or not the false positives demonstrated by the third picture are noticeable by the user or impact game-play. If all of your sprite images mostly fill the bounding rectangle then this simple collision detection may be good enough. But if you have a bunch of oddly shaped sprites that have lots of empty space within the bounding rectangle, your players may get annoyed by collisions that seem to happen against thin air.

Pixel Perfect Collision Detection

A more accurate method for collision detection is called *pixel perfect* collision detection. As you might guess from the name, this technique will only register a collision if any non-transparent pixel in the first image overlaps with a non-transparent pixel in the second image. If you recall our earlier lesson on pixel colors, you know that a pixel has four different color values: Red, Green, Blue and Alpha. The first three values determine the blend of colors in the pixel. The fourth value (the alpha channel) determines whether or not that pixel is transparent. A transparent pixel is not drawn on the screen.

Remember that image transparency is most commonly supported in the PNG and GIF image formats. JPEG images do not support transparency! You should be using PNG or GIF images for your games unless you know you don't want to use transparency or pixel-perfect collision detection.

We can use the alpha channel for a pixel to determine if a sprite has truly collided with another sprite. If a pixel one sprite overlaps a pixel in another sprite, we check the alpha channel value for each pixel. If they are both non-transparent, there is a true collision. If only one is transparent, or both are transparent, there is no collision. Only the left image below would be considered a collision because non-transparent pixels overlap.

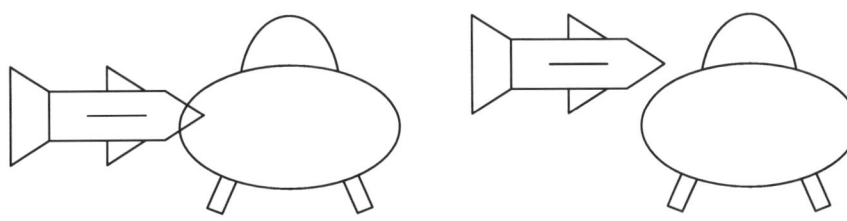

Although the pixel perfect collision detection works much better than the bounding rectangle detection, there are some drawbacks. The main problem is that checking every single pixel for collision is very time consuming, so frequent use can cause a program to slow down considerably.

The Combo Approach

Since pixel-perfect collision detection is so expensive, programmers will often adopt an approach combining both bounding rectangle and pixel-perfect techniques. Start with the simple bounding rectangle collision check. If the bounding rectangles of two sprites are colliding, *then* proceed to the more time-consuming pixel perfect collision detection. This will only use the costly pixel perfect detection when there is a chance of collision. The combination approach is an efficient algorithm and is used by our **Sprite** class.

Sprite Class Collision Detection

How does the **Sprite** class support collision detection? You can call the **IsCollided()** method on a **Sprite** and pass in a second **Sprite** as the parameter Here are the method details:

```
public bool IsCollided(Sprite otherSprite)
```

This method will start by performing bounding rectangle collision detection on the two sprites. If the bounding rectangles overlap, the more in-depth pixel perfect collision detection will be run. If a pixel-perfect collision is detected, **IsCollided()** will return **true**. If not, the method will return **false**.

We can call this method on one sprite (the rocket) and use another sprite (the ship) as a parameter like this:

```
bool isCollided = rocketSprite.IsCollided(shipSprite);
```

If the two sprites have hit each other (their non-transparent pixels have collided), the return value will be **true**; otherwise it will be **false**. Notice is doesn't matter on which sprite you call the function and which sprite you pass in as the parameter. If two sprites are collided then both results are **true**, and if they are not collided then both results are **false**.

Rotation, Scaling, and Collision Detection

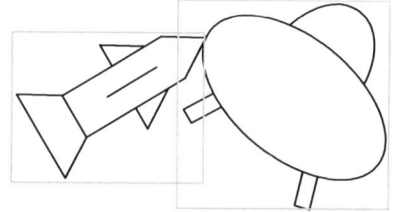

So far our collision detection examples have shown sprites without any rotation or scaling. It's pretty straightforward in that case to determine the bounding rectangle and figure out which pixels overlap. However if the sprites are rotated or scaled then the task becomes more complex! For starters, you can no longer determine the bounding rectangle simply using the **UpperLeft** coordinate and the image width and height.

Once you do have the bounding rectangle, it takes some advanced math to figure out which pixel in one sprite overlaps another pixel in a different sprite. One approach is to start with a pixel (X, Y) in the un-rotated normal-sized image and translate that coordinate to actual screen coordinates (X2, Y2), taking into account the rotation and scaling. Then translate those screen coordinates back into un-rotated coordinates for the second target image (X3, Y3). You can then compare the pixel at (X, Y) from the first image against the pixel at (X3, Y3) in the second image. The most effective way to perform the math is using matrix translations, details of which are beyond the scope of this course. Fortunately the **Sprite.IsCollided()** method handles all of the details for you, so you can still write games with rotated and scaled sprites and pixel-perfect collision detection!

There are a couple of related utility methods on the **Sprite** you might find useful:

```
public Rectangle GetBoundingRectangle()
public virtual void DrawBoundingRectangle(SpriteBatch theSpriteBatch,
                                          Texture2D borderTexture)
```

You can get the bounding rectangle taking into account rotation and scaling. You can also draw the bounding rectangle on the screen if you provide a texture. Generally there isn't a reason to do this within a final game but seeing the bounding rectangle during development may be insightful.

Activity Three: Feeling the Sting

In this activity you will check for collisions among the sprites in the Swarm game.

Your activity requirements and instructions are found in the "Chapter_07_Activity3.pdf" document located in your "TeenCoder\Game Programming\Activity Docs" folder. You can access this document through your Student Menu or by double-clicking on it from Windows Explorer.

Complete this activity now and ensure your program meets the requirements before continuing!

Lesson Four: Ending and Restarting the Game

All games must eventually come to an end. In most cases, this will be because the player has won or lost the game. The finishing touches shown at the end of a game are very important for a good player experience!

Game Over

Make sure that your game has logic to detect the end of a game and display some user feedback with congratulations (or sympathy) at the win or loss. Your player has been playing your game for some time – don't let them feel cheated at the end. If they have won the game, celebrate! Play a happy sound and show a message or an image on the screen. Let them know that they did a great job. If they lost the game, play a sad sound and send them a message challenging them to a new game. Always make sure that you give your player a chance to play again. After all, everyone wants a chance at a rematch!

Dynamic Difficulty Levels

A great way to keep a user interested in playing your game again and again is to change the difficulty level of the game based on the skill level of the player. If your player has lost the game you can decrease the level of difficulty automatically and give them a better chance at winning. If the player has won the game you can increase the difficulty to make the game more challenging. Most popular computer games have some concept of game level, which determines how difficult the game is to play.

Swarm Finishing Touches

You have now completed most of the core logic for the Swarm game! However you have a few finishing touches to complete the game experience. The Swarm game is over when either the player's smoke gun is hit by a bee shot, or the player has shot all of the bees on the screen. When the game is over, an appropriate win or loss message should be displayed at the top of the screen. If the user wants to play the game again, they should be able to hit the space bar and start the game again.

There are several parameters you can adjust to change the Swarm difficulty. You could increase or decrease the bee stinger shot speed or number of shots, increase or decrease the player smoke puff speed, change the smoke gun movement rate, add or subtract bees, make the bunkers larger or smaller, or make the bees move faster or slower. In the next activity you will adjust the bee movement speed based on the results of the previous game. The faster the bee movement, the less time you have to clear out the bees before they descend on your smoke gun. The slower the movement, the more time you have to clear out the bees.

Activity Four: Finishing Swarm

In this activity you will complete the end-of-game logic for Swarm. You will complete the **stopGame()** method plus tweak a few methods you have already completed in prior activities.

Your activity requirements and instructions are found in the "Chapter_07_Activity4.pdf" document located in your "TeenCoder\Game Programming\Activity Docs" folder. You can access this document through your Student Menu or by double-clicking on it from Windows Explorer.

Complete this activity now and ensure your program meets the requirements before continuing!

Chapter Review

- A game projectile has a position, size, direction, movement across the screen, and needs to collide with other objects. For this reason, projectiles are often represented as sprites.
- To keep a player from filling a game screen with repeated shots, the number of shots allowed at any one time is typically limited.
- When a projectile reaches the edge of the screen, you can make the object wrap, bounce, or vanish.
- Use the sprite's Time-To-Live (TTL) property to eventually eliminate shots that wrap around the screen or that should not cross the entire screen before vanishing.
- The **Update()** method provides a **GameTime** object with useful timing information, including the total elapsed game time, in milliseconds.
- *Collision detection* tells you whether or not two sprite images are touching on the screen.
- The simplest method of collision detection is called *bounding rectangle* collision detection. This method will register a collision if the bounding rectangles around each sprite overlap in any way.
- *Pixel-perfect* collision detection only detects a collision if a non-transparent pixel in each image overlaps. This is the ideal collision detection but it takes more time to process than the simpler bounding rectangles method.
- An efficient collision detection approach combines the speed of a bounding rectangle check first followed by a time-intensive pixel-perfect check when the bounding rectangles overlap.
- You should always end a game with some excitement. Your player should be congratulated if they won and consoled if they lost.
- You can change the difficulty level of a game to keep the player interested in playing again.

Congratulations, you have now finished your first fully functional computer game! You will return to Swarm to add special effects such as animation and sound effects during the next two chapters.

Chapter Eight: Animation

So far all images you have drawn on the screen have been static (unchanging). Your games will make a huge leap forward in believability when you animate the images to make them move in a realistic manner.

Lesson One: Animation Concepts

The word *animate* literally means "to bring something to life". *Computer animation* is the art of making still images appear to move and have life. Movies, television programs, and computer programs all animate images in a lifelike manner on the screen. Are the images on the screen really moving? Not really! The animations are made up of still images flashed past your eyes so fast that your brain blends the images together, giving the illusion of movement. Scientific research tells us that the eye needs to see somewhere between 18 and 24 images per second in order for this illusion to work. Good computer animation will show you a series of images at these speeds or higher. The reason no jerkiness or gaps between images is seen at higher speeds is due to "persistence of vision." From moment to moment, the eye and brain working together actually store whatever one looks at for a fraction of a second, and automatically "smooth out" minor jumps.

History of Animation

The phenomenon of "persistence of vision" was discovered by scientists in the 1800s. This discovery led inventors to create a machine called a zoetrope, or "wheel of life". A zoetrope is a cylindrical object that has vertical slits cut into its sides. On the inside of the cylinder is a series of images. When the cylinder spins, a person can look through the slits at the images on the inside of the cylinder. The spinning of the cylinder slits will keep the pictures from simply blurring together so that the user sees a rapid succession of images producing the illusion of motion.

Zoetropes provided viewers with the first "motion picture" of their time. These machines are still used today in exhibits and museums. There is even a life-sized zoetrope in the New York subway system. A wall along a Brooklyn subway was transformed into a zoetrope with 288 slits in the wall, each showing a separate image. As the subway passengers move by, the images appear to be in motion on the wall.

Another popular version of "persistence of vision" animation is the flipbook. The CrackerJack company popularized a form of art called flipbook animation in the early 1900s. Each box of CrackerJack candy contained a series of drawings in a tiny book. When the pages of the book were "flipped" or displayed very quickly one-after-another, the image would appear to be in motion. These simple animations were some of the cheapest movies of that time!

Flipbook animation is still a popular tool for teaching modern animation techniques. Some computer animators will test an animation by first drawing a series of rough images and then flipping the images to see if the end result gives the correct illusion of movement. The same theories of flipbook animation on paper will work for animation in a computer game.

2D vs. 3D Graphics

There are two distinct types of computer graphics: 2D (two-dimensional) and 3D (three-dimensional). Two-dimensional (2D) graphics contain "flat" images that have only a length and a width. These images can naturally be shown on a computer screen, which itself is a 2D surface.

Three-dimensional (3D) graphics are done with images that have three dimensions: length, width and depth. The three dimensions are then projected onto a 2D drawing surface according to some "eyeball" point of view. The resulting perspective image gives a very immersive, lifelike field of view for the computer user. 3D graphics have become popular in recent decades but are fairly complicated to draw on a computer screen.

In this course we will concentrate on 2D graphics. 3D graphics take quite a bit of math to understand and render, and the topic would fill up an entire book on its own! Fortunately with carefully chosen 2D graphics you can often achieve the illusion of a 3D environment with far less effort.

Animation Implementation

The simplest animation starting point involves movement only. You have already seen moving sprites in the Swarm game. When you move an object by re-drawing it in slightly different position you give the illusion that the object is sliding across the monitor. However, the image itself is still static.

In order to make an object realistically appear to move, you will need to both move and change the object at the same time. This means that you will need to pay attention to what objects really look like when they are moving and interacting with other objects. For example, let's say we are going to show a flying disc moving across the screen. We could show a single image in different positions:

This would make the disc move, but it wouldn't appear to by flying realistically. To make it more realistic, we could use these images:

Here, we have added a couple of special touches to make the flying disc seem more realistic. First, we added a stripe to the disc and rotated it a bit in each frame, so the disc appears to spin as it moves. Second, notice that the disc is tilting and wobbling a little. Have you ever noticed that about a flying disc? It rarely ever flies in a perfectly straight line. Instead, it wobbles and tilts, depending on how it was thrown. By adding these subtle little changes to our animation, it becomes much more life-like.

How many unique images or frames do we have in the above sequence? That's right, only four. The last image in the upper right is identical to the first image, so that last image is really just the first step in the next cycle. You may want to continually animate some object by repeating the same set of images over and over again. For instance, you may have a ball that is bouncing on the ground. You can probably accomplish that effect with only a handful of images. Be sure that your last image flows nicely back into your first image so the user doesn't see a jerky restart when the first image is displayed.

When you want to provide animations for your own programs, how should you obtain the image files? One option is to create your own! You can use the Paint program that comes with Windows or any of the many other free or commercial drawing programs available. You can also search online for sources of free or commercial animation files.

Lesson Two: Animation Textures

An animation consists of a series of images that are displayed in fast succession to simulate motion. In this lesson we will take a look at techniques to manage and load these images in an XNA game.

You learned how to add images as XNA Project Content in chapter four. These images were loaded into **Texture2D** objects, which could be displayed on the screen in a game's **Draw()** method. Animation requires multiple images, which can be handled a couple of different ways in a game program.

One approach to animation is to make a separate image file for each frame of the animation. This means that if we were using the flying disc example from our last lesson, we would need four different images:

  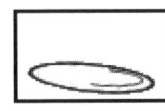 

Once we have these four images, we would need to load each of these images into a separate **Texture2D** object. When we want to implement the animation, we could select a different texture to draw each cycle, resulting in an animated disc flying across the screen.

This method is simple, but cumbersome. Since all of the images are separate files, we would have to add and keep track of four images in the Content pipeline, then load and manage four different **Texture2D** objects in our program. It can take more computer resources to manage four images instead of one. In addition, it's more difficult to draw a smoothly animated series of images if you are constantly flipping back and forth between different images in your graphics editor.

A better method of handling animation is to treat our series of images like a movie reel. A single movie reel contains all of the still images from the movie separated into frames, or single images. When it's time to show the movie, a projector will display one frame from the reel at a time, giving the illusion of motion.

We can adopt the movie reel concept to our own animated images. To do this, create a single image which contains all of the animation frames side-by-side in a single "strip". This type of image strip is just like the movie reel, containing all of our images from the beginning of our motion to the end. Notice that the physical image height is the same as the height of any one still image, but the image width is N times the width of any one still image, where N is the number of frames in the strip.

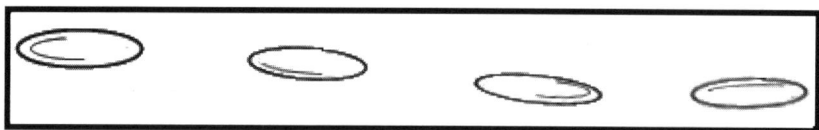

The game program will then work like a movie projector, showing one section of our animation "strip" at a time. It is much easier to load and manage one texture for a particular object.

Drawing Animation Strips

Let's take another look at the **SpriteBatch.Draw()** method we are using from within the **Sprite** class:

```
public void Draw (
    Texture2D texture,
    Vector2 position,
    Nullable<Rectangle> sourceRectangle,
    Color color,
    float rotation,
    Vector2 origin,
    Vector2 scale,
    SpriteEffects effects,
    float layerDepth)
```

So far we haven't paid too much attention to the **sourceRectangle** parameter. If you use **null** for this parameter then the entire texture image will be drawn. However you can specify any bounding rectangle you like that describes a subsection of the input image, and only that subsection will be drawn! In order to use an animation strip we will need to use this parameter to tell the **Draw()** method which of the animation frames within the strip to draw on the screen. The frame's bounding rectangle will be based on the width of the individual frame and the current frame number that we are drawing. Let's take a look at an example of this with our flying disc images.

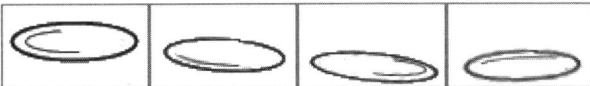

We've drawn boxes around the individual images to demonstrate where the frame boundaries are in the strip. In a real program, you would not have boxes in your strip image. Each of the frames should have the exact same width and height. In order to pass the frame location and size to the **Draw()** method, we need to create a **Rectangle** object. This rectangle will contain four pieces of information about the frame: the starting X-coordinate, the starting Y-coordinate, and the width and the height of the frame.

Let's say that in our flying disc strip, each frame has a width of 20 pixels and a height of 10 pixels. The upper-left corner of the entire strip (and the first frame) is point (0, 0). The starting X-coordinate for each frame can be calculated as: **X-coordinate = width of frame * frame number** (where frame number is zero-based). Since we will start our rectangle at the top of the strip every time, the starting Y-coordinate will always be zero. The height and width will always be 10 and 20 respectively. Here's how this information looks in our strip image:

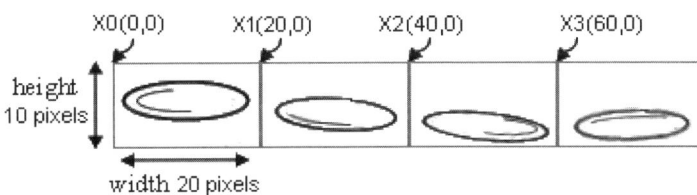

Note that our first frame is frame 0, not frame 1. Now we can create a **Rectangle** object to specify a particular frame in the animation strip:

```
Rectangle sourceRectangle = new Rectangle(width * frameNum, 0, width, height);
```

Now, to continuously loop the frames in our animation strip we merely need to increment the frame number (**frameNum** above) from 0 to N-1 and then wrap back to 0. We could also choose to perform a "short" one-time animation sequence from some starting frame through another ending frame and then stay on one static frame until the animation is called for again.

Lesson Three: Animation in the Sprite Class

In our last lesson we talked about how to create an animation strip and how to determine the bounding rectangle information for each individual frame. In this lesson we will take a closer look at how the **Sprite** class will handle animation for you.

Sprite Animation Properties

The **Sprite** class contains four internal properties to support animation strips:

```
private int numFrames = 1;
private int frameWidth;
private int currentFrame = 0;
private Rectangle imageRect;
```

The first property holds the number of frames that are contained within your animation strip. By default, this number is 1, which means that there is only 1 frame in the strip and the **Draw()** method will draw the entire image on the screen. This will work for any non-animated image, including all of the images you have loaded so far in previous programs! In fact the animation support has been in the **Sprite** class all along, and you may not have noticed. When you are using an animation strip this property will be automatically set to the correct number of frames when you load the image.

The second property is the width of an individual frame in the animation strip. The width will be automatically calculated based on the number of frames and the overall width of the animation strip. The third property tracks the number of the currently selected frame. The fourth property contains the bounding rectangle for the currently selected frame. The bounding rectangle is calculated based on the first three properties! All four properties are **private**, meaning you can't set them to arbitrary values from outside the **Sprite** class. The properties will be calculated or updated as necessary when the **Sprite** animation-related methods are called.

SetTexture() for Animation Strips

There are actually two different versions of the **SetTexture()** method to assign a texture to a **Sprite**.

```
SetTexture(Texture2D texture)
SetTexture(Texture2D texture, int frames)
```

You have been using the first form in your earlier programs, which defaults the number of frames to 1. The second version, which you will use to load an animation strip, tells the **Sprite** how many frames are in the strip. From the number of frames the **Sprite** can internally calculate the **frameWidth** property as follows:

```
frameWidth = spriteTexture.Width / numFrames;
```

The sprite's **imageRect** property is also initialized to the first frame:

```
imageRect = new Rectangle(0, 0, frameWidth, height);
```

This rectangle represents the first frame in the animation strip. The **Draw()** method will use this bounding rectangle to determine which portion of the image to draw on the screen.

Animate() and AnimationInterval

Once you have loaded an animation strip into a **Sprite**, you will need a way to cycle the currently displayed image through the different animation frames within the strip. The **Sprite.Animate()** method does just that:

```
void Animate(GameTime gameTime)
```

Each time you call **Animate()**, usually from within your **Update()** logic, the **Sprite** will check the current game time and advance to the next animation frame. How does the **Sprite** know how frequently you want to cycle through frames? By default the **Sprite** assumes that each time you call **Animate()**, regardless of the current game time, the frame should be advanced to the next image. **Update()** usually gets called 60 times a second, so if that is how fast you want your image to animate then you don't need to do anything special.

You may want to slow your animation down so it can be better seen. You can set the **Sprite.AnimationInterval** property to a number of milliseconds that must elapse before changing frames.

```
public int AnimationInterval = 0;
```

An update rate of 60 times a second gives an interval of 1000 / 60 − 17 milliseconds per frame. You can therefore set an interval larger than 17 milliseconds to slow down the animation. However you won't be able to animate faster than the **Update()** loop itself, so any interval less than 17 milliseconds will have no effect! The default value of 0 means the animation frame changes will occur at the same rate as your **Update()** logic.

Continuous and Short Animation

The **Sprite** class supports two types of animation: *continuous* and *short*. Continuous animation simply loops over the entire animation strip displaying each frame in turn. When the end of the strip is reached the **currentFrame** is reset back to 0 and the animation repeats. You can use continuous animation with the methods and properties already described. Just call **Sprite.SetTexture()** with an animation strip and number of frames, then call **Animate()** from your update logic. You can adjust the animation interval if desired.

Continuous animation is controlled by a **Sprite** property called **ContinuousAnimation** which defaults to **true** when you create the sprite.

An animation "short" is a brief one-time sequence of frames that may or may not cover the entire animation strip. Animation shorts can be used when you have an object that is usually static but might occasionally need to animate as a special effect. After the animation short completes you may want to revert to the original static frame or specify a new static frame. For example, in our Swarm game let's say we want to animate the destruction of the smoke sprayer if it gets hit by a bee stinger. We could use an animation strip where the first frame shows the normal smoke sprayer, and the remaining frames show the gradual collapse of the sprayer after taking a hit. The final frame would show the remains of the gun.

The smoker sprayer object would be loaded with the animation strip of 5 frames. Make sure you set **Sprite.ContinuousAnimation** = **false** when you plan to use an animation short, otherwise your short will animate right from the beginning! Then, when a collision is detected, you would call the **Sprite.StartAnimationShort()** method to begin the brief animation.

```
void StartAnimationShort(int startFrame, int stopFrame, int finalFrame)
```

The first and second parameters tell the **Sprite** on what frames to start and end the short animation. The final frame represents the frame that will be displayed after the animation sequence is complete. To animate the smoke sprayer given the animation strip shown above, you would use the following parameters:

```
smokeSprayer.StartAnimationShort(1, 4, 4);
```

The short animation will then cover the last 4 frames in the strip, and remain on the last frame when done.

One final public method that may be useful in your game logic allows you to determine if an animation sequence is currently running:

```
public bool IsAnimating()
```

This method will return **true** if the **Sprite** is under continuous animation or currently has an animation short running. You could use this method to determine if the **Animate()** method needs to be called.

```
if (smokeSprayer.IsAnimating())
    smokeSprayer.Animate(gameTime);
```

Chapter Eight: Animation

Example Animation

The **Sprite** animation methods make it very simple to use animation strips in your game project. Let's take a look at how our flying disc images would be continuously animated!

First, we will add the animation strip to our Content node as "FlyingDiscStrip". Then declare a **Texture2D** variable **discTexture** at the main game scope, and load the image into the variable in **LoadContent()**.

```
discTexure = Content.Load<Texture2D>("FlyingDiscStrip");
```

Now you can create a new **Sprite** called **discSprite** and set its position just like any other sprite:

```
Sprite discSprite = new Sprite();
discSprite.UpperLeft = new Vector2(100,100);
```

Next, set the texture into the **Sprite** and specify the number of frames in the strip:

```
discSprite.SetTexture(discTexture, 4);
```

This will initialize the sprite with our animation strip texture and set the **discSprite**.numFrames property to 4. Now when we call the **discSprite.Draw()** method the **Sprite** class will display the first frame of our animation on the screen.

To advance the animation to the next frame, we will need to call the **Animate()** method. In our **Update()** logic we can use the following lines of code to move and animate the image:

```
discSprite.UpperLeft.X += 5;
discSprite.Animate(gameTime);
```

Now our flying disc will move across the screen and its image will animate automatically!

Chapter Review

- *Computer animation* is the art of making still images appear to move in a lifelike manner.
- Smooth computer animation will show a series of images faster than 18 to 24 images per second.
- *Persistence of vision* is a phenomenon where the eye and brain work together to store images seen in a fraction of a second. The brain will smooth out the differences between the images giving the illusion of motion.
- Two-dimensional (2D) graphics are flat images with only a length and a width. Three-dimensional (3D) graphics have a length, width and depth. 3D graphics are projected onto a 2D image based on some eye viewpoint and then displayed on the flat computer screen.
- Realistic computer animation will attempt to copy the natural movements of an object.
- An *animation strip* is a long image that, like movie reel, contains a series of different frames representing the movement for an object. This method requires only one **Texture2D** object in code and is much easier to handle and maintain.
- To draw a single frame from an animation strip, you pass a "source rectangle" into the **Sprite.Draw()** method. This parameter causes only one small area (or frame) of the strip to be drawn on the screen.
- The **Sprite** class can handle either animation strips or regular images. To use an animation strip, you must specify the number of frames in the image during the **SetTexture()** method call.
- To move to the next frame in an animation strip, you can just call the **Sprite.Animate()** method.
- You can configure a **Sprite** for continuous (looping) animation over the entire set of frames.
- You can also launch an animation "short" sequence to show brief animated effects.
- Call the **Sprite.IsAnimating()** method to find out if the sprite is currently animating the image

Activity: Animated Swarm

In this activity, you will add some animation to the Swarm game! Specifically, you will animate the bees to make them appear to buzz back and forth on the screen, and animate the smoke shot fired from the smoke sprayer. You will also animate the destruction of the smoke sprayer when it gets hits by a bee stinger.

Your activity requirements and instructions are found in the "Chapter_08_Activity.pdf" document located in your "TeenCoder\Game Programming\Activity Docs" folder. You can access this document through your Student Menu or by double-clicking on it from Windows Explorer.

Complete this activity now and ensure your program meets the requirements before continuing!

Chapter Nine: Music and Sound Effects

So far we have learned about the graphics that make computer games look great. But there are other special effects important to games besides graphics. Sound and music, for instance, can turn a good game into a fantastic experience! In this chapter you will learn how to make sound effects and play background music.

Lesson One: Sound Files

Early computers used for the first games did not have sound cards. They only had a speaker capable of making beeping sounds. Originally this speaker was intended to offer simplistic feedback in the event of a computer error. But game programmers hijacked the PC speaker when they began writing games in the 1970s and 1980s. These early designers figured out that if you make slight changes to the duration and frequency (or pitch) of a sound, you can emulate musical notes. These notes were then used to make music and special effect sounds in a game. However, these sounds were not exactly high-quality and often required all game processing to stop while the sound was played.

In the 1990s, sound cards started becoming the norm in personal computers. These sound cards were add-on cards, which meant that they were typically installed after the computer was purchased. Sound cards were able to produce a much more realistic sound experience. Eventually, sound cards became so common that hardware manufacturers started including them on the motherboard itself. This ensured that the consumer had built-in sound capability as soon as the PC came out of the box. Many modern current computers have the ability to play true digital surround sound, just like any high definition receiver!

Of course, as a computer's sound hardware improved, so did the audio experience in computer games. Beeps and bleeps are no longer acceptable sound effects. Game consumers now expect a more intense experience, with explosion sounds, background music and constant sound feedback.

Sound File Formats

The sounds that we hear every day all start as changes in pressure in the human ear. The magnitude and frequency of these pressure waves combine to produce the full range of sounds humans can perceive. When a sound is recorded in digital form for a computer, these pressure waves are translated into digital wave forms. There are two main types of sound files on a computer: compressed and uncompressed.

Uncompressed sound files are often called Pulse Code Modulation (PCM) files. PCM is often used when the highest quality of sound is required and is often the format of choice for important or archived sounds. Common WAV files may contain uncompressed PCM. Unfortunately, to get the highest quality sound requires very large files, so uncompressed sound should be used with care. Most games will use uncompressed sound, especially for shorter effects, because they are very simple to play and have little impact on game speed.

Compressed sound files use complicated algorithms to pack more sound information in a smaller space. Compression algorithms allow for smaller file sizes, but do reduce sound quality. Some common compression formats include MP3 and WMA files. Compressed file formats became more important as the Internet inspired music file sharing. It takes much less time to upload a 2MB MP3 song vs. a 10MB WAV file!

Adding Sound to the Content Pipeline

Sound files are considered "content", just like images or fonts. The first step in using an uncompressed sound in an XNA game is to add the sound file to your project as Content. This is done the same way you added image files in previous chapters. The first thing you may want to do is add a sub-folder to the Content pipeline called "Audio" in order to keep your sound files more organized. To add a sub-folder, right-click on the "Content" node in the Solution Explorer and then choose "Add" and "New Folder":

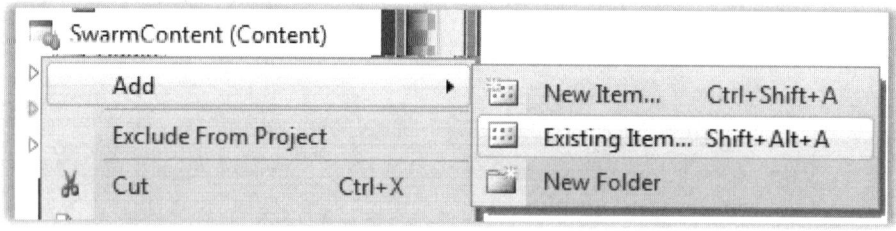

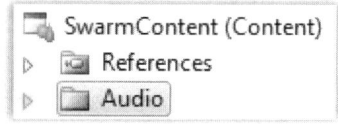 This will add a sub-folder named "New Folder", which you can rename to something more meaningful like "Audio".

Now let's say you want to add a WAV file called "buzz.wav" to your game project. To add the new sound, right-click on the "Audio" folder and choose the "Add" option and then the "Existing Item" option. Navigate to the location of your audio file, select the file and then click on the "Add" button. You should then see your sound in the Content Audio folder.

Lesson Two: Playing Sound Effects

Uncompressed sounds are commonly used in games and programs because they are high quality and do not require any special algorithms to play. The easiest method for playing a sound in XNA is with a class called **SoundEffect** from the **Microsoft.Xna.Framework.Audio** namespace.

SoundEffect Class

The **SoundEffect** class represents one sound file in your Content pipeline, just like a **Texture2D** class represents an image and a **SpriteFont** class represents a font. To load a sound from the Content pipeline, just create a **SoundEffect** variable like this in your code at the main class level:

```
public class Swarm : Microsoft.Xna.Framework.Game
{
    SoundEffect mySoundEffect;
```

Then in your game's **LoadContent()** method you can call **Content.Load()** method to load the sound file into the **SoundEffect** variable. The technique is just like loading images except the data type is **SoundEffect**:

```
protected override void LoadContent()
{
    mySoundEffect = Content.Load<SoundEffect>("Audio\\buzz");
```

You need to pass in any Content folder name you created with the sound file name, but do not include the sound file extension. XNA will be able to figure out what kind of sound file it is through the information in the Content tree. You should also notice that we cast the **Load()** call as a "**<SoundEffect>**". Now that the **mySoundEffect** variable is initialized, you can use it from any of your **Update()** logic by simply calling one of two **Play()** methods on the variable name.

```
public bool SoundEffect.Play()
public bool SoundEffect.Play(float volume, float pitch, float pan)
```

The first version of **Play()** with no parameters will simply play the sound with all default settings for volume, pitch, and pan. The three parameters in the second version allow you to alter the sound in different ways.

`float volume`	This parameter can range between 0.0 (silent) to 1.0 (full volume). Values between 0.0 and 1.0 play a softer than normal sound.
`float pitch`	This parameter can change the sound's octave. A value of -1.0 will turn the sound down one octave, 1.0 will bring it up one octave, and 0.0 will keep the normal octave.

| `float` pan | This parameter controls whether the sound comes from the left speaker (-1.0), the right speaker (1.0), both speakers equally (0.0), or any ratio in between (from -1.0 to 1.0). You could, for example, play an explosion sound only through the left speaker when the explosion occurs to the player's left, so the player's experience is more lifelike. |

Here's a quick example:

```
// play sound with all default parameters
mySoundEffect.Play();

// play sound at half volume, one octive higher, through right speaker
mySoundEffect.Play(0.5f, 1.0f, 1.0f);
```

Your game will now play the sound effect from beginning to end without any further effort on your part! But what if you want to have some control over the sound as it is playing? You may want to pause or stop the sound completely, especially if it's a lengthy effect and some condition within your game changes. That's where the **SoundEffectInstance** class becomes useful.

SoundEffectInstance Class

The **SoundEffect.Play()** method will internally create a **SoundEffectInstance** object. This object represents an actual playing sound. If you want to have fine control over the playing sound, or you want to play multiple instances of a sound from the same **SoundEffect** (perhaps with different parameters), you will need to create and use the **SoundEffectInstance** object directly. You will want to declare the variable at a class scope again within your main game object, so you can use it across multiple calls to **Update()**.

```
public class Swarm : Microsoft.Xna.Framework.Game
{
    SoundEffectInstance soundInstance;
```

When you are ready to launch a new sound in your game logic, call the **SoundEffect.CreateInstance()** method and store the result in your variable:

```
soundInstance = mySoundEffect.CreateInstance();
```

Now you have a firm grip on the actual sound that will be played! The sound is initially paused after you create a new instance. You can play, stop, pause, and resume the sound by making the corresponding calls on your **SoundEffectInstance** object.

```
soundInstance.Play();
soundInstance.Stop();
soundInstance.Pause();
soundInstance.Resume();
```

If your sound is a simple 2-second explosion, there is probably no need to monitor the instance of the sound effect. It will be done playing before you can pause, stop or resume it. However, if you are using the **SoundEffect** class to play a longer sound, you may want to create a **SoundEffectInstance** variable to have more control over the sound's playback.

The **SoundEffectInstance** object has useful properties you can set to control the output:

`float Volume`	Works just like the **volume** parameter to **Play**() described above.
`float Pitch`	Works just like the **pitch** parameter to **Play**() described above.
`float Pan`	Works just like the **pan** parameter to **Play**() described above.
`bool IsLooped`	If set to **true** prior to calling **Play**(), the sound will loop continuously instead of playing once through and stopping.

This example creates as **SoundEffectInstance**, sets some properties, and begins to play in a continuous loop. We assume that the **soundInstance** variable has already been declared elsewhere, and that **mySoundEffect** was declared and initialized with a valid **SoundEffect** object.

```
soundInstance = mySoundEffect.CreateInstance();
soundInstance.Volume = 0.5f;         // half volume
soundInstance.Pitch = 1.0f;          // one octave higher
soundInstance.Pan = 1.0f;            // play through right speaker only
soundInstance.IsLooping = true;      // continuous loop
soundInstance.Play();                // start sound!
```

 Between XNA 3.0 and XNA 4.0 the SoundEffect.Play() method definitions were changed. If you are looking at documentation or examples that do not match what we have described here, then you are probably looking at older XNA 3.0 materials!

Lesson Three: Playing Music

You may want to play longer music or songs in your game program. In this lesson, we'll take a look at a method to play any sound file (compressed or uncompressed). To play music you will use the **Song** class and the **MediaPlayer** class from the **Microsoft.Xna.Framework.Media** namespace.

Song Class

Music is a form of Content just like images, fonts, and audio files. You add music files to your Content pipeline just like any other type of content (right-click on the Content node and add the existing item). These music files are represented by the **Song** object in code, which is equivalent to **Texture2D** for images, **SpriteFont** for fonts, and **SoundEffect** for sounds.

As you probably have figured out already, you should declare a **Song** variable at your main game scope first.

```
public class Swarm : Microsoft.Xna.Framework.Game
{
    Song mySong;
```

Then, load the **Song** object from within the **LoadContent**() method like any other content:

```
mySong = Content.Load<Song>("Audio\\songName");
```

The **Song** class will not actually play a song! Instead it just holds available information about the song file.

Once you have loaded a **Song** variable, you can view any available information that was read from the WAV file. The following properties are part of a **Song**:

`Album` Album	Information about the song's album
`Artist` Artist	Information about the song's artist
`TimeSpan` Duration	The length of the song
`Genre` Genre	Information about the song's genre
`String` Name	The title of the song
`Int` TrackNumber	The song's track number on the album

Notice that most of these properties are themselves objects with sub-properties (e.g. **Artist** has an **Artist.Name** property, among others). For full details about each object properties please refer to the MSDN documentation.

MediaPlayer Class

The **MediaPlayer** class provides the methods and properties necessary to play **Song** objects. This class is a static class, which means you do not need to create a variable to use the **MediaPlayer** methods. The methods and properties for **MediaPlayer** are accessible by just using the name "MediaPlayer" and the dot operator. Let's take a look at the methods for the **MediaPlayer** class.

The **MediaPlayer.Play()** method will begin playing the specified **Song**:

```
MediaPlayer.Play(mySong) ;
```

The **MediaPlayer.Stop()** method will stop the current **Song** from playing:

```
MediaPlayer.Stop();
```

If you wanted to stop playing the current **Song** and then restart it later, you can use **Pause()** and **Resume()**.

```
MediaPlayer.Pause();
MediaPlayer Resume();
```

In addition to these methods, **MediaPlayer** has a couple of useful properties. These properties can be used to configure how the song is played.

`static float` Volume	Like the **SoundPlayer** volume control, this value is relative to the volume of the user's speakers. A value of 0.0 indicates that the volume is silent. A value of 1.0 indicates that the song is playing at full volume.
`static bool` IsMuted	This property can either be used to set the current song volume to muted, or check to see if the song is muted. This property is useful if you need to temporarily mute a song in the background so that the user can hear other instructions or sound effects in the game.
`static bool` IsRepeating	This property can be used to loop the song over and over. If this value is **true**, the song will play indefinitely on the player's computer. This is a great way to create a background sound for your game out of an MP3 or WMA file. This property can also be used to check the current repeat setting for the **MediaPlayer**.

We have really only scratched the surface of the **MediaPlayer**'s capability. The **MediaPlayer** can store a queue of **Songs** and play them in shuffled order or front to back, much like a MP3 player! We will not need this capability for our games, so you can refer to the MSDN documentation for more details.

Lesson Four: The XACT Tool

A **SoundEffect** class object is very simple to use, which is both a strength and weakness. You may find yourself looking for more advanced sound combinations and editing features. Fortunately XNA provides a built-in sound editor called the Microsoft Cross-Platform Audio Creation Tool (XACT). This free tool is automatically installed with the XNA Game Studio software. Let's take a quick tour of this valuable tool.

What is XACT?

Why do you need a separate tool for game audio? Consider that a game is made up of several fundamental parts: the program logic, the graphics (images), and the audio sounds or music. In large game software companies, these parts are all handled by different people with different skills. Programmers write the code for the game using (in our case) Visual C# software. Artists use their own professional image editing software to create realistic game images. Musicians or sound technicians compose the sounds and music for the game using XACT. The XACT tool can modify and blend different sounds together into useful combinations. Once this audio processing is finished, the final audio files are built and then handed off to the programmer, who can then plug the sounds into the game program.

XACT is a GUI-driven audio content creation system. Audio designers can load WAV files into groups, organize the files into discrete *cues* that can be activated by in-game events, and create transitions between cues. XACT also enables designers to define variables that can be changed in-game to modify audio settings. With these advanced tools, an audio designer might, for example, design a set of car engine sounds for a racing game. Through the use of a variable, then cause the car engine sounds to increase or decrease in pitch and volume as the variable is controlled in-game by the XACT engine.

XACT Walkthrough

We will not be using the XACT tool for any of the projects in this course. This tool is mainly used for complex games and a full tutorial could cover an entire book by itself! The following section will give you an overview of XACT and you are encouraged to learn more on your own if interested.

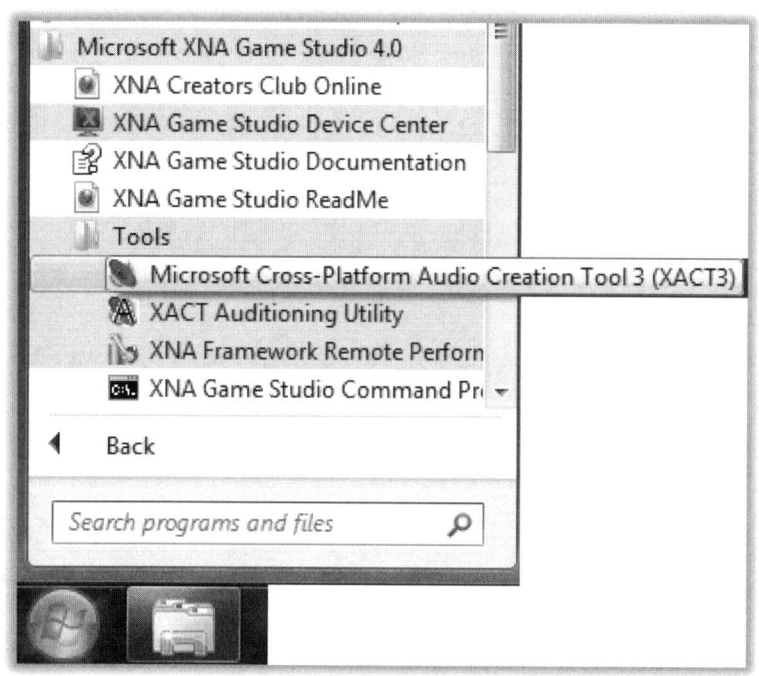

The XACT tool can be found on your Start menu under "Microsoft XNA Game Studio", then "Tools", then "Microsoft Cross-Platform Audio Creation Tool".

The main XACT window looks like this:

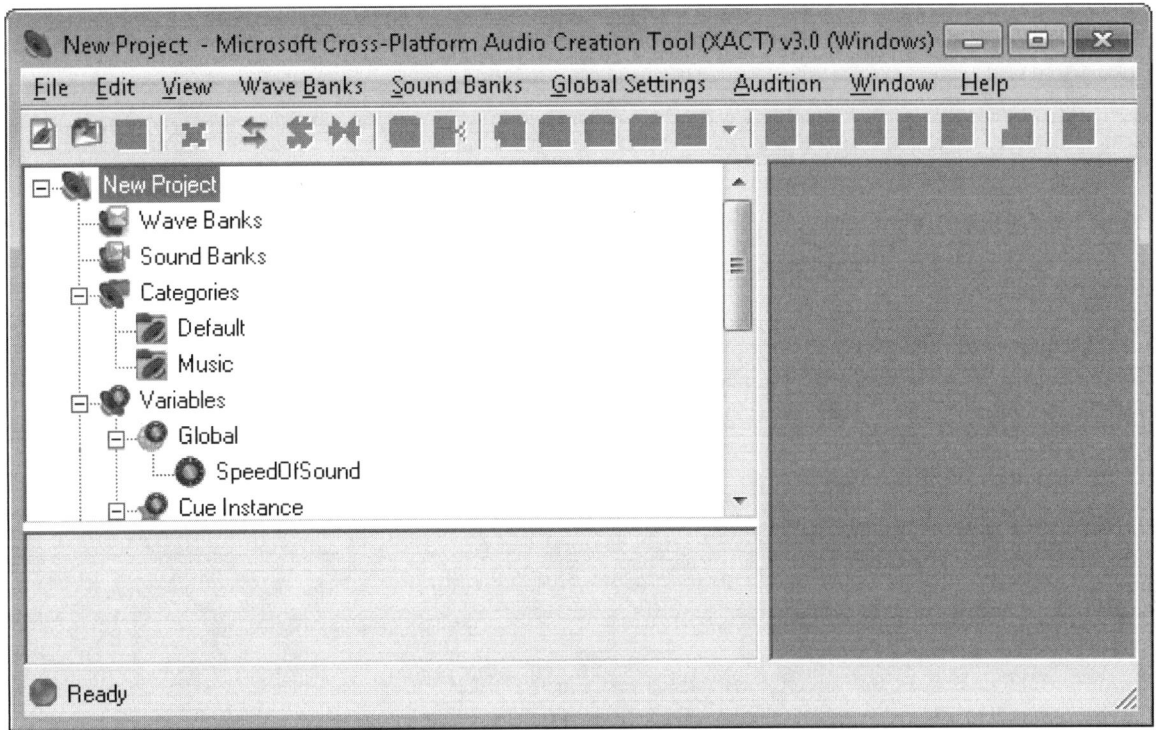

Within the XACT GUI you can create sound projects, add wave banks and sounds banks and then customize your sounds in various ways. The finished combinations and customizations of sounds are called "Cues", which can be played as one sound in your game program.

Once you have finished creating your sounds, you will save your XACT project. The XACT tool will create an ".xap" file which contains all the information about your sounds. When you add this file to your project, the Content Pipeline will automatically build your sound files at run time.

To initialize XACT support in your game, you must create a new **AudioEngine**, which works like the **GraphicsEngine** does for images. The **AudioEngine** keeps track of the game sounds and updates them when necessary. Next, you will load any wave banks you need by creating new **WaveBank** objects, and load any sound banks that you need by creating **SoundBank** objects. Once you load the necessary files, you can access your sound cues by calling the **SoundBank.GetCue()**. Each **Cue** instance that you retrieve is unique, even when you retrieve multiple cues with the same name. This allows multiple instances of the same **Cue** to exist and play simultaneously.

XACT is a powerful tool for XNA games. The ability to mix and combine sounds, and to add location features, like panning and Doppler effects, makes this tool very important for 3D games. If you plan on continuing your game programming education and moving into 3D games, the XACT tool is a must have!

Chapter Review

- Earlier computers only had a PC speaker capable of making beeping sounds.
- The advent of the sound card in the 1990s allowed game programmers to produce realistic sound.
- Uncompressed sounds are the highest quality and are easy to play, but have the largest file size.
- Compressed sounds have been packed into a smaller memory space and require less resources, but are not as high-quality as uncompressed sounds.
- Sounds are added to a project's Content pipeline in the same way as an image.
- The easiest method for playing a sound is to use a class called the **SoundEffect**.
- **SoundEffect** variables are initialized with the **Content.Load()** method just as an image. These sounds can then be played by calling the **SoundEffect.Play()** method.
- The **SoundEffect.Play()** method includes a version that allows you to change the volume, pitch and pan of the sound.
- A **SoundEffectInstance** object is created using the **SoundEffect.CreateInstance()** method. This object can be used to pause, play, stop or resume the sound as it is playing on the computer.
- A **Song** object contains information about a compressed sound file. A sound file can be loaded into a **Song** object using the **Content.Load()** method.
- The **MediaPlayer** class provides the methods and properties necessary to play **Song** objects. These methods include **Play()**, **Stop()**, **Pause()** and **Resume()**. The most useful properties are **Volume**, **IsMuted** and **IsRepeating**.
- Advanced sound editing for XNA games can be performed using the Microsoft Cross-Platform Audio Creation Tool (XACT), which is a free tool included with the XNA Game Studio installation.
- XACT is best used for complex games and is not used for the simpler games in this course.

Chapter Nine: Music and Sound Effects

Activity: Audible Swarm

In this activity you will add sound effects to the Swarm game. *Note: If you do not have a sound card in your computer, or your computer speakers are not properly hooked up or turned on, you will not be able to hear any sound!*

Your activity requirements and instructions are found in the "Chapter_09_Activity.pdf" document located in your "TeenCoder\Game Programming\Activity Docs" folder. You can access this document through your Student Menu or by double-clicking on it from Windows Explorer.

Complete this activity now and ensure your program meets the requirements before continuing!

Chapter Ten: Game Physics

The laws of physics determine how objects move, change speeds, and bounce or reflect off hard surfaces. You will often want to simulate these laws to govern sprite movement and make your games more realistic.

Lesson One: Velocity and Acceleration

In an earlier chapter we discussed velocity in the context of sprite movement. In this lesson we will look at how *acceleration* can change velocity over time.

Velocity

Recall from Chapter Six that *velocity* is a combination of *speed* (change in position per unit time) and *direction* (angle of movement). We also know that the velocity vector can be represented equally well by components in the X and Y direction instead of a speed and angle. We can always convert velocity representation between the (speed, angle) pair and the (velocity X, velocity Y) pair using some trigonometric functions.

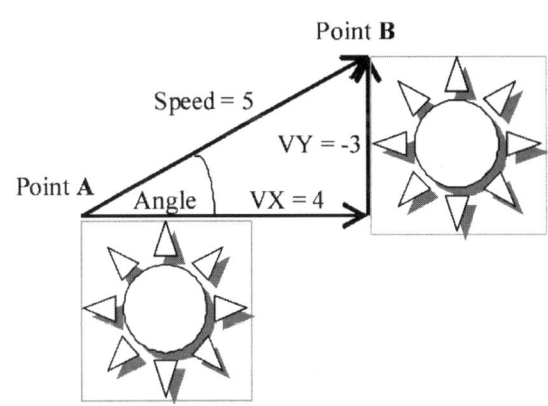

In trigonometry, if you know one side of a right triangle and the angle of one of its corners, you can calculate its other two sides. The diagram on the right shows how this calculation works when moving a sprite. The overall speed is 5 at an angle of 36.9 degrees. From these two values we can use some easy calculations to find the velocity in the X and Y directions:

```
Velocity X =  5 * Cosine (36.9°) =  4
Velocity Y = -5 *   Sine (36.9°) = -3
```

This means that if a sprite is moving with speed 5 at 36.9 degrees, we move the sprite by adjusting the upper-left corner position by 4 pixels in the **X** direction and -3 pixels in the **Y** direction. Remember that in computer terms the "up" direction is negative and the "down" direction is positive, which is opposite to the way that the math world works. This is why we use the negative value for our **Velocity Y** calculation.

What if we knew the velocity-X (VX) and velocity-Y (VY) components and wanted to calculate the speed and direction? The speed can be calculated by using *Pythagorean's theorem*. Pythagorean's theorem states that the square of the hypotenuse (diagonal edge) of a right triangle equals the sum of the squares of the two other sides of the triangle: $a^2 + b^2 = c^2$. In our case, the calculation is: $VX^2 + VY^2 =$ (overall speed of the sprite)^2. The square root of this result is our overall speed.

```
Speed = Sqrt(VX² + VY²)
```

Given the VX and VY components you can also determine the direction angle based on the tangent function. We know that for a right triangle, the opposite side (VY) divided by the near side (VX) equals the tangent of the angle. Therefore the inverse tangent (arctan) of the VY divided by VX equals the angle:

```
Angle = ArcTan( VY / VX )
```

This formula unfortunately isn't specific enough to determine which quadrant the angle actually resides in, since the input parameter can be positive or negative and there are two combinations of positive or negative VX and VY that will produce a positive or negative. Fortunately the .NET framework has another method called **Math.Atan2()** which handles this nicely!

```
double Math.Atan2(double y, double x)
```

The resulting value (in radians) has been assigned to the correct quadrant based on the positive and negative combination of the individual input parameters.

The **Sprite** has a static utility method that wraps up this calculation for you, accepting an input **Vector2** and returning the corresponding angle in degrees:

```
static public double CalculateDirectionAngle(Vector2 vect)
```

Acceleration

The speed of an object is the distance that the object can travel over a certain amount of time. For example, the speed of a car may be measured in the number of miles or kilometers it travels in an hour. *Acceleration* is a measure of how fast you are speeding up or slowing down. If you step on the gas pedal in a car, the car will increase its speed, or *accelerate*. If you step on the brake pedal, the car will slow down, or *decelerate*. The rate that the car speeds up or slows down is its *acceleration* or *deceleration*. So, for instance, if your car is traveling at 20 miles per hour and you accelerate 5 miles per hour, the car will end up traveling at 25 miles per hour (the original speed plus the acceleration).

Graphical objects on the screen can also accelerate and decelerate. Let's say you have a simple program in which a spaceship is flying through outer space. When the program starts the spaceship is moving at a speed of 5 pixels a second. Now let's say the ship is being chased by aliens. The player can hit the plus key (+) to accelerate the ship by 2 pixels a second for each key press. If the user hits the key 3 times then the ship's speed is accelerated to 5 + 2 + 2 + 2 = 11 pixels a second! Voila! The spaceship can escape the evil aliens.

You will typically want to accelerate an object in one of two ways. First, in many cases the acceleration is working along the same angle as the sprite is moving. The car example falls into this case, where acceleration (or breaking, which is just negative acceleration) always happens in whatever direction the car is heading. You can specify a single acceleration value that should impact the sprite's overall speed without changing the angle.

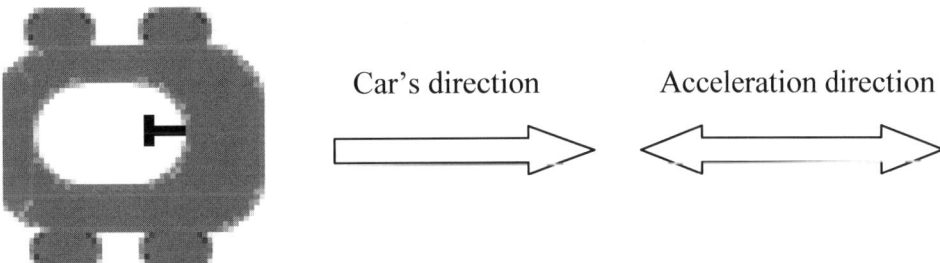

The **Sprite** class contains an **Accelerate()** method to accelerate (with a positive parameter) or decelerate (with a negative parameter) the sprite's speed along the current angle of travel.

```
void Accelerate(double acceleration)
```

Using trigonometry, the method calculates the X and Y components for the input acceleration based on the current direction angle and then adds these values to the current **Velocity.X** and **Velocity.Y** properties.

Just like velocity, acceleration can be represented as an acceleration magnitude and direction or as acceleration components in the X and Y directions (AX, AY). In order to adjust velocity by some acceleration, you can convert both velocity and acceleration to their X and Y components and then simply add the acceleration X to the velocity X and the acceleration Y to the velocity Y values.

```
Velocity.X = Velocity.X + acceleration.X
Velocity.Y = Velocity.Y + acceleration.Y
```

If you wish to accelerate a **Sprite** using the AX and AY components individually, of course there is method to accomplish this too!

```
void Accelerate(double AX, double AY)
```

This method will directly add the specified acceleration in the X and Y directions to the current velocity X and Y components.

Lesson Two: Gravity and Wind

Many computer games involve the use of objects that are either thrown or shot into the air. The movement of these objects may be influenced by gravity and wind effects.

Gravity

In the real world, every object that is launched or thrown into the air is influenced by the force of gravity. The Earth's gravity is a force which is constantly pulling everything towards the center of the earth (or, in terms of the computer screen, straight down in the positive Y direction).

When you throw a ball into the air it will travel up and away from you. As soon as it leaves your hands, gravity begins to work on the ball. No matter how hard you throw, the ball will eventually stop going in the upwards direction and will start moving down towards the ground. The arc that the ball follows from the time you throw it until the time it hits the ground is called a parabolic arc, which is shaped like an upside-down 'U'.

Let's take a look at a diagram that shows a ball moving under the force of gravity on the screen:

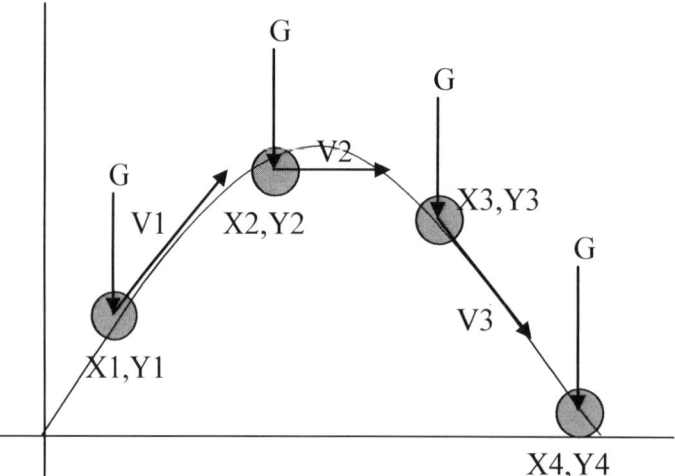

The original position of the ball is shown as point (X1, Y1). The ball has an initial velocity of V1, which is moving the ball in the negative Y direction (up), and positive X direction (to the right). We also have the force of gravity "G", which is pushing down on the ball. The effect is to reduce the upward velocity in the Y direction and leave the X velocity untouched.

The next position, point (X2, Y2), shows where the ball is after one or more iterations of the **Update()** method. At this point, gravity has slowed the Y velocity to near zero, and our ball is mostly moving in the positive X direction (still to the right).

The next position, point (X3, Y3) again shows the position of the ball after another timer tick or two. Now, gravity has reversed the Y velocity so that the direction is now positive (moving down on the screen). Finally, the last position of the ball (X4, Y4) shows the ball where it has landed on the "ground".

The curved line in the diagram shows the parabolic arc the ball would complete in the real world. Notice that the speed of the ball from left to right in the X direction is completely unaffected by the force of gravity. Gravity only acts to change the velocity in the Y direction. Also notice that the force of gravity "G" is a constant that affects the ball equally at each position.

We now know the values for both the X and Y acceleration components! There is zero (0.0) acceleration in the X direction because the X velocity does not change. The Y acceleration is a constant "G" representing the force of gravity. The second version of **Sprite.Accelerate**() accepting the component AX and AY values is ideal for our use in this situation.

So, to add the effects of gravity to a sprite flying through the air, we could use the following code:

```
mySprite.Accelerate(0.0f, 0.04f);
```

While gravity may be known as 9.8 m/s^2 in the real world, we don't have the concept of a "meter" on the computer screen. We are also applying this force 60 times a second (assuming default timing for the **Update**() function call). You'll have to play with several different AY values to find the strength of gravity value that "feels" right for your game environment. We picked 0.04f above. The size of the AY parameter will determine how quickly the object will fall back down to the ground.

Wind

Up until now we have only considered projectiles that are travelling through the air without any impact from the wind. Wind affects almost every projectile in the air. Golfers often check the wind before lining up their shots. Paper airplanes fly further if they are propelled by the wind, and baseball players may hit more home runs with the wind at their back than if the wind is blowing in their face. Adding the effects of wind for flying objects in a game may be a nice touch of realism or even be crucial to game-play!

So how do we add wind to a game? In the last section, we learned that gravity is a constant acceleration in the **Y** direction but did not affect the **X** velocity. The force of gravity caused our projectile to move in an arc on the screen. Wind, on the other hand, can be considered a constant acceleration in the **X** direction (assuming it is simply blowing left or right with no up or down-drafts). A wind blowing to the left would be a negative **X** acceleration, and wind blowing to the right would be a positive **X** acceleration.

The wind can have a powerful affect on the velocity and trajectory of a projectile. Consider the following illustration of a paper airplane in flight:

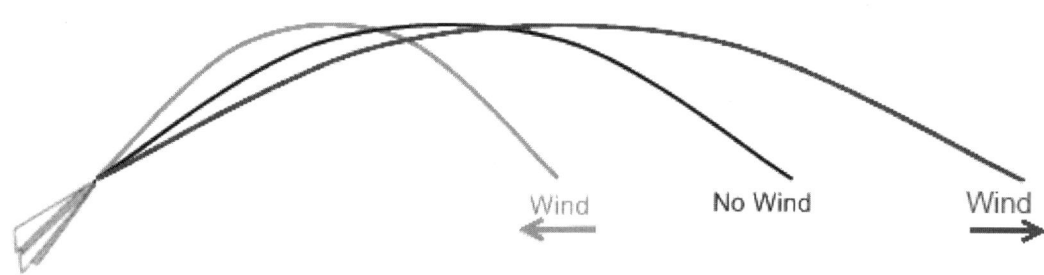

The paper airplane is thrown three different times with the same initial starting location, direction, and speed. The middle end-point represents the path that the airplane will take if there is no wind at all. With no wind, only the force of gravity affects the plane's path.

The right end-point shows the path the airplane will take if the wind is heading in the same direction as the airplane. This type of wind is called a *tailwind*, which is any wind travelling in the same direction as the projectile. The airplane will travel much further with a tailwind!

The left end-point shows the path the airplane will take when the wind is travelling in the opposite direction. This type of wind is called a *headwind*. With a headwind the airplane's flight will be much shorter!

How do you implement the effects of wind in your game? Easy! You already have an acceleration function that will split apart acceleration in either the **X** or **Y** direction. You added gravity to a projectile by specifying acceleration in the **Y** direction. The wind can just be thought of as acceleration in the **X** direction. A positive **X** acceleration will simulate a wind that travels from left to right on the screen. A negative **X** acceleration will simulate a wind that travels from right to left on the screen.

To add both gravity and wind effects to a sprite flying through the air, we could use the following code:

```
mySprite.Accelerate(0.03f, 0.04f);
```

A positive AX parameter (like 0.03) will give the effect of wind blowing from left to right on the screen. To add a leftward wind instead, just use a negative value like -0.03. Again, just like gravity, you'll have to play with the magnitude of this number to see what feels right in your game. Pick a value that is too high and you've just created a tornado that will overwhelm every projectile motion in your game!

Lesson Three: Reflection

We typically think of reflection when we look at our image in the mirror or in a calm lake on a sunny day. What we see in those cases is the reflection of light bouncing off of a surface and reflecting back at us. A ball that hits a flat surface will reflect in exactly the same way. We use the term *reflection* to describe what happens to the direction of the object while bouncing off a flat surface.

If you have ever bounced a ball off of the ground, you know the angle at which you throw the ball determines the direction it will bounce. If you throw it straight down the ball will bounce straight up. If you throw it at a large angle the ball will bounce back at the opposite angle.

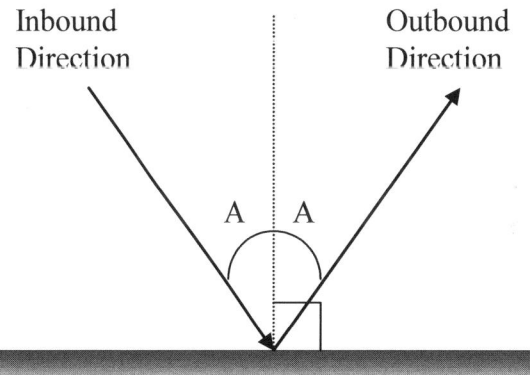

The angle of the reflection is determined by a law of physics aptly called the "Law of Reflection". This law says that any object that hits a flat surface at an angle will be reflected off of the flat surface at that same angle on the other side of a perpendicular (straight intersection) line. This is demonstrated in the picture to the right. The angle "A" the incoming object makes with the perpendicular line will be matched by the same angle "A" on the other side as the object leaves in the outbound direction.

The algorithm for creating reflection off a straight horizontal or vertical line in a game is simple. To reflect an object off any vertical line (such as the left or right side of the screen), we can just reverse the **X** direction of the object! Simply multiply the **X** direction with negative 1. To reflect an object off any horizontal line (such as the top or bottom of the screen), we can just reverse the **Y** direction of the object. This can be done by multiplying the **Y** direction with negative 1.

Let's take a look at an example that bounces a ball sprite off of the sides of the screen. The first thing we need to do is check to see if the ball has reached the left edge of the screen:

```
if (ball.UpperLeft.X <= 0)
{
```

When this condition is true, the ball's left edge has hit the left edge of the screen. In this case we want to bounce back to the right by multiplying the ball's **velocity.X** value with -1.

```
Vector2 velocity = ball.GetVelocity();
ball.SetVelocity(-velocity.X, velocity.Y);
```

Now let's check to see if the ball has hit the top of the screen:

```
if (ball.UpperLeft.Y <= 0)
{
```

When this condition is true, the ball's top edge has hit the top of the screen. In this case we want to bounce it back down the screen. To do this, we multiply the ball's **Velocity.Y** value with -1.

```
Vector2 velocity = ball.GetVelocity();
ball.SetVelocity(velocity.X, -velocity.Y);
```

Bouncing a sprite off the right or bottom of the screen is slightly trickier. In the above examples, we know exactly where the top and left sides of the sprite are located, using the **UpperLeft** property. Since we do not have a **LowerRight** property, we have to calculate the sprite's right and bottom coordinates before we compare them to the right and bottom of the screen.

To calculate the right side of a sprite, we take the left side of the sprite and add the sprite's width. The sprite's width can be obtained by using the Sprite class's **GetWidth()** method.

```
ball.UpperLeft.X + ball.GetWidth()
```

The coordinate for the right edge of the screen is simply the width of the screen, which we know from reading the **GraphicsDevice.Viewport.Width** value. Now, taking these two values, we can check to see if our ball has hit the right side of the screen:

```
if ( (ball.UpperLeft.X + ball.GetWidth()) > GraphicsDevice.Viewport.Width)
```

If the ball has hit the right side, we bounce the ball using the same X-reversal method as the left side.

To calculate the bottom of a sprite, we need to add the sprite's height to its top edge. We can get the sprite's height by using the **Sprite** class's **GetHeight()** method.

```
ball.UpperLeft.Y + ball.GetHeight()
```

We can also find the bottom edge of the screen from the **GraphicsDevice.Viewport.Height** value. Now we can check to see if the ball has hit the bottom of the screen:

```
if ( (ball.UpperLeft.Y + ball.GetHeight()) > GraphicsDevice.Viewport.Height)
```

If the ball has hit the bottom, we bounce the ball up using the same Y-reversal method as the top edge. Notice that we don't change the **velocity.X** value when we are bouncing off the top or bottom of the screen and we don't change the **velocity.Y** value when we are bouncing off the left or right of the screen.

Arbitrary Reflection Lines

You can also reflect against an arbitrary line that is not straight horizontal or vertical. The math involved is beyond the scope of this course, but we can certainly provide a nice function in the **Sprite** class to do the hard work! All you need to know is the slope of your reflecting surface, which is represented as a **Vector2**.

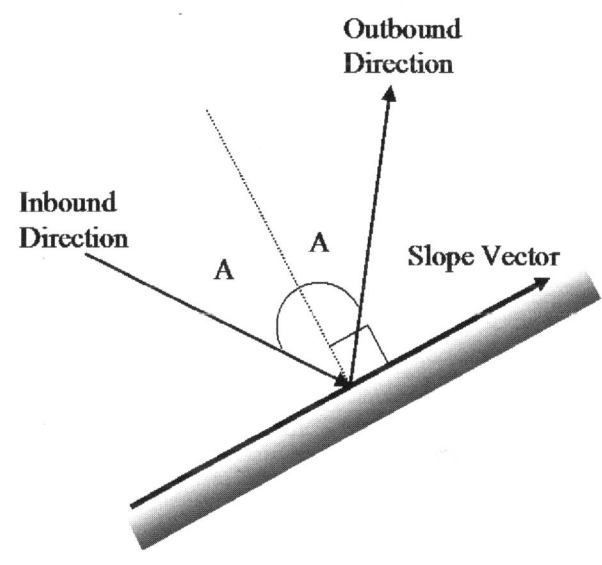

To obtain the slope, subtract any two known points along the reflecting surface from each other to form the vector. Let's say our surface runs from point (50,100) to point (500,600). To calculate the slope:

```
float dx = 500 - 50;                // difference in X coordinates
float dy = 600 - 100;               // difference in Y coordinates
Vector2 slope = new Vector2(dx,dy); // form slope vector
```

The **Sprite** class has a handy **Reflect()** method that will change the sprite's direction by reflecting its current velocity off the provided slope vector. Here is the method definition:

```
void Sprite.Reflect(Vector2 slope)
```

So when you have an actual sprite (such as **mySprite**) that needs to be reflected, calculate the slope vector of the reflecting surface and then call **Reflect()** with that slope:

```
mySprite.Reflect(slope);
```

Now **mySprite** has changed directions as if its current velocity hit the reflecting surface.

Chapter Review

- *Velocity* is a combination of speed and direction of an object. Velocity can also be represented by velocity components in the X and Y directions.
- You can convert between the two velocity representations with some trigonometry formulas.
- *Acceleration* is a measure of how fast you are speeding up or slowing down.
- Acceleration can be represented as a magnitude and angle or as acceleration components in the X and Y directions.
- During each **Update**() or unit of time you will add the acceleration X and Y components to the velocity X and Y components in order to change the velocity.
- The **Sprite** class contains two **Accelerate**() methods: one to cause acceleration along the current direction of travel, and one to apply separate X and Y acceleration components.
- A game program often mimics the effect of gravity and wind resistance on a projectile to give a more realistic motion to the object.
- Gravity can be thought of as simply acceleration in the positive (downward) Y direction.
- Wind is an acceleration in the positive (rightward) or negative (leftward) X direction.
- Reflection is the method by which an object is bounced off of a flat surface. This means the angle of direction changes (or the corresponding X and Y velocity components), but the speed does not change.
- To reflect a velocity vector against a vertical line, simply reverse the X direction of the object. To reflect off a horizontal line, reverse the Y direction of the object.
- Reflection of a sprite's direction against an arbitrary slope can be accomplished by calling the **Sprite.Reflect**() method.

Chapter Ten: Game Physics

Activity: Snowball Fight

In this activity, you will complete a game called Snowball Fight. Snowball Fight is a projectile game where two reindeer try to pelt each other with snowballs while hiding behind snow forts. You will be responsible for adding the physics-related code to this project!

Your activity requirements and instructions are found in the "Chapter_10_Activity.pdf" document located in your "TeenCoder\Game Programming\Activity Docs" folder. You can access this document through your Student Menu or by double-clicking on it from Windows Explorer.

Complete this activity now and ensure your program meets the requirements before continuing!

Chapter Eleven: Maze Generation

Mazes often appear in computer games, either directly as puzzles as indirectly as part of the environment thorough which a player is moving. In this chapter you will learn how to generate and solve mazes!

Lesson One: Maze Types

A *maze* is a graphical puzzle. The object of the puzzle is to navigate an uninterrupted path through a set of intricate pathways from the starting point to the goal.

What do all of these things have in common: a simple game in a child's book, a winding wall of towering hedges, or a misleading path through a hall of mirrors? They are all forms of mazes! The maze has been around almost since the beginning of recorded history. The first known maze was found in Egypt at around 500 BC. This Egyptian maze was constructed from brick and stone inside and underneath a great building. Not much remains of this early Egyptian maze now, but the love for mazes has continued to this day.

Uses of Mazes in Computer Games

Mazes have appeared in many forms in computer games over the years. A maze can be simply created and solved on the screen as a stand-alone puzzle game. The player is presented with a maze and is asked to trace a path from the starting point to the ending point. The parameters of the game may vary, but the overall idea is typically to find the shortest (or only) path from beginning to end.

Mazes can also be used as a background through which characters move as part of some larger game. The classic arcade game Pac-Man uses a maze to constrain the paths of the main character and ghosts as they chase each other. The maze in the background was not the main point of the game, but it made for a much more interesting game play!

Mazes are often the basis for complex floor plans or labyrinths, requiring the player to explore and navigate through to get to the next level. In 3D games instead of seeing an overhead view of your character, you could actually be immersed inside the maze from the character's point of view. The player can only see a short distance constrained by the walls of the maze, so there might be surprises around every corner. Unless the player builds a mental overhead map (or the game provides one) solving these mazes can be quite challenging!

Mazes can be categorized or described by many different properties. Each property will determine certain characteristics of the maze. We will cover some (but not all) of the main maze categories and properties.

Dimension

The first maze property is *dimension*. The dimension of a maze refers to the measure of its spatial configuration. A two-dimensional maze extends in two directions with a width and height. This is the type of maze that you would find in a book or on a piece of paper. A three-dimensional maze has three dimensions: height, width and depth. A 3D maze has multiple levels in which the pathways can travel up or down as well as along the ground. This is a much more difficult maze to solve. A third type of dimensional maze is commonly called a weave maze. Weaves are 2D mazes that have some pathways which tunnel under or over others. The result often looks like the pathways are woven together.

Routing

The second descriptive maze property is called *routing*. A maze can be routed in many different ways. A common type of maze routing that has only one path from any one point to another results in a *perfect maze*. In a perfect maze (see right) there are no open areas, inaccessible areas, or pathways that circulate back onto each other. There is only one solution for a perfect maze.

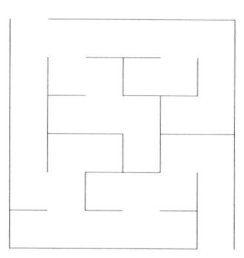

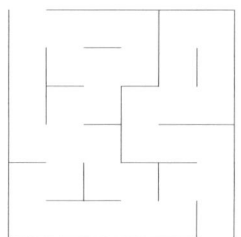

A maze that is *braid routed* does not have any dead ends (see left). This type of maze uses pathways that wind around and are constantly running back into one another. This feature causes the player to spend a lot of time going in circles. These types of mazes are often harder to solve than a perfect maze.

A *unicursal maze* is one that is routed without any junctions or branches (see right). A unicursal maze has a single, long winding pathway that snakes throughout the maze. There is no mystery to a unicursal maze as there is only one path to take (albeit a complicated, twisty path!)

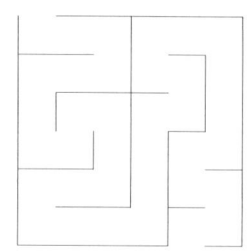

Texture

The *texture* of a maze refers to how the pathways are constructed. This category has four main factors: *run*, *elitism*, *bias*, and *river*. The "run" factor of a maze indicates how long the straight sections are before a player is forced to turn. A maze with a low run factor will have short straight-aways, while a high run maze will have long passages that cut across most of the maze.

The "elitism" factor of a maze's texture is an indication of the length of the solution with respect to the size of the maze. A high-elite maze will have a short and direct solution, while a low-elite maze will make the player wander through most of the maze before finding the exit. A good-quality high-elite maze can be much trickier to figure out than a simple low-elite maze.

The "bias" factor of a maze's texture is a reference to the direction that a player will tend to travel. A maze with a horizontal bias will cause the player to travel through long left to right passages, with short up and down passages. A vertical bias (see right) will have long up and down passages and short left to right passages. It is usually more difficult to travel against the bias than with the bias. In another words, it is difficult to go up or down in a horizontally biased maze and difficult to go left or right in a vertically biased maze.

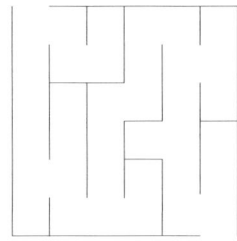

The "river" factor determines how strongly the maze flows before reaching dead ends. A low-river maze will have many short dead ends, while a high-river maze will have longer paths with fewer dead ends. The example above shows a high-run (long passageway), low-elite (long solution), and vertically biased texture.

Lesson Two: Generating a Perfect Maze

The perfect maze is the simplest maze to create and solve using a computer. In this lesson, we will take a look at some algorithms for generating the perfect maze. There are many different algorithms that can be used to generate a perfect maze. We will only cover four of the most common approaches.

Prim's Algorithm

Prim's algorithm was developed in three stages by three different men. A Czech mathematician named Jarnik in 1930 and a computer scientist named Prim in 1957 independently created versions of the algorithm. In 1958, another man named Dijkstra further refined the method. Prim's algorithm is occasionally called the DJP method to honor all three men.

Each cell in Prim's algorithm can have one of three types: "in", which means the cell is already part of the maze, "frontier" meaning the cell is not part of the maze, but is adjacent to an "in" cell, and "out", which is a cell that is not "in" and does not have any "in" neighbors. When Prim's algorithm begins, all of the cells in the maze are walled off on all four sides and are labeled "out".

In the first step you pick a random starting cell. This cell is marked as "in" (I) and all of its neighbors are marked as "frontier" (F). A "frontier" neighbor is picked at random and the wall between the two cells is broken down. The neighbor cell is now set to "in" and all of its neighbors are set to "frontier". This process repeats until there are no more "frontier" cells or "out" cells left in the maze. The demonstration maze to the right is partially complete, with many "out" (O) cells left to clear. A maze created by the Prim algorithm tends to be "low river" with many short dead-ends, but the algorithm executes quickly.

Kruskal's Algorithm

Kruskal's algorithm was developed in the 1950s by an American mathematician named Joseph Kruskal. The Kruskal algorithm creates a maze in a random, not sequential fashion. Where most maze generation algorithms will create a maze by flowing from one cell to an adjacent cell, Kruskal's method chooses cells at random, creating pathways in a disjointed, sporadic way. The end result however is still a perfect maze!

Kruskal's algorithm, like Prim's, assumes that all cells start with walls on all edges. The first step in Kruskal's algorithm is to assign every cell in the maze a unique ID. In the example to the right we have numbered the cells 1 through 36 to start. A cell wall is then chosen at random and the IDs of the two adjacent cells are checked. If the adjacent cells have different IDs, the wall between the cells is knocked down. All cells in the grid matching the higher of the two numbers are given the lower of the two numbers. All cells with matching numbers in the grid indicate there is a pathway between those cells. If adjacent cells already have the same ID, the wall is left alone.

1	2	3	3	5	6
7	2	9	3	11	12
13	14	15	3	17	18
19	14	14	14	23	24
25	14	14	28	29	30
31	32	33	28	35	36

This method repeats until all of the cells have the same ID number. This indicates that there is a pathway between every cell in the maze. You can see in the example that we have started to build some longer connected passageways that are currently disjoint, but that will eventually be connected by knocking down a wall between the different IDs. This algorithm yields mazes with a low "river" factor, but not as low as Prim's algorithm. Kruskal's algorithm is speedy but not quite as fast as Prim's, and it uses a relatively large amount of memory to complete.

Recursive Division

The *recursive division* algorithm is different from previous algorithms as it starts without any walls on any of the cells. Instead of concentrating on breaking down walls, recursive division focuses on creating walls.

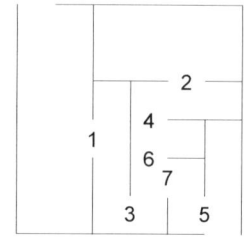

The recursive division algorithm starts by creating either a horizontal or vertical wall stretching across the entire maze. An opening in this wall is created in one randomly selected cell. Each side of the wall is considered a separate chamber that will be subdivided again by a different horizontal or vertical wall, again with a randomly chosen opening. This method is repeated until all of the sub-chambers within the maze are small enough. In the example to the right we have numbered the walls created in sequence where the opening on that wall was chosen. You can see that we have not yet finished dividing some larger chambers to the left and top.

When you are using recursive division, you should consider the size of your maze. If the maze is wider than it is tall, you should make sure that you are creating more vertical walls than horizontal walls and vice versa. The recursive division algorithm is one of the fastest maze generators available. However, it does tend to create very long or tall passages in the maze.

Recursive Backtracker

The recursive backtracker algorithm is a very commonly used algorithm for maze generation. It is fairly fast, with only Prim's algorithm being slightly faster, and results in a perfect maze with a very high river factor. This is the algorithm that we will use for maze generation in this course!

Like Prim's and Kruskal's algorithm, recursive backtracker starts with walls on all four sides of every cell. A random cell is selected as the starting point. This cell is marked as "visited" and the neighbor cells are checked to see if any have not yet been "visited". If a neighbor cell has not been "visited", the wall is broken down between the initial cell and the neighbor and the neighbor cell is marked as "visited". If all the neighboring cells have been "visited", we move back to the previous cell 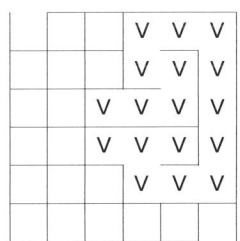 and try again. This method is repeated until all cells have been "visited". In the example to the right we chose a starting square near the middle and began visiting adjacent cells, only backtracking to a previous cell if we hit a dead end with nowhere else to go.

Lesson Three: Solving a Perfect Maze

In the previous lesson we talked about algorithms that can be used to *create* mazes. In this lesson, we will take a look at some algorithms that can be used to *solve* mazes. There are many different algorithms that can be used; we will cover four of the more common techniques.

Wall-Follower

The *wall follower* algorithm is a very simple algorithm which runs fast and uses very little extra memory. First, start in a random direction along a passage. When a junction is reached, always turn in the same direction. If you choose to always go right, you are using the "right-hand" wall follower. If you choose to always go left, you are using the "left-hand" wall follower algorithm.

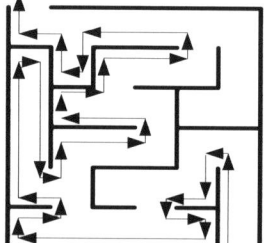

This method can also be used by a human in a physical maze, like a garden or corn maze. You start at the entrance and put your hand on either the left wall (as shown in the example) or right wall of the maze. If you keep your hand on this wall as you walk through the maze, you will almost always find your way to the exit.

This algorithm will work for a perfect maze, but may not work for any maze that has circuits or switchbacks or ends in the middle of the maze. In those cases, you could find yourself going around in circles forever or coming back to the start of the maze without ever finding the exit. The wall follower algorithm is simple and fast, but does not often give the shortest path from start to end. Instead, it tends to wind around, backtracking often before finally finding the solution.

Random Mouse

The *random mouse* algorithm is by far the simplest of all maze solution algorithms. Unfortunately, it's also a slow, inefficient algorithm that is not guaranteed to find a solution.

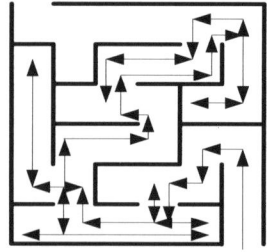

The random mouse algorithm is so named because it follows the same logic as a simple mouse that has been placed inside a maze. The mouse travels straight until it reaches a junction. A random direction is chosen and the mouse moves straight until it reaches another junction. This method continues until the maze exit is found. You can see in our example the poor mouse has made a bunch of random choices, often covering the same ground, and still hasn't found a way out yet!

This algorithm does not try to keep track of what cells have already been visited, or what direction the solution is heading. Instead it just makes random directional changes until a solution is found.

Recursive Backtracker

The *recursive backtracker* solution algorithm is very similar to the recursive backtracker maze generation algorithm. This method will not always find the shortest solution, as it may have to backtrack from time to time, but it will always find a solution for a perfect maze.

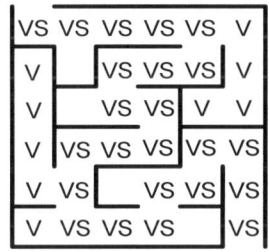

The recursive backtracker starts at the maze entry point and marks this cell as "visited" (V) and as "part of the solution" (S). The next step is to check to see if any of the neighboring cells have not been "visited" and do not have a wall between them and the initial cell. If there is no wall and the neighbor has not been "visited", move to that cell and mark it as both "visited" and as "part of the solution". If you hit a dead end, remove the current cell from "part of the solution" and backtrack to the previous cell. When finished, the cells marked as "part of the solution" (S) form the path through the maze. You will be using the recursive backtracker algorithm in the activity for this chapter!

Dead End Filler

The *dead-end filler* algorithm works by filling in all of the dead ends in a maze. This algorithm creates a very fast solution without using a great deal of memory.

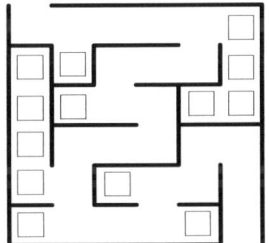

This method works iteratively over the whole maze. The maze is searched and any dead-end cells are marked as not part of the solution. This will include filling in dead-end cells as well as any passages that become parts of dead-ends when other dead-end sections are removed from the solution. The end result is a single unique solution (for a perfect maze) or multiple solutions (for an imperfect maze).

The dead-end filler algorithm will not work for all types of mazes. It will have trouble finding a solution in a braided maze that has no dead ends!

Chapter Review

- A *maze* is a graphical puzzle where the goal is to navigate an uninterrupted path through a set of intricate pathways from the starting point to the goal.
- Mazes can be used as stand-alone games or as backgrounds or navigation for computer games.
- The *dimension* classification of a maze refers to its spatial configuration (e.g. 2 or 3 dimensions).
- A maze's *routing* classification describes how the maze's paths are followed from beginning to end.
- A *perfect maze* is a maze that has only one solution and no dead areas.
- The *texture* of a maze refers to the *run* (length), *bias* (direction), *elitism* (solution complexity) and *river* (dead end frequency).
- There are many different algorithms dedicated to either building or solving the perfect maze.
- *Prim's algorithm* creates a perfect maze by slowly carving a pathway through a series of closed cells.
- *Kruskal's algorithm* creates a perfect maze by randomly linking adjacent cells at random locations.
- *Recursive division* builds a maze by starting with a blank grid and subdividing chambers with walls and random openings.
- *Recursive backtracking* builds a maze by carving out walls in a random direction, and moving backwards to an available wall when a dead end is reached.
- The *wall-follower* algorithm is a simple method of maze solving. This method just follows either a right or left side wall until it reaches the end of the maze.
- The *random mouse* algorithm chooses a random direction at every junction in a maze. This is the least efficient maze solution algorithm without any memory of prior steps.
- The *dead-end-filler* algorithm solves a maze by repeatedly sweeping the entire maze and filling in dead ends. Other cells become new dead ends that will be filled also, until only the solution remains.
- The *recursive backtracker* algorithm solves a maze by walking through pathways building a solution path. When a dead end is reached the dead end is removed from the solution and the algorithm backtracks to the previous juncture.

Chapter Eleven: Maze Generation

Activity: A-Maze-ing Backtracker

In this activity you write *recursive backtracker* algorithms to create and solve a perfect maze. You will use recursion to write a method for creating the maze on the screen, and then write a recursive method for solving the maze, showing both the final path and any backtracking that was necessary to solve the maze.

Your activity requirements and instructions are found in the "Chapter_11_Activity.pdf" document located in your "TeenCoder\Game Programming\Activity Docs" folder. You can access this document through your Student Menu or by double-clicking on it from Windows Explorer.

Complete this activity now and ensure your program meets the requirements before continuing!

Chapter Twelve: Menus, Overlays and Deployment

This chapter will cover several topics that will become important as your games grow larger and you want to distribute them to other people to play.

Lesson One: Title Screens and Option Menus

So far we have created games with only one screen. Most games, however, will used several different screens. Title screens, options and menus screens, and main game-play screens may look very different. In this lesson you will learn how to create multi-screen games.

Title Screens

A *title screen* is shown when a game first starts. Title screens will typically display a graphic that introduces the game or shows author and publisher information. A title screen can also be used to hide the time that it takes to initially load the game onto the game console or computer. Large games may take many seconds to load. Games can hide this load time by showing the player an interesting graphic introducing the game while initialization continues in the background.

Title screens can be displayed until a player presses a "start" button or until a certain amount of time has passed. Screens that display for a certain amount of time and then disappear automatically are also referred to as "splash screens", because they are splashed onto the screen and then wiped away when the game begins.

Menu and Option Screens

Menus allow the player to navigate through game choices. You might choose to start a new game, exit the program, or perhaps transition to an options screen.

```
Press Space Bar to start
Press "O" for options
Press ESC to exit
```

Option screens contain areas where the player can set various game parameters. There are many different options that a player might choose such as the number of players in the game, the difficulty level, a course selection, audio or video options, personalization settings, and so forth.

Some option screens may only make sense right after the title screen, before the main game-play has started. These screens allow the player to select the important parameters such as the number of players or game scenario that cannot be changed once the game starts. Other options like audio and video settings might reasonably be changed at any time during a game. Allowing those option screens to be displayed during game play gives the player the ability to change certain aspects of the game on the fly.

When an option or menu screen is shown during game play, the game should generally be paused in the background until the screens have disappeared. This prevents the player from missing out on the game while they change a game option. In this case, the option and menu screens are often created as transparent or semi-transparent overlays on top of the paused game screen. Being able to still see the main game underneath the options gives the player confidence that their game is indeed paused in the background.

Lesson Two: Handling Different Screens

Now that we know the importance of multiple game screens, how can we process and display all of these different screens? Each screen may look substantially different, so attempting to draw everything from within one **Draw()** method would be quite complicated. Each screen may also have different user input, so the **Update()** logic will become very cumbersome if crammed within one method.

Tracking the Current Screen

Clearly you will need to execute different logic based on the current screen. In order to distinguish what screen you are handling, you can create an enumeration of all possible screens at the beginning of your **Game** class. The following example defines a game with four screens:

```
enum GameScreen
{
    TITLE = 0,
    OPTIONS = 1,
    PLAYING = 2,
    GAMEOVER = 3
}
```

Then, declare a member variable at the top of your **Game** class to track the currently displayed screen:

Chapter Twelve: Menus, Overlays and Deployment

```
public class BumperCars : Microsoft.Xna.Framework.Game
{
    GameScreen currentScreen;
```

In your game, set your current screen to one of the enumerated screen values whenever your player switches to a different screen. Now you have a specific guide to tell you which types of user input you should be processing and what screen output to draw at the current time.

Screen-Specific Update() Logic

Within your **Update**() method you will have game logic plus handling of user input. The nature of the logic and the user input may change drastically depending on which screen is displayed. A straightforward organizational approach would be to declare a separate version of the update method for each screen:

```
void updateTitle(GameTime gameTime)
{
    // game logic and input handling specific to the Title screen
}
void updateOptions(GameTime gameTime)
{
    // game logic and input handling specific to the Options screen
}
void updatePlaying(GameTime gameTime)
{
    // game logic and input handling specific to the Playing screen
}
void updateGameOver(GameTime gameTime)
{
    // game logic and input handling specific to the GameOver screen
}
```

Your main **Update**() method becomes a simple selection procedure based on the current screen:

```
protected override void Update(GameTime gameTime)
{
    if (currentScreen == GameScreen.Splash)
    {
        updateSplash(gameTime, currentKeyboard);
    }
    else if (currentScreen == GameScreen.Menu)
    {
        updateMenu(gameTime, currentKeyboard);
    }
    else if (currentScreen == GameScreen.Playing)
    {
        updatePlaying(gameTime, currentKeyboard);
    }
    else if (currentScreen == GameScreen.GameOver)
    {
        updateGameover(gameTime, currentKeyboard);
    }
    base.Update(gameTime);
}
```

Now your entire program will seamlessly switch to the correct update logic based on the current game screen. Within the individual update methods your game logic should allow the user to switch screens (by setting a new **currentScreen**) based on whatever criteria are appropriate for that screen.

Here is an example **updateTitle**() method that will keep a splash screen displayed for 5 seconds and then automatically switch to the menu screen:

```
private void updateTitle(GameTime gameTime)
{
    // keep the splash displayed for a few seconds
    if (gameTime.TotalGameTime > TimeSpan.FromSeconds(5))
    {
        // switch to the menu screen!
        currentScreen = GameScreen.Menu;
    }
}
```

Now that you have your **Update**() logic well-organized, let's turn attention to the rendering of each screen.

Screen-Specific Draw() Logic

Much like your **Update**() method, the nature of your **Draw**() logic may need to change significantly for each screen. Let's split the **Draw**() logic into dedicated functions for each screen.

```
private void drawSplash(GameTime gameTime)
{
    // do whatever you need to draw the Splash screen here
}
private void drawMenu(GameTime gameTime)
{
    // do whatever you need to draw the Menu screen here
}
private void drawPlaying(GameTime gameTime)
{
    // do whatever you need to draw the Playing screen here
}
private void drawGameOver(GameTime gameTime)
{
    // do whatever you need to draw the GameOver screen here
}
```

Now as you are no doubt expecting, we'll use the main **Draw**() method to choose between the individual screen methods based on the **currentScreen** variable.

```
protected override void Draw(GameTime gameTime)
{
    GraphicsDevice.Clear(Color.Azure);
    spriteBatch.Begin();                    // prepare to draw all images

    if (currentScreen == GameScreen.Splash)
    {
        drawSplash(gameTime);
    }
    else if (currentScreen == GameScreen.Menu)
    {
        drawMenu(gameTime);
    }
```

```
            else if (currentScreen == GameScreen.Playing)
            {
                drawPlaying(gameTime);
            }
            else if (currentScreen == GameScreen.GameOver)
            {
                drawPlaying(gameTime);
                drawGameOver(gameTime);
            }
            spriteBatch.End();                       // done drawing all images
            base.Draw(gameTime);
        }
```

Notice that we began and ended the **SpriteBatch** in this outer function so we wouldn't have to do it within each screen rendering method. However you could begin and end within each method if that made more sense for your game. You might also choose to clear the screen to a different color within each method.

Also notice that for the **GameOver** case, we chose to draw both the playing and game over screens. In effect this keeps the last playing screen visible (where maybe the player just won or lost in spectacular fashion) and superimposes the game over message on top of that background.

Let's take a look at some sample code that will draw a simple title screen consisting of a black background, a sprite image, and a string with instructions for continuing:

```
        void drawTitle(GameTime gameTime)
        {
            GraphicsDevice.Clear(Color.Black);
            mySprite.Draw(spriteBatch);
            spriteBatch.DrawString(gameFont, "Press Spacebar to Continue",
                              new Vector2(150, 250), Color.White);
        }
```

Remember if your title screen requires a key press to continue the game, make sure you check for this key press in the **updateTitle()** method and change the **currentScreen** variable accordingly.

Here's another example where we display a simple menu screen consisting of two choices:

```
void drawMenu(GameTime gameTime)
{
    GraphicsDevice.Clear(Color.Black);
    spriteBatch.DrawString(gameFont, "Press 1 for 1 Player",
                            new Vector2(150, 200), Color.White);
    spriteBatch.DrawString(gameFont, "Press 2 for 2 Player",
                            new Vector2(150, 250), Color.White);
}
```

The player has two possible selections: press "1" for a single player game, or "2" for two players. If your player will be using an Xbox controller instead, make sure to offer button presses like "A" for single player and "X" for two players.

Regardless of which button or device the player is using, make sure to use the **Update()** method to check for the correct condition. When the player presses the right key or button, then set the options and change the screen accordingly.

Lesson Three: Displaying Scores and Overlays

One of the most important aspects of any game is the ability to keep track of scores and display key player information. You can display this information simply by writing text directly onto the screen.

Scores and other information should be displayed in an area where the text will not interrupt or block the game play. In addition, if you change screens during game-play, try to keep the same information in the same spot and general format on every screen. This ensures that the player does not have to search the screen for important information during the game.

Player 1 Score: 2
Player 2 Score: 0

Some simple scores can be written to a corner of the screen using the **SpriteBatch.DrawString()** method, like this:

```
spriteBatch.DrawString(gameFont, "Player 1 Score: " + unit1.Score,
                        new Vector2(10, 10), Color.Red);
spriteBatch.DrawString(gameFont, "Player 2 Score: " + unit2.Score,
                        new Vector2(10, 30), Color.Red);
```

Displaying Overlays

You can also show game information with a graphical *overlay*. An overlay is often thought of as a "game dashboard". Just like car dashboards show information about the current status of the car, a game dashboard can be used to display game status information like speed, score, maps and player objectives. A good overlay makes the information display seem more integrated into the game.

An overlay image can be anything from a small corner graphic to a full screen frame around the game screen. A combination of graphical overlay and text is often used to give up-to-date information to the player. Fancy borders or game board backgrounds can also be purely decorative.

In this example we have shown a car dashboard overlay that could be drawn on top of the road or racetrack. The overlay contains information about the car's current speed and engine RPMs.

The overlay image (and any information contained within the image) should be drawn as the last item in the **Draw()** method. Or use the "depth" property to order images back to front so the overlay is on top of any other game graphics and is fully visible to the player.

Lesson Four: Distributing Games

Once you have created your game program masterpiece, there is only one thing left to do: share it with the world! In this lesson, we will discuss ways to distribute your completed game program to other players.

Game Files

An executable program file is created for you every time you build your project. This file is called <Game Name>.exe and can be found buried deep in your project files in the "\<Project Name>\<Project Name>\bin\x86\Debug" directory. You can verify this by looking at the Cat and Mouse game files that were created in an earlier chapter. In the "\Cat and Mouse\Cat and Mouse\bin\x86\Debug" directory, you will find the file "CatAndMouse.exe". You can run this file directly on your computer by double-clicking on it.

Chapter Twelve: Menus, Overlays and Deployment

But what if you wanted to share the game with your little brother? Can you just copy the "CatAndMouse.exe" file to his computer? The answer is no! An XNA program (and almost all other types of programs) will require extra files, images and libraries to be installed on a computer before a program can be run. These files are commonly called *dependencies*, since a program is dependent on them to run properly.

XNA games created with the Game Studio version 4.0 and higher require the following dependencies to be installed on any computer running an XNA game:

.NET Framework	All C# programs require the .NET Framework to be installed on a computer before the C# program will run. The .NET Framework was installed for you (if not already present) when you installed Visual C# 2010 Express. However your players may need to install the .NET Framework with a free download from Microsoft.
XNA Framework Redistributable 4.0	You have been using XNA objects from the XNA runtime library to create your games. These objects must be deployed on the target computer by installing the XNA Framework Redistributable 4.0, which is also a free download from Microsoft.
Content Files	Content files are your images, sounds, fonts, etc. that are required for your program to run properly. These files are bundled by the Game Studio compiler into a format that the XNA game can understand and utilize. Content files are typically located in the "Content" subdirectory from where your ".exe" file was built.

Distributing to Other XNA Developers

If you are sending your game to other XNA developers, we know they will already have the XNA Game Studio installed. Therefore they also already have the .NET Framework and XNA Framework installed. This means we only need to package the game file and our Content files for distribution!

To use this method, open your project, right-click on the project name in the Solution Explorer and choose "Package as XNA Creators Club Game" from the pop-up menu.

Once you choose this option, your project will compile and build. When this process is complete, you will see the "Finished…" message in the bottom left corner of the screen.

The result of this build is a single file called "<Game Name>.ccgame". You can find this file in your \<Game Name>\<Game Name>\bin\x86\Debug" folder. This file can then be copied and sent to any other XNA Game Studio user.

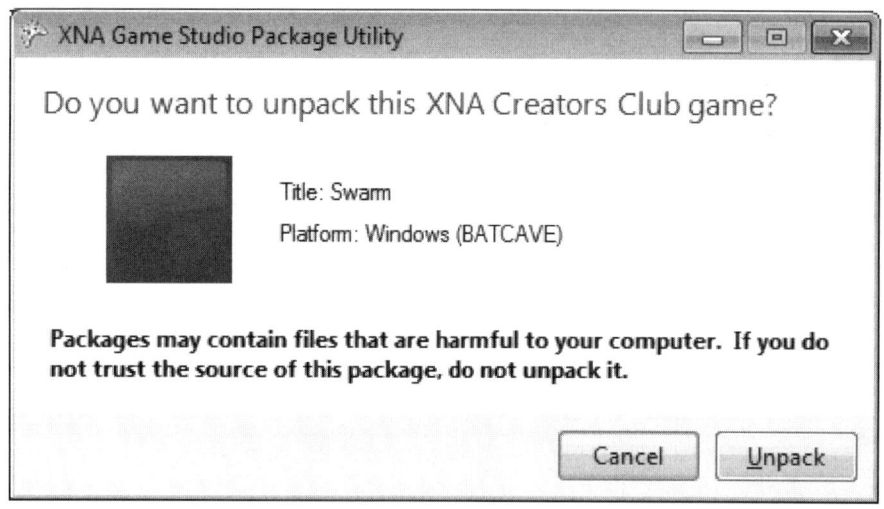

Once this file is copied to another developer's computer, they can just double-click on the file, which will display screen shown to the left.

If you are sure that the "ccgame" file came from a trusted source, it is safe to click on "Unpack". If you have downloaded the file from an unknown or un-trusted source, you may want to run a virus check before unpacking the files.

The "Unpack" button will create all of the files for this game on the user's computer. These files will include a "<Game>.exe" file and all the necessary Content files to run the game.

Distributing to the Public

The method described above is great for simple distribution to another XNA Game Studio developer, but what if you just wanted to distribute your game to any user? To do this, we will use another method commonly referred to as "Publishing". This method will create a "setup.exe" file which will allow you to distribute the game to any user, regardless of whether they have the .NET or XNA software already installed.

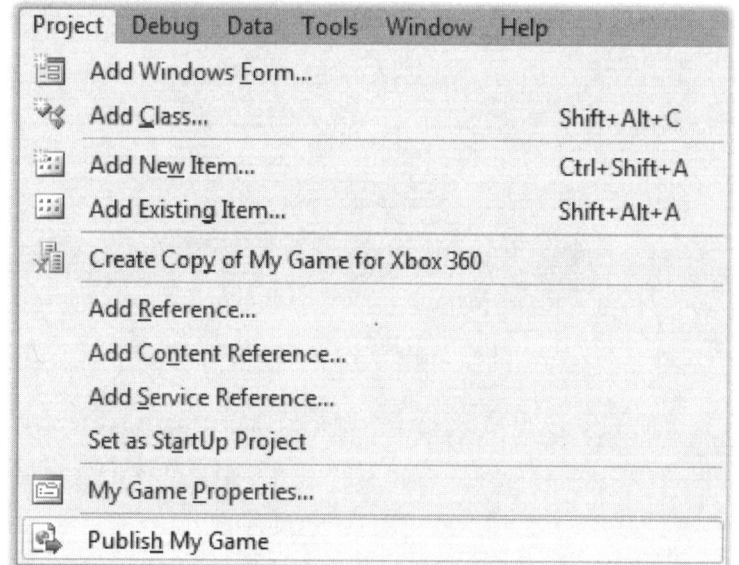

To publish your game program, open the game project and then click on the "Project" menu and select "Publish <Game Name>".

Chapter Twelve: Menus, Overlays and Deployment

You will then see a screen like the one shown below:

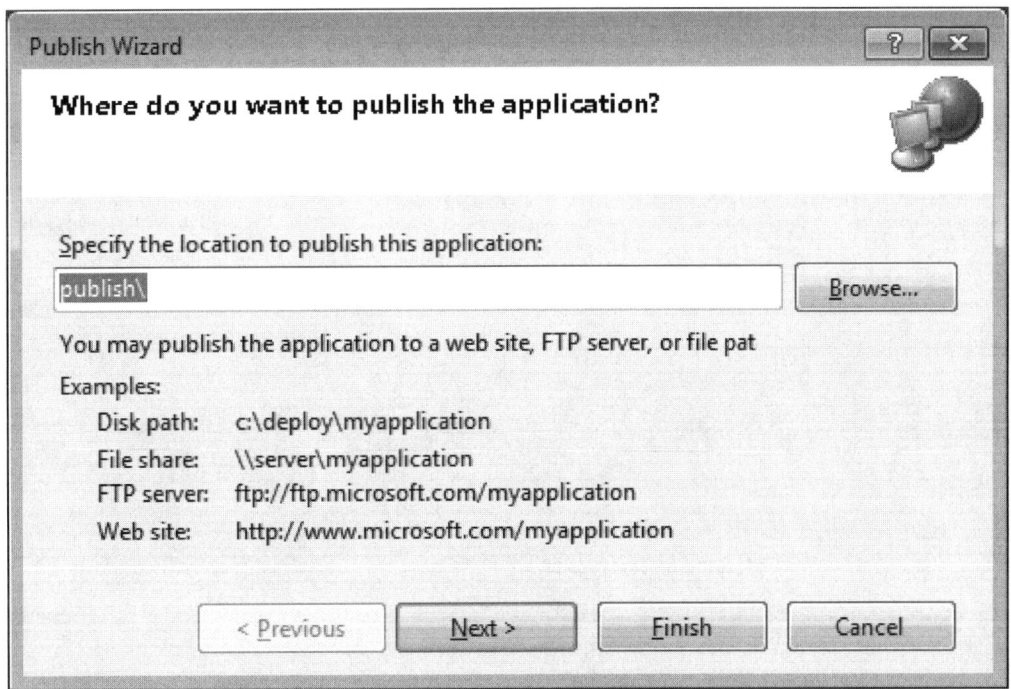

From here, you can choose where you want to output the setup files for your game program. The simplest method is to output to a location on your computer's hard drive (e.g: "C:\My Game"), but you can also choose to send them straight to a website or an FTP server.

Choose the location on your hard drive where you want your setup files to go, and then click the "Next" button. You will then see the screen shown to the right.

On this screen, you need to decide how you will distribute your game. You can distribute the game from a web site on the Internet, from a network drive (the UNC path or file share) or from a CD-ROM or DVD-ROM. The last option is the most popular, since it will allow you to save the files to a CD or DVD and distribute them personally. You should note that this method will not burn the resulting setup files onto a disc, but will just create the files on your hard drive which can then be copied or burned to a disc later.

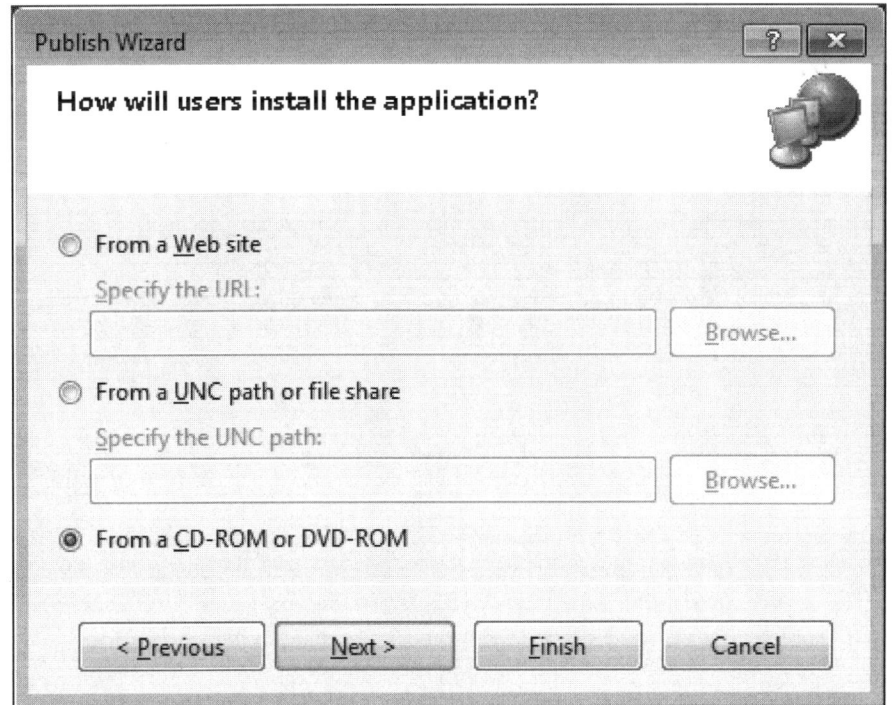

183

The next screen will allow you to set a place where the game program can check for updates. This is a great feature if you want your users to be able to download any fixes or patches for the game when the game is installed. This is optional and we will not be using it in our programs, so just click "Next".

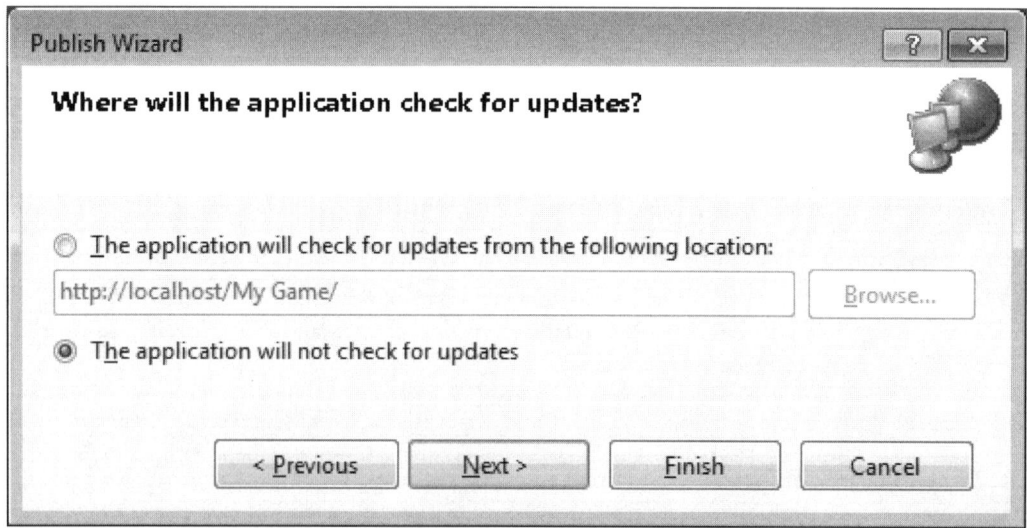

The final screen is shown below. This screen will just allow you to double-check all of your settings before the setup files are created.

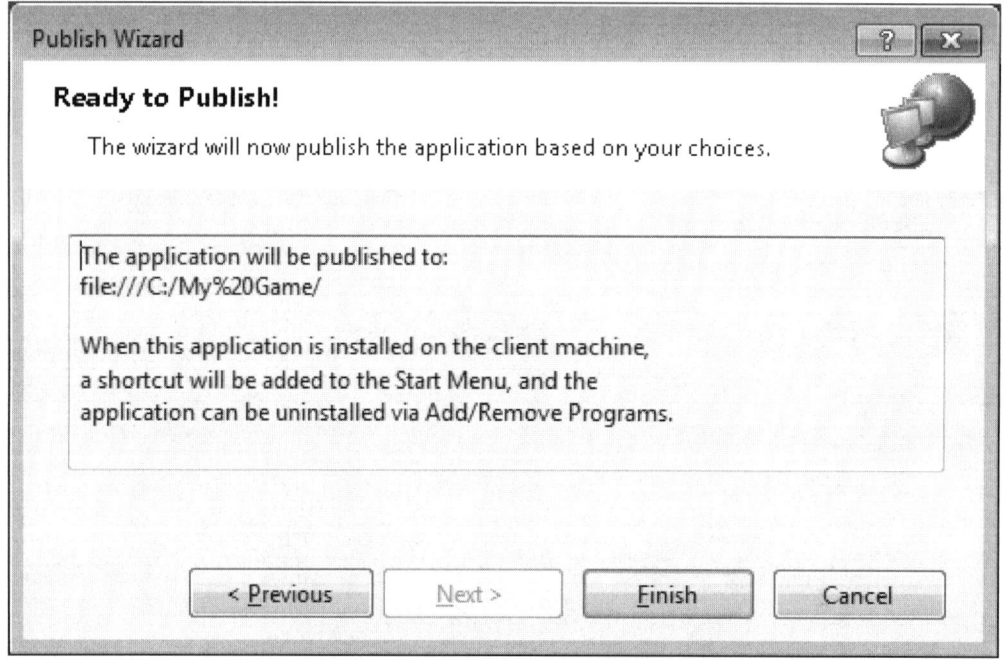

Once you click on the "Finish" button on the above screen, the project will be compiled, built and setup files will be created. At the end of this process, you will end up with files in your target output directory like this:

Chapter Twelve: Menus, Overlays and Deployment

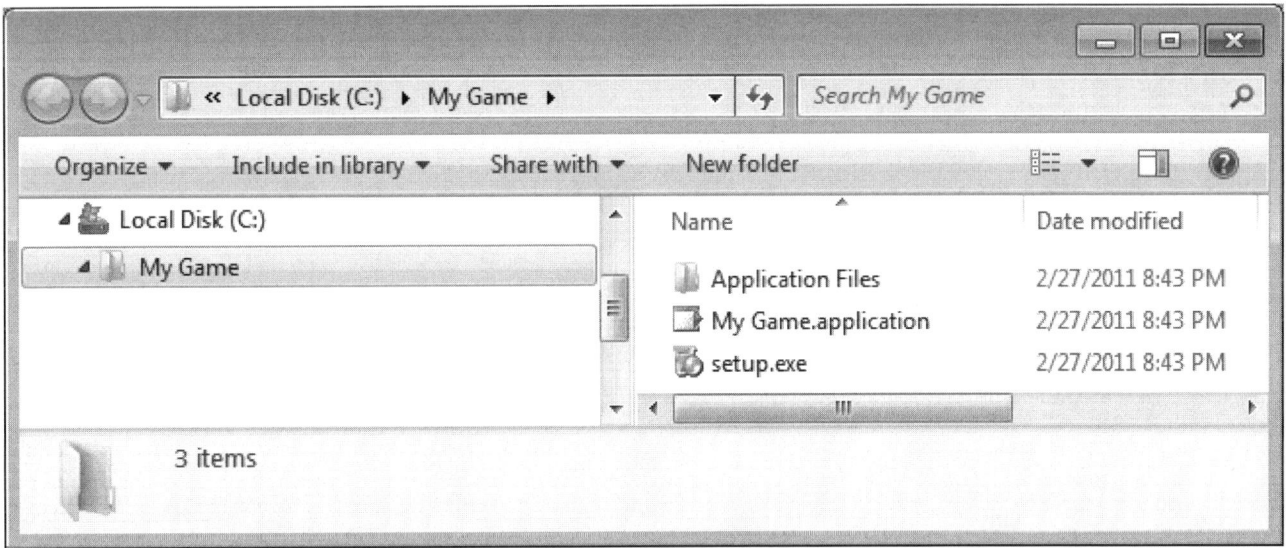

You can now take these files and place them onto a CD, DVD, flash drive, ZIP file, etc. and distribute them to whomever you wish. When the "setup.exe" file is run on the user's machine, it will install all the necessary files (including the .NET Framework and XNA Framework Redistributable package) and add a shortcut to the Start Menu. The game can then be played right from the Start menu!

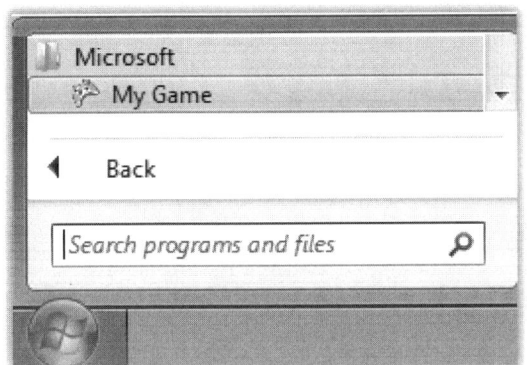

You should note that this method does not create an "Un-Install" program. Your users will have to go to the Control Panel screen and choose "Add/Remove Programs" or "Programs and Features" to remove the game once it is installed.

Other Methods of Distribution

The methods of distributing a game program described so far are the simplest and easiest for you to use. However, you may find that these methods don't offer the flexibility or choices that you need to install (or uninstall) your game program. If this is the case, you may need to try a different distribution tool. There are many good tools on the market today, including professional packages that cost money or freeware tools geared more for individual users. These tools offer more features than those built into the XNA IDE but they are more difficult to configure and use. We recommend using the packing and publishing features that come with the XNA Game Studio unless you have a strong motivation to use some other a 3rd party tool.

Chapter Review

- Most game programs contain more than one screen.
- A *title screen* is a screen that is only shown when a game is first started. These screens are often used to hide the loading of resources at the beginning of a game.
- *Menu screens* are used to allow the player to navigate through option screens or to start the game.
- *Option screens* contain areas where the player can set various game options.
- When an in-game option screen is displayed, the game should usually be paused. In this case, the option screens are often created as overlays on top of the paused game screen.
- If a screen requires input from the player, the on-screen instructions should be clear.
- You can define an enumeration to represent each of your game screens, and keep track of the current screen in a variable.
- Use a different **Update()** and **Draw()** method for each of your game screens to help keep your game program organized and easy to read.
- You will generally want to display player scores and key information on-screen in some fashion.
- You can simply write text to the screen with **SpriteBatch.DrawString()** to display player scores.
- A graphical overlay is often thought of as a "game dashboard" where game information is displayed in a graphical manner at the top or bottom of the game screen.
- The distribution of game files requires more than just copying the "game.exe" file to another player's computer. There are dependent files and game components which must also be installed.
- You can package an XNA game for other XNA developers, assuming they have the .NET Framework and XNA Framework Redistributable packages.
- To distribute your game program to the general public, you will need to "publish" the game.
- The Publish Wizard in XNA Game Studio will create a set of game files and a "setup.exe" file, which can be used to install the game onto any other Windows computer.

Activity: Tic-Tac-Toe

In this activity, you will practice your multiple-screen and overlay skills on a simple tic-tac-toe game.

Your activity requirements and instructions are found in the "Chapter_12_Activity.pdf" document located in your "TeenCoder\Game Programming\Activity Docs" folder. You can access this document through your Student Menu or by double-clicking on it from Windows Explorer.

Complete this activity now and ensure your program meets the requirements before continuing!

Chapter Thirteen: Multiplayer Games

Playing a computer game by yourself is fun, but it's often great to play a game against a friend! Nothing beats the thrill of being able to zoom past or beat a human opponent instead of a simple computer player.

A multiplayer game can take several forms. The simplest form of multiplayer game is the turn-by-turn game. In this type of game two or more players take turns playing on the same computer or game console. All players share the same type of input – keyboard, mouse or game controller. We already created this type of multiplayer game with the Snowball Fight from an earlier chapter.

In this chapter we will cover another type of multiplayer game: the split screen game. A split screen game divides the game screen into two or more sections, with each section showing a single user's point of view. Split screens allow two or more players to move around independently in an environment that may be larger than a single physical screen.

Lesson One: Handling Multiple Inputs

In a split screen game, all players are playing the game simultaneously. This means that each player must have a unique method of providing input to the game. There are a few different ways to allow multiple players to interact with a game at the same time.

Keyboard Input

The computer keyboard was the first type of input for computer games. In one-player games, the movement of game characters is usually done with the arrow keys. The up arrow move the character up on the screen, the down arrow moves the player down and the left and right keys move the character either left or right.

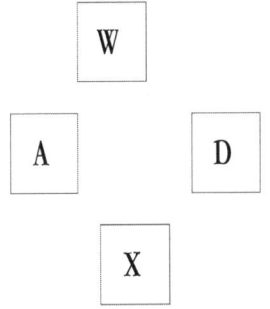

In two-player games, each player must have a unique set of keys. Up/down/left/right movement is traditionally done with keys "W", "A", "D", and "X" for the left player. If you look at these four letters on your keyboard, you will see that they form a sort of cross configuration on the opposite side of the keyboard from the arrow keys. The "W" key is used to move up, the "X" key will move down and the "A" and "D" keys will move left and right respectively.

189

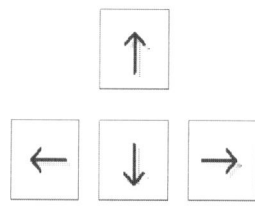

For the right-side player the arrow keys work nicely to move in the up/down/left/right directions. You can use any combination of non-traditional movement keys for your players. However, you will want to make sure that those keys make sense for the direction that the player is trying to move. For instance, the "up" key should be higher on the keyboard than the "down" key. The "right" key should be on the right side and the "left" key should be on the left side. This is more intuitive and easier for the player to learn.

It is difficult to allow for more than two players when you are using a keyboard for game input. You can assign any set of keys to any player, but the keyboard quickly becomes crowded when more than two sets of hands are using it at one time. You can decide which player uses which set of keys to move their characters based on the location of the player's split screen on the computer monitor. If a player's split game screen is on the left, they should use the leftmost set of keys (W A D X). If a player's game screen is on the right, they should use the rightmost set of keys (the arrow keys).

Mouse Input

It is difficult (if not impossible) to allow two users to share a mouse in a simultaneous game. Even if you could connect two mice to a computer, your game program will not be able to discern the difference between the mice. A mouse click from mouse #1 and a mouse click from mouse #2 will be treated as the same mouse click. However, you can always allow one player to move around the game using the mouse and another to move using the keyboard. We used this method in our Cat and Mouse project in an earlier chapter.

Xbox 360 Controllers

The use of gamepad controllers in Windows games allows for interesting input options. This is especially true when dealing with multiplayer games. Game controllers in multiplayer games give each player the same set of controls for the game. The gaming experience for one player is the same for another player within the same game. This is also a great way to add more than two players. An XNA game can handle up to 4 controllers at a time (this is the most that are allowed to connect to an Xbox game console), without any crowding around a single keyboard! You can plug more than one controller into a Windows PC with multiple USB ports. Please note that the XNA Framework will currently only recognize Xbox 360 game controllers.

Each game controller is controlled with a **GamePad** class object. When retrieving the current controller state you simply need to specify the index of the player you are checking.

```
GamePadState currentState1 = GamePad.GetState(PlayerIndex.One);
GamePadState currentState2 = GamePad.GetState(PlayerIndex.Two);
GamePadState currentState3 = GamePad.GetState(PlayerIndex.Three);
GamePadState currentState4 = GamePad.GetState(PlayerIndex.Four);
```

Don't forget to check each game pad state's **IsConnected** property to see if the controller at the specified index is currently hooked up and enabled.

You can assign any function to the buttons on an Xbox controller in your game. However, there are some traditional button assignments for the controller:

- Start button = Start
- Back button = back or quit
- Left thumbstick is directional movement
- Right thumbstick moves camera view
- Directional pad navigates menus
- Letter buttons for common tasks, like shooting
- Trigger buttons are also used for shooting

By using traditional button assignments, new players can learn to use your game more quickly. Regardless of what keys or mouse movements you have chosen to use in your game, you should always process all input within the **Update()** method (or one if its child functions). Checking for multiple player inputs is exactly the same as checking for single player input. You just have more keys or buttons to observe and you need to make sure you are routing the commands to the right player based on the input assignments.

Lesson Two: Scrolling Games

Scrolling games are very popular two-dimensional games that have been around since the early arcade days. The first arcade games had a very serious limitation: the game world was limited to the size of the arcade machine screen. Even though early games used the screen space in very creative ways, this small game world quickly became an issue for hard-core gamers. The answer to this problem was the scrolling game.

A scrolling game has a relatively large game world. The player is only shown a small section of the world at a time. This section is often the "camera view" for the player. When the player moves his or her character, the background of the game will "scroll", showing a new section of the world. In many cases the player character is not actually moving on the screen. Instead the background (the game world) is moving, giving the illusion of character movement! Scrolling games can scroll either vertically, horizontally or in both directions, although choosing one direction is easier to program.

An early popular example of a horizontal scroll game was the arcade game "Defender". In this game a player controlled a spaceship by moving the joystick left or right. The background would scroll in the opposite direction of the joystick movement, making it look like the spaceship was "flying" through space. This added a lot of visual excitement and game potential, so the technique was widely copied in later arcade games.

The placement of a game character on the screen in a scrolling game depends on the objective of the game. If the character needs to navigate a series of obstacles in a racing game, the view in front of the game character is traditionally larger than the view behind the character. This allows the player to adjust for new obstacles as they come into view on the screen.

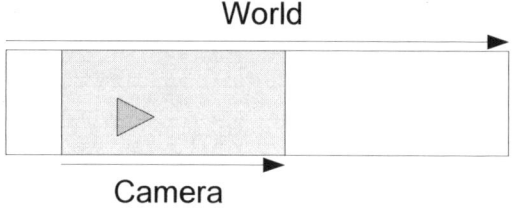

The *parallax scrolling* technique uses different rates of scrolling movement for different objects on the screen. For example, a racing game might occur on a background that contains an image of a dirt road. The road is scrolling at a certain rate, which makes the car look as though it is traveling at a certain speed. As the player races up the road, they must navigate barrels that roll into view. The barrels are rolling at a different rate of speed than the road, which gives a rudimentary illusion of 3D depth in a 2D game. In another example, mountains off in the distance may be scrolled very slowly, while a closer object such as a tree moves by quickly as the player's car proceeds down the road.

Game Tiles

A scrolling game can use a technique for creating the game world called *game tiles*. Game tiles are small subsections of a game world. These tiles can be put together in various (and often infinite) ways in order to create any number of unique game worlds. This method is extremely flexible and prevents a game from needing to load and track giant image files. Loading large files will slow down a game program. Instead we can use a small number of tiles that are drawn multiple times as the player moves through the environment.

Consider the small sampling of "road" tiles below.

Each tile would be a separate image loaded into the game. Or you could come up with a fancier **Sprite** class to display a single tile from a larger tile strip or grid, similar to animation! By arranging these tiles in different combinations you can construct a racetrack or road system of great complexity. This example only shows a small number of tiles you might design for a road segment; imagine what you can do with a few dozen tiles!

Chapter Thirteen: Multiplayer Games

World Coordinates and Screen Coordinates

Since a scrolling game uses a larger game world than the screen size, we need to use two different coordinate systems to keep track of the game character both on the screen and in the world. The *world* coordinates contain the player's position on the overall game world. The *screen* coordinates contain the location of the player on the actual computer screen.

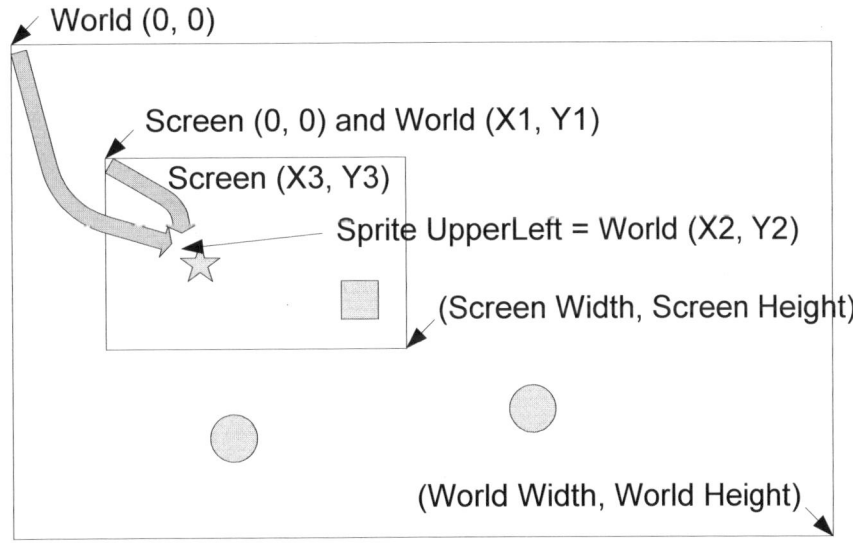

In the diagram above the outer rectangle represents the entire world with coordinates that range from (0, 0) in the upper left to (world width, world height) in the lower right. All sprites in the world, including our hero "Super-Star" (at world coordinates X2, Y2), a friend "Square Peg", and two evil villains "Circular Logic" are located somewhere in the world with world coordinates relative to the upper left world location at (0, 0).

The smaller inner rectangle represents what you can actually display on the computer screen given the screen width and height. The upper left corner of the screen resides at some world coordinate (X1, Y1). All images drawn on the screen must be drawn in terms of screen coordinates, where (0, 0) is the upper-left corner of the screen and (screen width, screen height) is the lower right corner of the screen. Some sprites such as our two circles may be so far away in the world that they are not visible at all and hence not drawn on the screen.

In order to make the scrolling game work properly, you must be able to calculate your sprite's screen coordinates from its world coordinates. For simplicity a game sprite can always keep track of its **Sprite.UpperLeft** position in world coordinates such as the (X2, Y2) point shown above. When you know the sprite's upper left world coordinates and the screen's upper left world coordinates, you can easily calculate the screen upper left coordinates for the star sprite, marked (X3, Y3) in the example above.

```
X3 = X2 - X1;      // Sprite upper-left screen X-coordinate
Y3 = Y2 - Y1;      // Sprite upper-left screen Y-coordinate
```

In English this code means "The sprite's screen coordinates equal the sprite's world coordinates minus the upper-left corner of the screen's world coordinates."

After this calculation, any sprite that has an upper-left screen position that is less than (-sprite width, -sprite height) is considered out of the field of view completely and is not drawn on the screen. Any sprite that has an upper-left screen position that is greater than (screen height, screen width) is also out of the field of view completely and is not drawn. All other sprites are drawn at the calculated position on the screen. Your sprite should be partially displayed on the screen if it's partially overlapping on any screen boundary.

What happens if your game scrolls in a purely horizontal or vertical direction? A horizontal scroller has a screen height equal to the world height, because the screen view can't be moved up or down. A vertical scroller has a screen width equal to the world width, because the screen view can't be moved left or right.

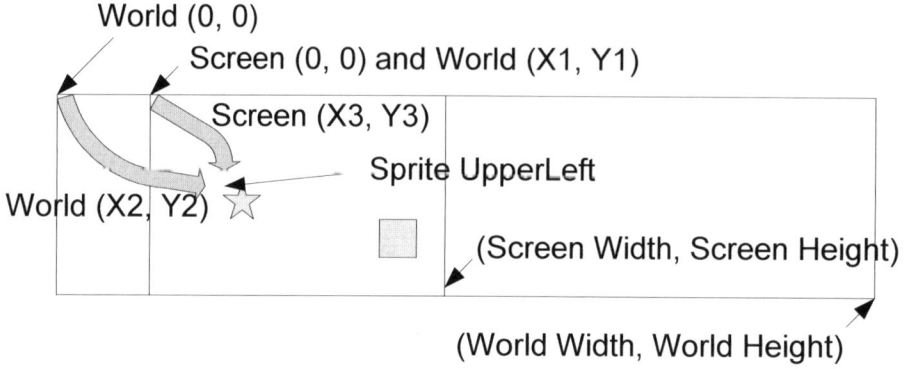

In this horizontal example you can see that the sprite's Y-coordinate is the same in both world and screen coordinates, because Y3 = Y2 – 0 = Y2. In this case the value you store in the sprite's **UpperLeft.Y** property is both the screen and the world coordinate. You can envision the same rules apply to a vertically scrolling game! The sprite's X-coordinate will be the same in both world and screen coordinates because X3 = X2 – 0 = X2.

Lesson Three: Viewports and Cameras

A multiplayer game like Snowball Fight has two or more players sharing the same game screen. This is fine for stationary games, but what if we have a scrolling game? What if one player wants to explore the map and the other wants to stay in one place? If you use one game screen for both players, they are tied to each other for the duration of the game. That's no fun!

A multiplayer scrolling game can be implemented as a split screen game unless there is a strong reason to keep the players together within the world. For each player in the game we can split off a part of the screen dedicated to one player's view of the game. That way each player can scroll anywhere in the world and see the resulting environment within their own view, without impacting what the other players are doing.

Viewports

XNA contains a class called the **Viewport** which makes splitting the screen very simple. A **Viewport** refers to a section of the computer or console screen. Every game contains a default **Viewport** object called **graphics.GraphicsDevice.Viewport**. In a normal game, this default **Viewport** covers the coordinates for the full screen or window from position (0, 0) to (screen width, screen height). We have often used the default **Viewport** properties to determine the width and height of the game window!

The **Viewport** class will split a game screen into different areas. Once the screen is split, each section will contain its own coordinate space. This means that the upper-left corner of the **Viewport** will always be (0, 0) no matter where the **Viewport** exists on the screen. A **Viewport** that starts in the middle of the screen still has an upper-left value of (0, 0). The example below shows viewports splitting the screen in half vertically.

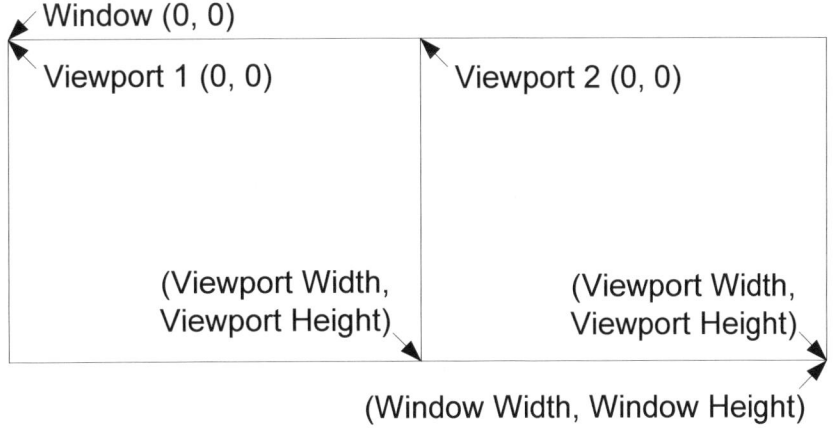

When you draw into each viewport you are using screen coordinates that range from (0, 0) to (viewport width, viewport height)!

Let's take a look at the code required to split a game screen. First, we need to create a **Viewport** object:

```
Viewport rightViewport = new Viewport();
```

Now we have a new **Viewport** to use, but we need to initialize it with some more information. The **Viewport** object contains several properties which determine the position and size.

```
rightViewport.X = 400;        // screen coordinate of viewport left side
rightViewport.Y = 0;          // screen coordinate of viewport top side
rightViewport.Width = 400;    // viewport width
rightViewport.Height = 600;   // viewport height
```

The X and Y values will set the upper-left position of the **Viewport** on the screen. The **Width** and **Height** values will set the **Viewport** width and height in pixels on the screen. The code shown above will create a **Viewport** that represents the right side of an 800 x 600 pixel window.

To create a **Viewport** for the left side of the screen, we could use the following code:

```
Viewport leftViewport = new Viewport();
leftViewport.X = 0;
leftViewport.Y = 0;
leftViewport.Width = 400;
leftViewport.Height = 600;
```

Now we have two viewports which split the screen into two vertical sections. In order to draw anything into one these viewports, we will need to set it as the current **Viewport** for the game. To do this, we can use the following line of code in our **Draw()** method:

```
GraphicsDevice.Viewport = leftViewport;
```

After this statement, anything that we write to the screen will be placed into our left-side **Viewport**. It's important to remember that our new viewports only extend 400 pixels across and 600 pixels down on the screen. If we tried to draw a sprite at coordinate (400, 100), the sprite will not appear in either viewport!

It's always a good idea to keep track of the original **Viewport** values. To do this, we can save the original values before we change to another **Viewport**. This way, we can easily change back to the original **Viewport** when we have completed our drawing tasks in the new viewports.

```
Viewport original = GraphicsDevice.Viewport;

GraphicsDevice.Viewport = leftViewport;
// do left viewport drawing here

GraphicsDevice.Viewport = rightViewport;
// do right viewport drawing here

GraphicsDevice.Viewport = original;
```

The Camera Class

Now that you have separate viewports in your game, you will need a way to keep track of what part of the world each player is seeing. Remember that you'll need to know the viewport's upper left corner in world coordinates, plus the width and height of the viewport. One common approach is to define a **Camera** class to keep track of these values and provide some other useful view-related methods. In a scrolling game, the **Camera** moves with the player so that the view is updated as the player moves around the screen.

There is no pre-defined **Camera** class in XNA, but we can easily create our own:

```
class Camera
{
    // the world position of the upper-left coordinate of the camera
    public Vector2 UpperLeft = new Vector2();

    // these members are used to keep the camera view within
    // valid world coordinates
    public int ViewWidth = 0;
    public int ViewHeight = 0;
    public int WorldWidth = 0;
    public int WorldHeight = 0;

    // this method will prevent the camera's display from straying
    // outside the bounds of world coordinates
    public void LockCamera()
    {
        // details below
    }
```

```
    // this utility method will return true if the specified object is at all
    // visible within the camera view
    public bool IsVisible(Vector2 objectUpperLeft,
                          int objectWidth, int objectHeight)
    {
        // details below
    }
};
```

Our **Camera** class also defines two useful utility methods:

LockCamera()	This method will automatically adjust the **UpperLeft** position to ensure that the viewable area is entirely within the world coordinate space.
IsVisible()	This method will return **true** if the object (specified by upper left position, width, and height) is at all viewable within the visible area.

The **LockCamera()** method will keep the camera's viewable area from straying off of the game world. Any time you adjust the **Camera.UpperLeft** coordinate there is a danger that you have specified a position where some part of the screen has no corresponding world coordinates. For instance, if you set **Camera.UpperLeft** to (-10, -10) then the first 10 pixels across the top and left side of the view have no corresponding world coordinates, so it's tough to draw anything there! Or, you could set **Camera.UpperLeft** to (world width -10, world height -10) and have only a small 10 x 10 pixel area of valid world coordinates visible in the upper left corner.

Here is the code behind **LockCamera()**:

```
public void LockCamera()
{
    if (UpperLeft.X < 0)                                    // check left edge
        UpperLeft.X = 0;
    if ((UpperLeft.X + ViewWidth) > WorldWidth)             // check right edge
        UpperLeft.X = WorldWidth - ViewWidth;

    if (UpperLeft.Y < 0)                                    // check top edge
        UpperLeft.Y = 0;
    if ((UpperLeft.Y + ViewHeight) > WorldHeight)           // check bottom edge
        UpperLeft.Y = WorldHeight - ViewHeight;
}
```

LockCamera() makes sure that the camera never has an X position value that is less than 0, or large enough such that the right edge of the viewport will fall off the right edge of the world. Similarly the Y position should not be less than 0 or large enough such that the bottom edge of the viewport will fall off the bottom edge of the world. Any time you update the **Camera.UpperLeft** property you should call **LockCamera()** afterwards to ensure the viewport remains within the world boundaries.

The **Camera.IsVisible()** method will tell you if an object or region specified by the given upper left position, width, and height has any overlap with the camera's current view.

```
public bool IsVisible(Vector2 objectUpperLeft,
                      int objectWidth, int objectHeight)
{
    // all coordinates are in world coordinates
    Rectangle cameraRect = new Rectangle((int)UpperLeft.X, (int)UpperLeft.Y,
                                         ViewWidth, ViewHeight);
    Rectangle objectRect = new Rectangle((int)objectUpperLeft.X,
                                         (int)objectUpperLeft.Y,
                                         objectWidth, objectHeight);

    return cameraRect.Intersects(objectRect);
}
```

IsVisible() will build two bounding rectangles; one for the camera view and one for the object or area specified by the input parameters. Then it will return **true** if the rectangles intersect. Why would you use this method? Imagine you have a very large world populated with many objects, but only a small fraction of the objects can be seen in the viewport. You don't want to blindly call **Draw()** on each object, since most of them are completely off the screen! That would be a big drain on your computer's resources. Instead you can quickly check to see if any part of the object is visible within the camera view before you render it.

```
if (myCamera.IsVisible(mySprite.UpperLeft,
                       mySprite.GetWidth(), mySprite.GetHeight()))
{
    mySprite.Draw(spriteBatch);
}
```

Using the Camera

At the start of your game, create a separate **Viewport** and **Camera** object for every player in the game. Initialize your viewports with the location and dimensions you want them to occupy on the screen. Then initialize the corresponding **Camera** objects with the viewport's width and height, the world width and height, and the camera's initial **UpperLeft** position in world coordinates.

How do you determine the camera's **UpperLeft** position at the beginning or at time later? It depends on what your player should be seeing! You could create a game with a large map, and allow the player to pan their camera across the entire map without moving the player's character at all. More commonly, especially in scrolling games, you will fix the camera's position based on the sprite representing the player!

To do this, simply update your player's sprite normally based on its movement parameters (position, velocity, acceleration) or by directly setting the sprite's upper left position. Then, calculate the **Camera.UpperLeft** based on the new sprite location. Let's say your main character is riding around in the **Sprite** called **myShip**. You have created a horizontal scrolling game where the ship is heading toward the right, and you want to keep the ship located about 25% of the way from the left side of the screen.

```
myShip.Move();
myCamera.UpperLeft.X = myShip.UpperLeft.X - (myCamera.ViewWidth / 4);
myCamera.LockCamera();
```

First we moved the ship normally. Then we set the camera's X-coordinate so the left viewport edge positions the sprite a quarter of the view width from the left side. Then for safety we called **LockCamera()** to make sure we're still within world coordinates. We have not touched the camera's Y coordinate, which for our horizontal scroller will always equal zero. This

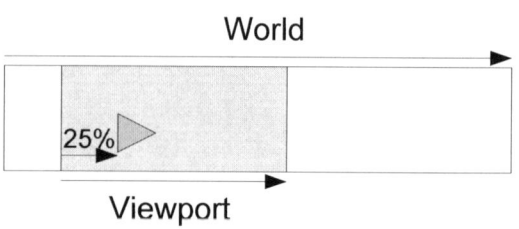

allows the player's ship to move up and down on the screen without moving the camera up and down too. As the ship moves horizontally through world coordinates, the **Camera** will naturally follow along!

Drawing an Object with World Coordinates

Sharp readers may have been impatiently wondering, "How do we draw a sprite at the right spot on the screen if the **Sprite.UpperLeft** is in world coordinates instead of screen coordinates?" Recall our statement in the first lesson regarding conversion of world coordinates to screen coordinates:

The sprite's screen coordinates equal the sprite's world coordinates minus the upper-left corner of the screen, in world coordinates.

We are conveniently tracking the upper-left corner of the screen (viewport), in world coordinates, within the **Camera.UpperLeft** member. We have the sprite's world coordinates in **Sprite.UpperLeft**. So all that's left is a simple subtraction to convert the sprite's world coordinates to screen coordinates! The **Sprite** class has a version of **Draw()** that does this for you.

```
public void Draw(SpriteBatch theSpriteBatch, Vector2 cameraUpperLeft)
{
    UpperLeft -= cameraUpperLeft;
    Draw(theSpriteBatch);
    UpperLeft += cameraUpperLeft;
}
```

This method will temporarily convert the **Sprite.UpperLeft** from world to screen coordinates, draw the image on the screen, then restore the **Sprite.UpperLeft** to the original world coordinates. All you have to provide is the camera's upper left coordinate and the **Sprite** will be automatically drawn in the right spot on the screen!

```
myShip.Draw(spriteBatch, myCamera.UpperLeft);
```

Chapter Review

- A multi-player game can involve turn-taking or simultaneous game play.
- You can handle multiple player input in different ways in a Windows game: via the keyboard, mouse and keyboard or multiple game controllers.
- The keyboard is large enough to allow two users to simultaneously press their own set of buttons.
- Multiple game controllers have the advantage of allowing all players to have the same set of controls.
- It is difficult (if not impossible) to allow two users to share a mouse simultaneously in a game.
- Scrolling games allow the game "world" to be larger than the player's computer screen. By scrolling the background as the player moves around, the "world" can be as large as your imagination allows.
- *Parallax* scrolling uses different rates of movement for objects different distances away. This gives a 2D game a simplistic illusion of depth.
- Game *tiles* are small, interchangeable pieces of a game world. These tiles can usually be put together in many different ways in order to create a large number of unique game worlds.
- Scrolling games require the use of both world coordinates and screen coordinates. The world coordinates contain the player's position on the overall game world. The screen coordinates contain the location of the player on the actual computer screen.
- The **Viewport** class is used to split a game screen into different sections, usually one for each player. Each viewport has its own width and height and location on the screen.
- Our **Camera** class is a convenient way to keep track of the viewport's current position within world coordinates. Each player will generally have one **Viewport** and corresponding **Camera**.
- The **Camera** contains utility methods to keep the viewport area safely within world coordinates and determine if an object is visible in the view.
- A version of our **Sprite.Draw()** method will accept the camera's upper left position in world coordinates and automatically draw the **Sprite** in the right location on the screen.

Activity: Star Racer

In this activity you will be working with a game called Star Racer, where two ships race through an asteroid field to the finish line. You will implement the separate viewports and cameras for each player.

Your activity requirements and instructions are found in the "Chapter_13_Activity.pdf" document located in your "TeenCoder\Game Programming\Activity Docs" folder. You can access this document through your Student Menu or by double-clicking on it from Windows Explorer.

Complete this activity now and ensure your program meets the requirements before continuing!

Chapter Fourteen: Artificial Intelligence

In this chapter we will discuss artificial intelligence, or AI. Computer games use AI to provide computer opponents in games that may require more than one player or to make objects behave in a lifelike manner.

Lesson One: Understanding AI

You may have heard the term *artificial intelligence* many times in fictional settings – Hollywood movies and science fiction books all love a smart robot or a scary computer program bent on world domination. These artificial life forms display human-like intelligence, emotions, and adaptability. In reality, however, this type of artificial intelligence does not exist! The human mind is the most powerful computer in the known universe. We have the amazing ability to react to our surroundings, adjusting and adapting with ease. Modern machines are much more powerful than the earliest computers, but they are no match for the human brain.

All computers will do exactly what they are programmed to do. The nature of the program may be complex enough that it's hard to predict or understand why software behaves the way it does. Complex programs are also more likely to contain bugs that make the behavior even more unexpected. However, despite your Aunt Bethel's firm belief, there are no gremlins running around in the machine making it do things of its own free will! Nor can machines evolve new capabilities out of thin air, although some neural networks can "learn" how to do things based on many attempts to solve a problem.

The artificial intelligence we need for computer games has little resemblance to a Hollywood super-robot. Game AI is a simpler, more focused algorithm that that makes computer games more believable and fun. Here are some examples of things you can do with AI in computer games:

- Control an opposing fighter plane in a dogfight simulation
- Provide a computer opponent in a card game
- Allow non-playing-characters (NPCs) in a role playing game to "converse" with you
- Control a bird's flight pattern and behavior as part of background scenery

As you can see, some types of AI are very simple and some are very complex. However they are all focused on doing one task – and only doing that task well enough to make the human player have fun! One game may have many types of AI routines to control different objects. You might not think of a function to make a fish decide whether or not to bite your lure as AI. However if the goal is to simulate lifelike behavior for an object, then the routine can be classified as game AI. More complex AI will result in a better simulation of real behavior, while very crude AI might produce behavior that is unnatural or predictable.

Characteristics of AI Algorithms

When deciding to implement AI for an object in your game, it pays to keep in mind some key requirements. Ask yourself if your AI approach meets all of these criteria:

Believable	Does your AI produce behavior that a human player can enjoy? In most cases you are not trying to fool the human into thinking another human is playing. You are just trying to provide a reasonably lifelike approximation of the real thing in order to make the game entertaining. If you make a bird fly in a square pattern on the screen, that's not very believable. But if you make the bird fly around randomly and occasionally sit in a tree, great! That's what birds do. Even if your bird does the exact same sequence over and over again, chances are your player won't notice or care because the bird is being reasonably lifelike.
Challenging	Does your AI appropriately challenge a human player? It should not be a trivial exercise for a human to beat a computer opponent; otherwise the game gets boring very quickly. Likewise a computer opponent shouldn't wipe the floor automatically with the hapless human every single time! Games should provide AI that is not too hard and not too easy, encouraging user to keep playing and improve their own skills. The best games will offer levels of AI difficulty – easy modes for novice players just learning the game, normal and hard modes for more experienced users, and maybe even "insane" challenges for the expert player!
Programmable	Is it possible to write code to represent your AI algorithm? If your plan for writing a computer card player relies on studying the human's facial expressions to determine if they are bluffing, you probably won't get very far. However if you plan to make the computer AI "count" cards and calculate odds based on the computer's infallible memory of what's been played, that's more achievable.
Computable	Some AI algorithms are very short, simple, and impose little load on the computer resources (memory and CPU). However it's possible to design algorithms that will completely chew up your available CPU and use more memory than is available on the system. For instance, computer chess programs that challenge grandmasters often require specially built hardware and software with enormous computing resources to look ahead through millions of permutations to select the next move. When designing your AI algorithm, keep in mind that games tend to be resource "hogs" requiring lots of CPU and memory to run, so don't make it significantly worse with a poorly designed AI routine.

Lesson Two: Developing an AI Algorithm

During your initial game design you should plan which objects might require some AI guidance. Remember that AI can be used for anything from providing more realistic background scenery to providing a challenging computer opponent. This lesson will focus on the latter case – how can we make the computer mimic a human opponent?

We'll use a Tic-Tac-Toe game as a running example. The object of Tic-Tac-Toe, of course, is to put three X's or three O's in a line vertically, horizontally, or diagonally on a 3x3 grid. Two players take turns placing one X or O in a square, with the X player going first.

Think like a Human

How do we teach a computer to play a game? First, think about how you would play the game yourself! What options would you have on your turn? If you are playing a card game your options might be restricted to selecting the next card to play. But if you are playing a large strategy game you may have many different things you can do, possibly at the same time. Make a list of your options at each point where a decision needs to be made and then think about how you would make that decision yourself as a human player.

Next, think about the information you would need to remember about what has been going on in the game so far. Often your next move can be effectively calculated just based on the current state of the game (the specific cards showing on the table, where the checkers pieces are placed on the board, etc). However you might really want to know what has happened in the past, such as which cards that have been played already! You may also need to remember if you have selected some overall plan in the past (such as "reach the top of the hill") so your next decision would move you closer to that goal.

For a Tic-Tac-Toe game our decision each turn will be pretty simple. We need to select an empty square to place or X or O (depending on which player is AI-controlled). We would give highest priority to any square that would immediately win the game! Next, if such a move is not available, we should move to block a square that our opponent could use to win the game on the next move. Otherwise we need to pick a square that gives us progress towards our goal of three marks in a row.

Flowcharts

When designing an algorithm it is often useful to visualize a logical sequence of steps in a picture called a *flowchart*. A flowchart is a visual representation of a process that makes it easier to understand. While some flowcharts can become very complex with many different symbols, we will use just two different shapes. A rectangle will represent an action to be taken. A diamond will represent a question or a decision that we have to make. Arrows connecting the shapes will indicate the program flow, and words written along the arrows will show relevant decisions or actions.

Here is an example flowchart representing the Tic-Tac-Toe AI we described above.

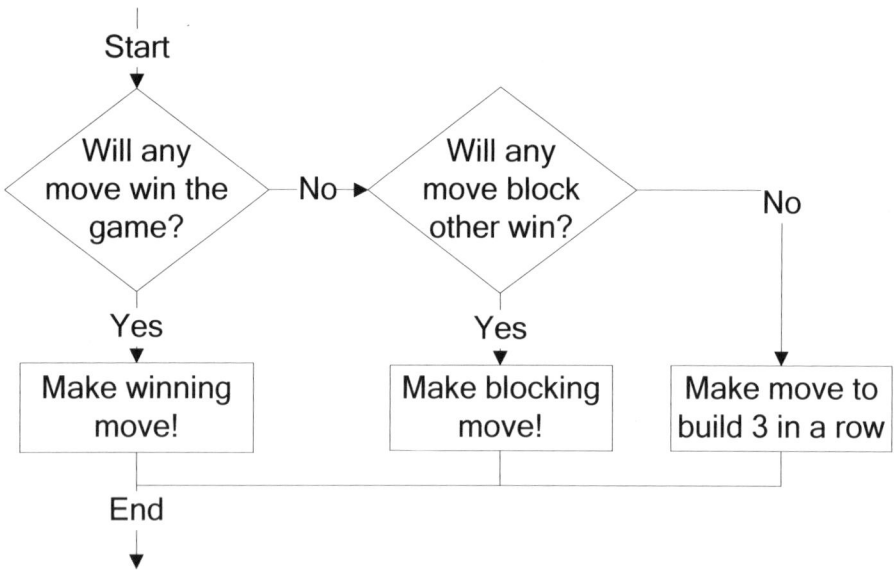

Sometimes a flowchart may show you where additional detail is necessary. For instance, the "Make move to build 3 in a row" rectangle above may take some more thought, and possibly even a small flowchart by itself to figure out the next best move.

Use of flowcharts is certainly not limited to artificial intelligence! Most algorithms can be reasonably represented by a flowchart. Flowcharts are great design tools when you are trying to figure out how some algorithm or piece of logic should work.

Special AI Data Structures

Recall that a key part of game design is your game state: a set of data structures that represents everything about your game. Until this point your game state has contained whatever minimal information that was necessary to operate the game. If you wrote a checker game then your game state would contain all of the remaining pieces and their locations for each player, plus some indication of the current player's turn. The Swarm game kept track of all the bees on the screen, the shots in mid-air, the state of the beehives, the speed of the bees, and so forth.

It is possible that your AI algorithm can operate strictly on the existing game state with no new information. However some AI may require you to build additional data structures to keep track of information useful to the AI. For instance a real-time strategy game AI might want to keep track of the last place any of its army units came into visual contact with opposing units. A path-finding AI also might keep track of the dead ends it has previously encountered in a labyrinth.

Luckily, our Tic-Tac-Toe game is simple enough that no extra data structures seem to be necessary. You certainly don't need to remember the order of previous moves – looking at the current state of the 3x3 grid is enough to select the next move. However, you may choose to construct a data structure to help you select the next move! It might be effective for you to pre-calculate all possible permutations of X's and O's on the grid and pre-select the most optimal next move for each configuration.

Cheating AI

At some point you will likely have to ask yourself: should my AI cheat? Instinctively you might think "No, of course not"! A chess AI cannot move the King piece like a Knight without invaliding the entire game. But the answer is not necessarily that simple. Keep in mind that the main objective of your AI is to make a *believable* game for the human player, yet still be a *programmable* and *computable algorithm*. In order to be believable of course your AI should not violate any central game rules. If you are playing a board game then don't steal money from the bank when you are running low!

However, it can be possible for the AI to cheat in ways that are not obvious to the user, or do not significantly impact game play – yet make your algorithm easier to write and require fewer computing resources to run. It's also possible that your algorithm would not normally pose any challenge to the human player unless you give it some extra "edge" to even things out. This type of cheating is generally OK as long as your game is fun for the real players. For instance, a strategy game may require a very complex algorithm to compete effectively with a human. But a simpler algorithm could still give a fun challenge if you give the AI player an extra percentage of resources, or slightly faster response times, or complete visibility of every piece on the game board that might normally be hidden to human players. A cheating AI, so long as the game is fun, is not a moral dilemma – it's an effective programming response to the disadvantages computer code may have when faced with a human opponent!

Lesson Three: Simple Movement Algorithms

Movement algorithms deal with how an artificially intelligent sprite moves around in the game world. These algorithms can typically be broken down into three main categories: chasing, evading and random movements.

Chasing Algorithms

The Chase algorithm usually involves two objects: a *predator* and a *prey*. The predator's main function is to find and move towards the prey. On a 2D computer screen this means we need to examine the X and Y coordinates of both predator and prey. A simple technique might be to simply compare the X and Y values of each object and increment the predator towards the prey position, as shown in the following pseudo-code:

```
    If (predator X position > prey X position)
        Move predator one step left
    Else if (predator X position < prey X position)
        Move predator one step right

    If (predator Y position > prey Y position)
        Move predator one step up
    Else if (predator Y position < prey Y position)
        Move predator one step down
```

If the predator is currently left or right of the prey it will take a step in the correct horizontal direction. Similarly if the predator is above or below the prey it will step in the correct vertical direction. The movements are combined to step along a diagonal line if the prey's X and Y coordinates both are different than the predator.

While this simple algorithm would work, look at the resulting path a predator might take:

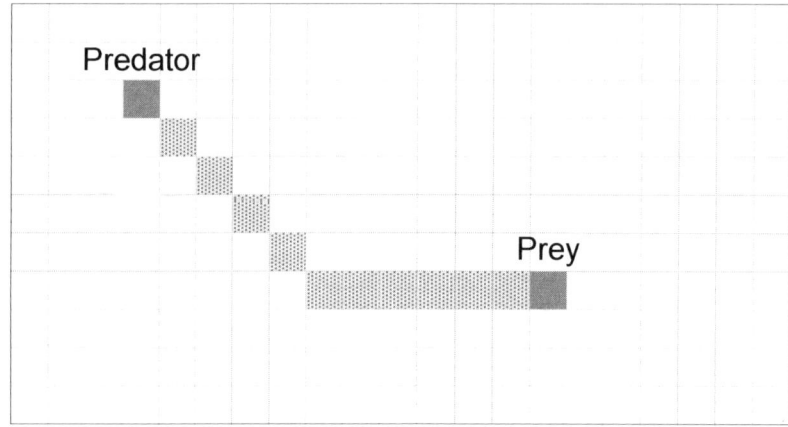

As you can see, the predator will find the prey using the simple algorithm, but the movement is not very realistic. If you are pursuing someone, chances are that you will choose a more direct line to your prey. To achieve this direct line, we can calculate the angle to the prey and take a step in a direct line along that angle.

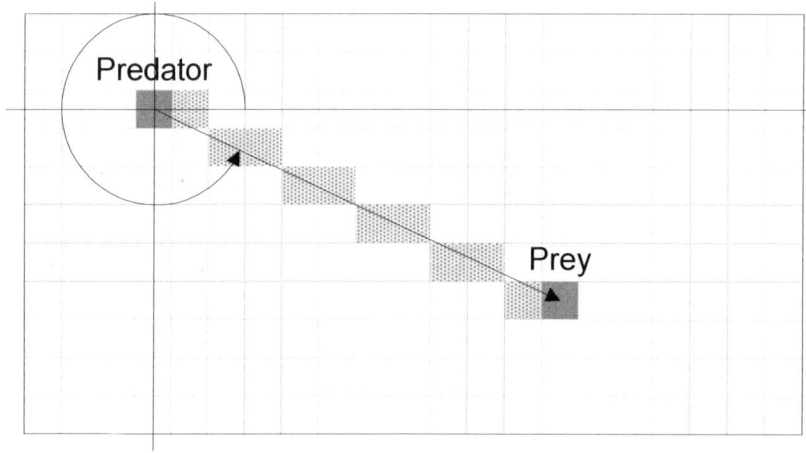

The angle can be determined by forming a vector from the predator to prey. Assume the predator is located at the origin by subtracting the predator's X and Y coordinates from the prey's coordinates. The resulting X and Y values form a vector pointing to the prey. You can then calculate the angle itself with some trigonometry. Fortunately the **Sprite** class has a method to perform this calculation for you!

```
static public double CalculateDirectionAngle(Vector2 vect)
```

Given an input vector this method will return the corresponding angle between 0 and 360 degrees. Here's an example, assuming predator and prey are both **Sprites**:

```
// form vector from predator to prey
Vector2 direction = new Vector2(prey.UpperLeft.X - predator.UpperLeft.X,
                                prey.UpperLeft.Y - predator.UpperLeft.Y);

// get the angle to the prey
double angle = Sprite.CalculateDirectionAngle(direction);

// set the predator's direction directly towards the prey
predator.SetDirectionAngle(angle);

// go get 'em!
predator.Move();
```

Evading Algorithms

The Evade algorithm is just the opposite of the Chase algorithm. We still have two objects: the predator and the prey, but this time we are concentrating on getting away, not chasing. You could use the same simple technique as we discussed for the Chase algorithm; just move the prey instead of the predator!

```
    If (predator X position > prey X position)
        Move prey one step left
    Else if (predator X position < prey X position)
        Move prey one step right

    If (predator Y position > prey Y position)
        Move prey one step up
    Else if (predator Y position < prey Y position)
        Move prey one step down
```

Of course this simple Evade routine would produce the same awkward diagonal and straight patterns as the before, so you'd want to use the more realistic technique. Find the angle between the predator and prey using the same logic as above, and then keep moving the prey in that direction. Depending on the situation you may also want the prey to move in a random or erratic direction to attempt to fool the predator. Otherwise if the predator is faster and is using the same directional algorithm, the predator will certainly catch up!

Random Movement Algorithms

Random movement algorithms allow a sprite to move in a random pattern or direction on the screen. This technique can be used to add some interest in a game. For instance, our random-moving asteroids added a challenge to our Star Racer game. Randomly moving background sprites could just add some ambiance to a game, like crowds of people walking by a game character on a busy street. Whatever the reason, a Random Movement algorithm will choose a randomly selected direction and speed to move a sprite around the screen.

To pick a random direction, just select a random number between 0 and 360 to represent your angle. To pick a random speed, select a random number between 0 and your maximum object speed. You can then call the **Sprite.SetSpeedAndDirection()** method to get the object going in your chosen direction.

Depending on the object you may want to vary the random speed and direction at certain time intervals. Keep in mind that your direction and speed may need to obey some reasonable constraints! Don't make a cloud randomly float faster than the jet your player is piloting. A little creativity with the movement of the minor or cosmetic objects in your game can go a long way towards enhancing game-play; just make sure the background activity is not too distracting.

Lesson Four: AI for Star Racer

In this lesson you will implement a very simple game AI for the Star Racer program from an earlier chapter. If you want to play the game by yourself, it would be great to have a computer opponent to race against! Your first version of the Star Racer game AI will be very simple, and then we'll describe how you can make it smarter for the activity at the end of the chapter.

The game AI will control the second starship if the user selects a one-player game from the menu. In that case the normal keys will not work for the starship. Movement will be determined by your AI encoded in a function called **DoSimpleAI()**. Open your StarRacer game project from the previous chapter and find this method now.

```
void DoSimpleAI()
{
}
```

Chapter Fourteen: Artificial Intelligence

This method in the starter activity does not contain any logic. It's up to you to make the starship move in a way that will provide a challenge for the human player piloting the first starship.

Now, recall that to develop a game AI you need to start by thinking like a human. If you are in a race and need to get to the finish line first, what's your biggest priority? Speed! If at any point you are moving less than your maximum possible speed, your natural reaction should be to speed up. So, your **DoSimpleAI()** method can consist solely of a check to see if the second starship is moving at less than maximum speed and accelerate if needed.

Go ahead and implement your **DoSimpleAI()** method as described above. Check the `StarShip2.GetVelocity().Y` against the `StarShip2.MaxSpeed` and, if the Y velocity is less, call **Accelerate()** on the sprite just as if a human player had hit the up arrow key. Use a zero value for the X acceleration and (**-ACCELERATION_FACTOR**) for the Y acceleration.

That's it! Now you can run the StarRacer program and select the one-player game. You should see the computer player immediately accelerate to maximum speed and stay there. If the ship hits an asteroid it will just keep blindly trying to move ahead until the asteroid is out of the way.

Let's review this AI against our four desired characteristics.

- **Believable**? Probably not, no race pilot is just going to go straight ahead regardless of obstacles!
- **Challenging**? Possibly, try it and see. Can you beat the computer AI yourself? Most likely you can, although the AI might get lucky depending on the asteroids.
- **Programmable**? Certainly yes, this was an easy fuction to write.
- **Computable**? Also yes, this function took no significant computing resources to complete.

Since we only hit two out of our four goals, we should figure out a better AI that will produce a more believable and challenging result. That will be the subject of your activity at the end of this chapter!

Chapter Review

- Computer games use *artificial intelligence* (AI) to provide computer opponents in games that may require more than one player or to make objects behave in a lifelike manner.
- AI can be used for anything from creating more realistic background scenery to providing a challenging computer opponent.
- Game AI algorithms are focused pieces of logic that make computer games more believable and fun.
- A good AI algorithm should be believable, challenging, programmable and computable.
- A computer opponent should take into account how a human player would play a game and what information the human player would understand about the game.
- When designing an algorithm it is often useful to visualize a logical sequence of steps in a picture called a *flowchart*.
- A computer opponent should always follow the important game rules. However there may be situations where a cheating AI makes an algorithm much more efficient without drastically changing the game play.
- Movement algorithms deal with how an artificially intelligent sprite moves around in the game world. These algorithms can typically be broken down into three main categories: chasing, evading and random movements.
- Chasing and Evading algorithms both involve a predator and a prey. The Chase algorithm has the predator moving towards the prey and the Evade algorithm has the prey moving away from the predator. The implementation of these algorithms is very similar.
- Random movement algorithms allow a sprite to move in a random pattern or direction on the screen.
- Random movements can be set by choosing a random direction (angle) and speed.

Chapter Fourteen: Artificial Intelligence

Activity: Star Racer AI

In this activity you will write a better game AI for the Star Racer computer pilot. In the last lesson you should have already created a function called **DoSimpleAI()** that simply accelerated the second racer straight ahead. Now, to make the AI more believable and challenging, let's make the AI try to avoid asteroids that might slow it down!

Your activity requirements and instructions are found in the "Chapter_14_Activity.pdf" document located in your "TeenCoder\Game Programming\Activity Docs" folder. You can access this document through your Student Menu or by double-clicking on it from Windows Explorer.

Complete this activity now and ensure your program meets the requirements before continuing!

Chapter Fifteen: Final Project

In this chapter you will be creating a final project. This game will demonstrate most of the concepts and techniques that have been presented in this course. It's time to show what you have learned about game programming!

Lesson One: Bumper Cars Overview

The final project game is a one or two-player game called "Bumper Cars". Each player controls their own car on the screen. These cars can move around the screen and bounce off of each other and the "walls" around the edge of the screen. A single golden coin will appear in a random location on the screen. The first person to drive their car over the coin gets a point. As soon as a point is scored, another coin will appear in another random location on the screen. This process continues until one of the players reaches 10 points.

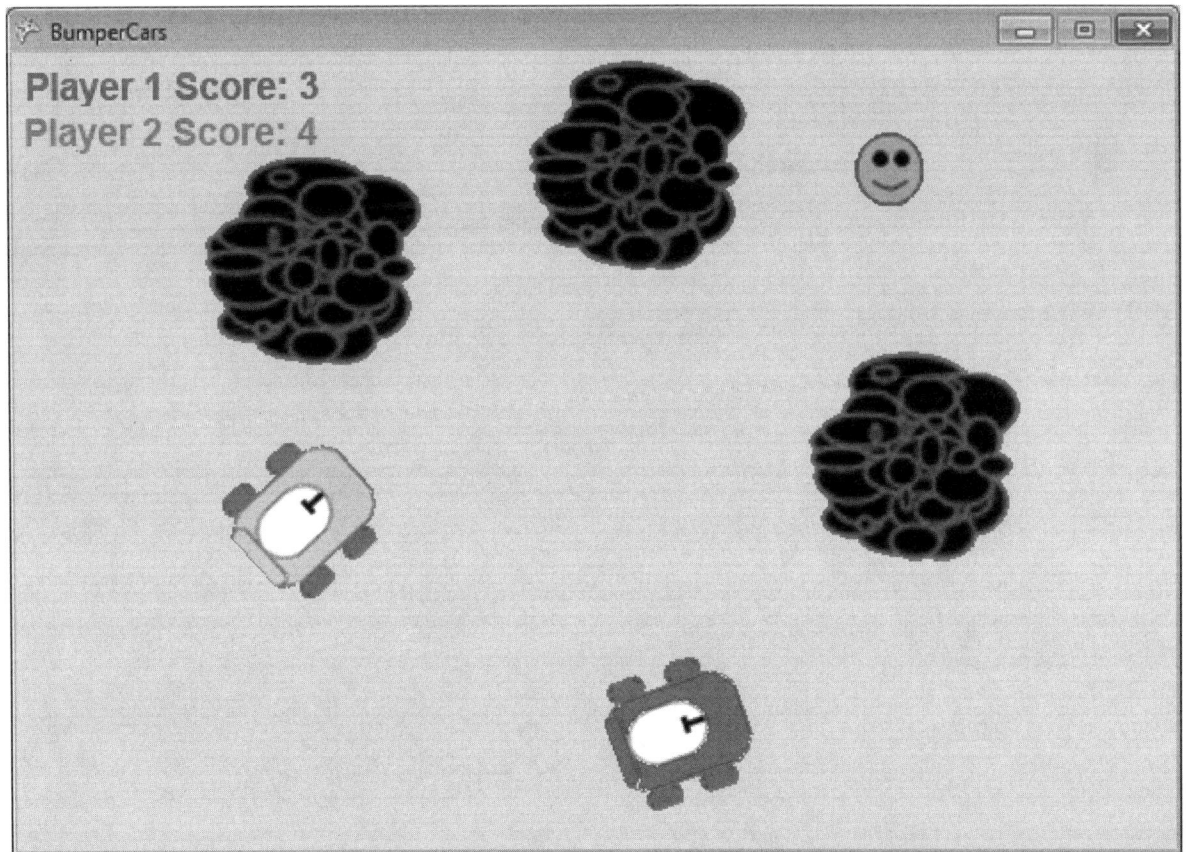

TeenCoder™: Game Programming

The game is made more difficult by the appearance of random oil slicks on the screen. These oil slicks will appear in random locations on the screen and will "dry up" after a period of time. Once an oil slick dries up, another oil slick will appear in a different location on the screen. If a bumper car runs over the oil slick, the car will slow down dramatically. A bumper car will also slow down if it hits any side of the screen.

Final Project Concepts

In this project you will apply your knowledge in the following areas:

Sprites and Animation	Each element on the screen will be represented as a **Sprite**, which can be moved, rotated and animated when necessary.
Movement and Acceleration	The bumper cars will need to move, accelerate and decelerate.
User Input	This game involves multiple player input using the keyboard. You will need to decide what keys belong to each player and will need to handle these key presses in your program.
Collision Detection	Bumper cars will be colliding with each other, the side walls of the screen, oil slicks and golden coins.
Sound	Every great game involves sound, and Bumper Cars is no different!
Menus and Options	The Bumper Cars game will require the player to navigate between screens using menus.
Artificial Intelligence	You will be creating a game that can be played as a multi-player game or a single-player game that involves a computer opponent.

Getting Started

There is no starter activity for this project. You will create the game project from beginning to end! However, some individual game elements are provided that will save you time and coding. These files can be found in your "\TeenCoder\Game Programming\Activity Starters\BumperCars" directory.

Sprite.cs	This file contains the same **Sprite** class you have been using throughout the course. All of the on-screen elements in Bumper Cars will be **Sprite** objects.
Car.cs	This file contains a **Car** class which is a subclass of **Sprite**. The **Car** class contains some extra properties and methods that make it easier to implement the two bumper cars.
Images\	All of the images that you will need are included in the "Images" subdirectory. This includes the bumper car, oil slick, and golden coin images. Of course, if you are artistically inclined, you are free to use your own images!
Sounds\	All of the sound files that you will need are included in the "Sounds" subdirectory.

Chapter Fifteen: Final Project

Activity One: Project Kick-Off

In this activity you will create your new Bumper Car project and begin loading content.

Your activity requirements and instructions are found in the "Chapter_15_Activity1.pdf" document located in your "TeenCoder\Game Programming\Activity Docs" folder. You can access this document through your Student Menu or by double-clicking on it from Windows Explorer.

Complete this activity now and ensure your program meets the requirements before continuing!

TeenCoder™: Game Programming

Lesson Two: Menus and Controls

Bumper Cars has a simple menu system. There are three game screens: Menu, Playing, and GameOver. The following flowchart shows how the player can transition between screens with certain commands or conditions.

You will implement this menu system in the next activity using the familiar pattern we developed in the Menus and Overlays chapter.

Activity Two: What's on the Menu?

In this activity you will create the menu system for Bumper Cars based on the flowchart in the lesson.

Your activity requirements and instructions are found in the "Chapter_15_Activity2.pdf" document located in your "TeenCoder\Game Programming\Activity Docs" folder. You can access this document through your Student Menu or by double-clicking on it from Windows Explorer.

Complete this activity now and ensure your program meets the requirements before continuing!

Lesson Three: Adding Cars

Now it's time to get some action on the Playing screen by adding some bumper cars.

The Car Object

Each bumper car will be represented by a **Car** object, which was provided for you in the starter files. Let's take a closer look at what the **Car** class provides for you.

```
public class Car : SpriteLibrary.Sprite
{
    public int Score = 0;

    public void Steer(double angleChange)
    public bool MoveAndReflect(float screenSizeX, float screenSizeY)
    public bool CheckBump(Car car2, int screenWidth, int screenHeight)
}
```

There is one **public** property on the car: **Score**. This convenient integer variable can be used to keep track of the player's current score.

There are three public methods on the car. The **Steer()** method will adjust the direction of the car by turning either left or right by the specified angle change (in degrees).

The **MoveAndReflect()** method should be used to move the bumper cars around on the screen. It works as the normal **Sprite.Move()** method does, except when the car hits the edge of the screen it will *reflect* off the side instead of wrapping or vanishing. Hitting the edge of the screen will also slow down the car significantly. You have to provide the screen width and height to this method in order to determine when to reflect the car. This method will return a **true** value if the car reflected off of a screen edge or **false** if the car did not reflect.

The **CheckBump()** method replaces your normal collision detection routine between the two cars. This method will determine when the cars are close enough to have collided and bounce them away from each other as if they were billiard balls! After you move both calls, call **CheckBump()** on one car and pass in the other car for comparison. It doesn't matter which car you use to call the method. The method will return a **true** value if a "bump" occurred or a **false** value if no "bump" occurred.

Car Controls

Each bumper car will need four inputs: steer left, steer right, accelerate (speed up), and decelerate (slow down). You are free to choose your own inputs for any combination of mouse, keyboard, and game controller, though we recommend the following keyboard layout for two players:

Command	Player 1	Player 2
Steer left	'A' key	Left arrow key
Steer right	'D' key	Right arrow key
Speed up	'W' key	Up arrow key
Slow down	'X' key	Down arrow key

The game works smoothly if you simply recognize these keys when they are held down. There is no need to process discrete key-presses as you would for menu selections.

Cars can't change directions instantly, they can only steer left and right by some amount. When you detect a steer left or steer right command, call the **Steer()** method on the corresponding **Car**. You will need to choose some constant value to represent the angle change, in degrees, that each steer command will handle. Similarly you need to decide by what amounts the speed up and slow down commands will accelerate the car.

Note: If you are using Xbox gamepads in this game, all of the steering should be done with the left thumb-stick control. When the thumb-stick is tilted to the left or right, the player's car should steer left or right. When it is tilted up, the car should speed up, and when it is tilted down, the car should slow down. Just as with the keyboard input, there is no need to keep track of an old gamepad state when you are processing continual input.

Activity Three: Start Your Engines

In this activity you will add the bumper cars to the screen and put them under user control.

Your activity requirements and instructions are found in the "Chapter_15_Activity3.pdf" document located in your "TeenCoder\Game Programming\Activity Docs" folder. You can access this document through your Student Menu or by double-clicking on it from Windows Explorer.

Complete this activity now and ensure your program meets the requirements before continuing!

Lesson Four: Oil Slicks and Coins

Once you get the bumper cars bouncing merrily around the screen, it's time to give them something to chase and something to avoid. In this lesson and activity you will add the oil slicks and the spinning coin.

Spinning Coin

The spinning coin is simply an animated sprite with 5 frames:

You will want to define a **Sprite** for the coin in the main game object and also define a method to place the coin in a random location on the screen as needed. The coin should be continuously animated with an `AnimationInterval` of 200 milliseconds.

Oil Slicks

Oil slicks are static (non-animated) images that appear on the screen for a period of time and then disappear. You can choose how many you'd like to keep on the screen at one time, though we recommend 3 or 4 to start with.

You can keep track of the last time an oil slick appeared and create a new one in a random location every 5 seconds or so. When you create a new oil slick, make sure to get rid of the oldest one so the screen doesn't become impassable. One straightforward implementation would be to keep a **LinkedList**<**Sprite**> of oil slicks. You can add new sprites to the beginning and trim the older ones off the end.

Activity Four: Hazards and Rewards

In this activity you will complete all remaining game logic to make a fully functional two-player game! This includes adding in the oil slicks and spinning coin, collision detection and score keeping, and game over logic.

Your activity requirements and instructions are found in the "Chapter_15_Activity4.pdf" document located in your "TeenCoder\Game Programming\Activity Docs" folder. You can access this document through your Student Menu or by double-clicking on it from Windows Explorer.

Complete this activity now and ensure your program meets the requirements before continuing!

Lesson Five: Bumper Cars Sounds Effects

You can't have cars crashing around an arena, skidding on oil slicks and racking up points without making any sound! The "Activity Starters\BumperCars\Sound" directory contains sound files to be used in the following conditions:

bumpercar_oilslick.wav	Play this sound whenever a bumper car hits an oil slick.
bumpercar_bounce.wav	Play this sound whenever a bumper car bounces off another car or a wall.
bumpercar_coin.wav	Play this sound whenever a player gets a coin.
background_music.wav	Play this sound in a loop for the game's background music. Make sure to turn down the volume so that other sound effects can be heard.

Two of these sounds ("bumpercar_bounce" and "bumpercar_coin") you can simply **Play()** without tracking a **SoundEffectInstance** afterwards. The "background_music" should be played in a continuous loop at half volume.

The "bumpercar_oil" slick sound will be the trickiest. You can't simply **SoundEffect.Play()** the sound each time the car sprites collide with an oil slick. The collision will be continuous over a long period of time (many **Update()** methods) as the car makes its way through the oil. You don't want to restart the sound by calling **Play()** each time! Therefore you should create an instance of the "Bumpercar_oil" sound effect and call **Play()** on that one instance when collided. If the sound is already playing, calling **Play()** again on the **SoundEffectInstance** will not have any effect.

Activity Five: Make Some Noise

In this activity you will add sound effects to the Bumper Cars game.

Your activity requirements and instructions are found in the "Chapter_15_Activity5.pdf" document located in your "TeenCoder\Game Programming\Activity Docs" folder. You can access this document through your Student Menu or by double-clicking on it from Windows Explorer.

Complete this activity now and ensure your program meets the requirements before continuing!

Chapter Fifteen: Final Project

Lesson Six: Add Artificial Intelligence

For the last feature in your Bumper Cars project you will enable the one-player option. This means the second bumper car will be controlled by game AI.

As in previous chapters, if a player is controlled by AI instead of a human you will bypass the normal user inputs and call a method such as **DoAI()** to calculate the player's next move. How exactly should that next move be determined? You can create your own AI algorithm or follow our suggestions below!

Let's think about how you would control the car as a human. If you see the coin to the left, you would steer left until you are heading straight for it. Similarly if you see the coin off to your right you would steer right until it was in your sights. If the coin is directly behind you then you can turn around in either direction. This is similar to the predator and prey chase algorithm, except you are driving a car that cannot instantly determine a new angle – you have to steer towards the goal instead.

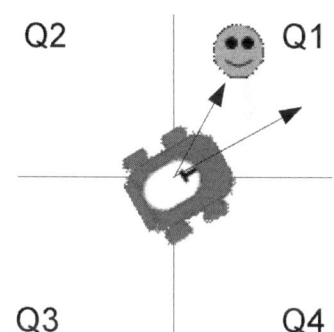

A car's **velocity** vector also defines its current direction angle relative to the X axis. You can make a second vector from the car to the coin by assuming the car is at the origin, and subtracting the coin location from the car location. This second vector gives you the angle to the coin from the X axis. You can use **Sprite.CalculateDirectionAngle()** to get the angle of that vector.

If both angles are in the same quadrant (shown as Q1, Q2, Q3, or Q4), you can simply compare the two angles to determine which way to steer. If the angle to the coin is greater than the angle of car travel, turn left. If the angle of the coin is less than the car direction, turn right.

However, consider what happens when the vectors point into different quadrants. Keep in mind that angles in Q1 are 0° → 90°, in Q2 are 90° → 180°, in Q3 are 180° → 270°, and in Q4 are 270° → 360°.

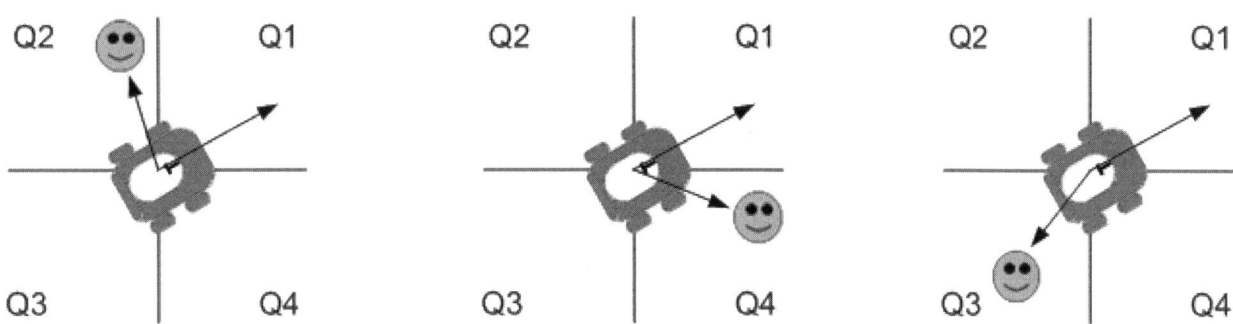

Initially the math looks identical. In the first diagram you want to turn to the left because the coin angle is greater than the car angle. But look at the second diagram! The coin angle is also greater than the car angle (because angles in the fourth quadrant are 270 → 360°) but you really need to turn right! Clearly you cannot blindly perform some math on the vector angles without understanding which quadrants they are in.

However, we can reasonably say that if the coin angle is one quadrant counter-clockwise from the car angle, then turn left. If the coin angle is one quadrant clockwise from the car angle, turn right. If the coin angle and the car angle are in opposite quadrants (e.g. Q1 and Q3) then you can reasonably turn either direction without wasting too much time.

The proposed bumper car AI algorithm can be summarized as:

1. Determine the vector from car to coin, and also obtain the car's velocity vector.
2. Find the angle of the vector to the coin and the angle of the car's velocity vector.
3. Identify the quadrant (Q1, Q2, Q3, or Q4) of each angle
4. If the two quadrants are the same
    a. Turn left if the coin angle is larger than the car angle
    b. Turn right if the coin angle is smaller than the car angle
5. Else if the coin quadrant is to the counter-clockwise direction from the car quadrant
    a. Turn left
6. Else if the coin quadrant is to the clockwise direction from the car quadrant
    a. Turn right
7. Else the coin is in the quadrant behind the car
    a. Turn in any consistent direction
8. If we are going less than the maximum speed
    a. Accelerate!

This algorithm does not take into account all behavior a human driver might show. The computer will not steer around oil slicks or attempt to bump the opposing car. You may choose to add these features if you feel ambitious, but remember you are trying to write AI that is just good enough to keep the human player entertained and still be easily programmable.

Chapter Fifteen: Final Project

Activity Six: Racing Buddy

This is the last activity for the final project! Your task is to implement game AI for the second bumper car when the one-player game is chosen from the menu.

Your activity requirements and instructions are found in the "Chapter_15_Activity6.pdf" document located in your "TeenCoder\Game Programming\Activity Docs" folder. You can access this document through your Student Menu or by double-clicking on it from Windows Explorer.

Complete this activity now and ensure your program meets the requirements before continuing!

Congratulations, you have now completed a complex project from scratch and have demonstrated your understanding of the major topics covered in this course. You are now well-equipped to begin writing your own games!

What's Next?

Congratulations, you have finished the *TeenCoder™: Game Programming* course! You now have a fundamental understanding of many crucial game programming topics and can begin writing your own simple computer games. You are encouraged to continue learning new techniques through online resources such as Microsoft's XNA community website.

You have now completed a full year of the TeenCoder™ curriculum. If you are interested in a career in computers, the concepts and skills you learned are a solid foundation for further study. We also offer a TeenCoder Java series that will teach you to write Java programs and Android smart-phone applications.

Our two KidCoder™ series for 4th+ grade students focus on other programming topics. The KidCoder Visual Basic series gives you some of the same graphical Windows capabilities in an easy-to-use language. The KidCoder Web Design series will teach you simple HTML, CSS, and JavaScript techniques so you can build your own websites.

We hope you have enjoyed this course produced by Homeschool Programming, Inc. We welcome student and teacher feedback at our website. Please also visit our website to request courses on other topics or see what new courses are available!

http://www.HomeschoolProgramming.com

Index

.NET Framework 24
acceleration 152
alpha channel 58
angles, degrees and radians 72, 109
animation 127
    continuous and short 133
    frames 131
    realistic touches 129
    strip images 130
ApplyChanges() function 53
artificial intelligence 205
    cheating 209
    data structures 208
AudioEngine object 147
BlendState enumeration 70
Bumper Cars game 217
ButtonState enumeration 85
Camera object 197
chase algorithm 209
collision detection 120
    bounding rectangle 120
    pixel perfect 120
    with rotation and scaling 122
color models 56
    CMYK model 56
    RGB model 57
Color object 58
content pipeline 63
    adding folders 64
    adding images 65
    adding sounds 140
Content.Load() function 65
data types 16
debugger 18
display modes 53
distributing XNA games 181
Draw() function 42
    drawing images 66
    drawing text 74
DrawString() function 76
else if keyword 17
else keyword 17
enumerator 18
evade algorithm 211
file I/O 19
flow control 16
flowchart 207, 220

fonts 74
for() loop 17
Form object 38
full screen mode 52
functions 18
game content 32
game dependencies 181
game design 31
game engine 33
game executable 180
game logic 34
game loop 44
    timing 45
Game object 39
    constructor 40
game over 124
game proposal 31
game scores 179
game state 33
game tiles 192
game types 20
    arcade games 20
    board games 21
    first person shooter (FPS) 22
    MMORPG 22
    real time strategy (RTS) 21
    role playing game (RPG) 21
    sports 21
GamePad object 90
    GetState() function 90
GamePadState object 90, 91
    IsConnected property 91, 191
GameTime object 118
    ElapsedGameTime and **TotalGameTime** properties 118
    TotalMilliseconds property 118
GraphicsAdapter object 54
GraphicsDevice.Viewport.Height property 53
GraphicsDevice.Viewport.Width property 53
GraphicsDeviceManager object 40, 52
gravity 154
HiDef and Reach graphics settings 43
history of Windows 15
if keyword 17
image formats (GIF, PNG, JPG) 59
image location coordinates 50
image rotating 71
image scaling 70

231

inheritance	19
Initialize() function	40
installing	
course files	27
MSDN C# Help Library	29
Visual C# 2010 Express	29
XNA Game Studio 4.0	30
instructional videos	4
IsFullScreen property	55
IsMouseVisible property	85
keyboard input	79
keyboard modifiers	84
Keyboard object	80
KeyboardState object	80
GetPressedKeys() method	81
GetState() function	80
IsKeyDown() function	80
IsKeyUp() function	81
Keys enumeration	79
layer depth	69
linked lists	106
LoadContent() function	41
logical expressions	17
loops	17
math operators	17
Math.Atan2() function	152
mazes	163
dead-end filler	169
dimension	164
Kruskal's algorithm	166
Prim's algorithm	165
random mouse	168
recursive backtracker	167, 169
recursive division	166
routing	164
texture (run, elitism, bias, river)	164
wall follower	168
MediaPlayer object	145
Play(), **Stop**(), **Pause**(), **Resume**() functions	145
menu screens	173
Microsoft.Xna.Framework namespace	39
Microsoft.Xna.Framework.Audio namespace	141
Microsoft.Xna.Framework.Input namespace	79
mouse cursor	85
Mouse object	85
GetState() function	85
SetPosition() function	88
MouseState object	85
multiplayer keyboard input	189
multiplayer Xbox 360 controllers	190
multiple screens	173
drawing	177
tracking	174
updating	175
object-oriented programming (OOP)	19
option screens	174
origin	68, 72
overlay (dashboard)	180
parallax scrolling	192
persistence of vision	127
pixel colors	57
pixels	49
PlayerIndex enumeration	90, 190
polymorphism	19
PreferredBackBufferHeight property	53
PreferredBackBufferWidth property	53
private keyword	19
project, creating new XNA project	36
public keyword	19
publishing XNA games	182
Pulse Code Modulation (PCM)	140
Pythagorean's theorem	151
random movement	212
reflection	157
scale	68
screen coordinates	49
scrolling games	191
Song object	144
sound files	139
SoundBank object	147
SoundEffect object	141
Play() function	141
Play() parameters volume, pitch, pan	141
SoundEffectInstance object	142
looping sound	143
split screen game	189
sprite	95
Sprite object	95
Accelerate() function	153
Animate() function	133
animation properties	132
AnimationInterval property	133
bouncing	112
CalculateDirectionAngle() function	152
Draw() function	99
GetBoundingRectangle() function	122
GetCenter() function	101
getting and setting direction angles	111
GetWidth() and **GetHeight**() functions	101
initializing	105
IsAlive property	98
IsAnimating() function	134
IsCollided() function	121
LayerDepth property	98
MaxSpeed property	110
movement	109

Index

movement functions	111
Origin property	98
Reflect() function	159
RotationAngle property	98
Scale property	97
SetSpeedAndDirection() function	110
SetTexture() function	97, 99, 132
SpriteTexture property	97
TTL property	98
UpperLeft property	97
Velocity property	110
wrapping	112
SpriteBatch object	40
Begin() function	66
Draw() function	67, 130
End() function	66
SpriteEffects object	68
SpriteLibrary namespace	95
SpriteSortMode enumeration	70
Star Racer game	203
string data type	17
numeric character index	18
Swarm game	102
System.Collections namespace	18
System.IO namespace	19
System.Math object	17
Texture2D object	65
title screens	173
ToggleFullScreen() function	56
ToString()	18
transparency	58
UnloadContent() function	41
Update() function	41
user input	17
variables	16
Vector2 object	51
velocity	151
while() loop	17
wind	155
window mode	52
window size	53
Windows programming in C#	16
working directory	30
world coordinates	193
converting to screen coordinates	200
XACT sound tool	146
Xbox 360 controller (gamepad)	88
directional pad	90
letter buttons A, B, X, Y	89
shoulder buttons	90
start and back buttons	89
thumbsticks	89
trigger buttons	90
vibration	92
Xbox Live Indie Games	24
XNA Creator's Club	24
XNA Framework	24
XNA Game Studio 4.0	25
XNA namespaces	38
zoetrope	127
Z-ordering	69